Teresa
of Avila's Way

THE WAY OF THE CHRISTIAN MYSTICS

GENERAL EDITOR

Noel Dermot O'Donoghue, ODC

Volume 13

Teresa
of Avila's Way

by

J. Mary Luti

A Michael Glazier Book
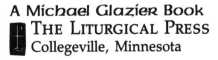
THE LITURGICAL PRESS
Collegeville, Minnesota

BX
4700
.T4
L83
1991

Cover design by Don Bruno
Woodcut by Robert McGovern

A Michael Glazier Book published by The Liturgical Press

1   2   3   4   5   6   7   8   9

Library of Congress Cataloging-in-Publication Data

Luti, J. Mary, 1947–
   Teresa of Avila's way / by J. Mary Luti.
      p.   cm. — (The Way of the Christian mystics ; v. 13)
   "A Michael Glazier book."
   Includes bibliographical references.
   ISBN 0-8146-5548-3
   1. Teresa, of Avila, Saint, 1515–1582. 2. Christian saints—Spain—Avila—Biography. 3. Mysticism—Spain—History—16th century. 4. Mysticism—Catholic Church—History—16th century. 5. Catholic Church—Doctrines—History—16th century. I. Title. II. Series.
BX4700.T4L83 1991
282'.092—dc20   91-7114
[B]   CIP

For Mudge and Bill

*"To have had virtuous and God-fearing parents
along with the graces the Lord granted me
should have been enough for me to have led a good life,
if I had not been so wretched."*

Teresa of Avila
The Book of Her Life, 1:1

CONTENTS

Preface

This book means to capture something of Teresa of Avila's way of living the Christian gospel in her place and time. It should serve as an introduction to her inner life, her encounters with God, her growth in grace, her gradual transformation into a holy one, a saint of the Christian community. Although it presents the reader with a view of a woman who sought full Christian maturity (Teresa would have said "perfection") as a nun, it is written with the knowledge that in the centuries since her death her way has proven attractive to others whose callings have little to do with monastic life. More than anything else, this book seeks to convey to the reader the sense of vitality and urgency that characterized Teresa's challenge to her contemporaries, a challenge to take God up on the eternal invitation to intimacy with the divine—for the sake of our soul, and Teresa would add, for the sake of the Church and world, for the glory of God.

Teresa of Avila was a mystic, a woman of prayer whose life was an icon of her contemplatively-experienced, loving union with God. Her extraordinary inner life is well documented, especially by Teresa herself in her books on prayer. As a teacher of contemplative prayer and spiritual guide, she has few rivals in the Christian tradition.

Anyone who has even a passing acquaintance with Teresa's life is aware that her journey with God was marked by mystical phenomena such as visions, voices, raptures, elevations, healings, the ability to read hearts, and the like. Teresian commentators have always highly valued and emphasized these unusual occurrences, viewing them as indicators of her personal sanctity and guarantors of the credibility of her extensive written teachings on the spiritual life. To the hagiographers Teresa was above all the "Seraphic Virgin," aflame with mystical love, and "Mystical Doctor," guided by the Spirit to reveal compellingly the mysteries of God's action in the human soul in teachings that would endure forever. And it is certain that Teresa the mystic, or better, Teresa of the mystical *experiences,* has always appealed to the religious imagination as something of a divine prodigy.

From her own writings we know that Teresa esteemed these dramatic mystical phenomena for the way they increased her love of God. She believed, for she herself had had experience of it, that these gifts carried with them a particular efficacy that could touch and transform areas of a person's being that had resisted years of human effort and desire. She taught her disciples to accept and embrace, sometimes even to seek, such gifts without scruples of vainglory; for if genuine, these phenomena could be trusted to lead the soul into greater union with God and help fashion within it a more perfectly resolute human will, strong with the determination to serve *God's* will in all things.

Nonetheless, we do well to remember that Teresa was also adamant never to *equate* the contemplative life with unusual occurrences, and she never calculated her own or another person's holiness by adding them up. She knew that the presence or absence of these gifts in the life of a Christian seriously seeking God could have ambiguous significance and that much discernment and experience had to be brought to bear before one could feel confident that self-delusion or, as she believed, even demonic trickery, was not at play.

Thus, although she esteemed mystical phenomena, she was also cautious about them. And she was cautious not only because such experiences could be counterfeited by the soul or by the devil, but also and especially because she understood the mystical life to involve much more than peak experiences. The secondary mystical phenomena are, in the words of one scholar of the subject, "the overflow" of God's much deeper work of grace in the person's life.[1] And that deeper work concerns only love. For Teresa, the marks of true Christian intimacy with God were first, last,

---

[1]Harvey D. Egan, S.J., *Christian Mysticism, The Future of a Tradition* (New York: Pueblo, 1984) 305. (Hereafter, *Christian Mysticism.)*

and always the marks of concrete love: the bearing of the cross, the service of neighbor. Sensation was not what she was seeking but transformation in God for the sake of God's service. A far cry from the isolated, even selfish pursuer of divine delights or the stressed-out modern seeking spiritual relaxation through meditation techniques in order to feel better about life, Teresa was a person in whom grace was at work in an extraordinarily profound way, creating the full new humanity promised in Christ, in whom union with God and love of others were neither separate categories nor successive experiences. In short, mystical (or contemplative) prayer, complete with its attendant extraordinary phenomena, was one important way in which Teresa entered the Christian mystery. But that mystery was for her a whole *way of living* in which all the experiences of prayer, ordinary and extraordinary, personal and corporate, were always understood as an integral piece of a much larger life.

That is why in this volume I have chosen to present Teresa the mystic without isolating those unusual experiences for extensive description or theological analysis.[2] I have not ignored them, to be sure, but have chosen not to dwell on them so that the reader's attention may be directed more broadly to the way in which those experiences and others worked together to create a life, a *whole* and *integrated* life that Teresa lived in union with God. It seems to me, for example, that Teresa's ecclesial activism, her life as a reformer and social critic, and her literary life are at once the fruits of her mystical encounter with God and inextricable aspects of mysticism itself, understood as a way of being, knowing, seeing, and acting in the world.

My approach to Teresa in this volume is to a complex human person living a whole life in a particular time and place, a woman who, I hope the reader will see, was capable both of transcending and challenging her culture and, at times, of being hoodwinked by it. Few things can be said of such a person baldly. In writing this book, then, I have tried to keep Teresa's place and time, her heritage, and her spiritual and ecclesial assumptions before the

---

[2] Readers interested in more complete theological explanations of Teresa's mystical gifts and the secondary mystical phenomena in general may wish to consult the Bibliography at the end of this volume. Teresa's own writings, especially her *Life* and *The Interior Castle*, are the best places to begin.

reader's eyes as much as possible, even though doing so required lengthy contextualization in places. It may even appear at times that the point gets lost in digression, but Teresa had a similar problem as she tried in her works to paint a full picture of the soul's life with God. In Teresa's case, the reader's patience is always rewarded and her point is always made, enormously enriched. I hope the same thing will happen with this book.

Further, in the course of examining aspects of Teresa's life with God, I have been, when it seemed pertinent, frank about Teresa's sore spots as a human being, not out of an iconoclastic impulse but rather because her own desire was to be seen by posterity as an ordinary sinner redeemed by a gracious God, not as a perfect and unreachable star. The great things God did for her seemed all the greater precisely because she was and always remained, in her view, undeserving. Teresa knew about and bemoaned a great many of her imperfections; others she was not aware of at all. Most commentators have not, until recently, been willing to point them out either, perhaps because they feared that to say she could be at times angry, resentful, envious, and unfair in her appraisals of people, among other failings, might detract from her glory as a saint and reduce her divine dimensions.

I believe, however, that Teresa's power to attract and engage other human beings does not depend on her having been "good" but on her having tried to be faithful. Most people I know who encounter Teresa for the first time find it immensely comforting and encouraging to read, for example, that not until her late forties was she able to approach her appointed prayer time each day without a certain reluctance. They find some solace and realism too in the picture of the old and worn out Teresa who even in the last months of her life was experiencing frustration and bitter disappointment in friendships, heartaches for which her own short-sightedness or stubbornness was at times, at least in part, to blame. Teresa's trust in God's mercy and her courageous perseverance in joy and hope, faith and service through the pain of her own sin and the sin of the world can readily inspire, teach, and support all modern Christians for whom the quick fixes thrust upon us today are rapidly losing appeal.

In the same vein, I have tried in a variety of ways throughout the book to let the reader know the difference I think it makes to our apprehension of her inner life that Teresa was a woman.

Her self-understanding and her opinions about the female sex are generally those of a sixteenth-century nun living in a culture whose ideology of women and male-female relationships sharply circumscribed women's lives. Her God was decidedly masculine, even if not every metaphor she used to talk about God was male. Her language about women is at times most unflattering and seems to assume a good many of the misogynist axioms of the patriarchal culture that nurtured her.

But within the assumptions that ruled men's and women's lives and relationships in sixteenth-century Castile, many women, Teresa among them, found it possible to achieve, create, enjoy and use power, and exercise formative influence on the world around them, in ways that, at times, conformed to outward expectations concerning their roles and capacities, and at times broke or reconfigured those arrangements. Moreover, many women did not internalize, to use the modern word, *everything* the stereotypes imposed; the writings of some hispanic nuns in this period, for example, reveal a sometimes stunning consciousness of the difference between their own experience and the assumptions of the dominant male culture. The historically conscious and alert reader of Teresa's works will quickly learn that Teresa played fast and loose with the conventions of gender even as she observed them, that she was aware of certain aspects of the reigning ideology of gender *as ideology,* and that she frequently adopted a polemical stance with respect especially to those that made women *apostolically* useless and invisible. This particular sort of marginalization especially angered her, but it also fueled her creativity, as we shall later describe (Chapter 6).

It is true that *laypersons* in general (especially the uneducated), and not only women, enjoyed little esteem in the Catholic Church of Teresa's day. As laity, they had no authority or meaningful apostolic role in the eyes of the Church; if not theologically trained (and most were not), anything they might say or do in the realms of the spirit and of doctrine could, if it deviated from accepted norms, be regarded as audacious at best, erroneous or heretical at worst. Lay men, as well as all women, risked running afoul of the authorities if they presumed to interpret Scripture, undertake novel reformist activity, teach the faith, or speak as spiritual persons in public on behalf of God.

Nonetheless, it remains the case that women carried a particular burden of suspicion when it came to matters of religious authority, apostolic activity, or spiritual credibility. Even the most uneducated layman was at least a male, and that meant that he was by nature more credible than a woman, and that at least in theory he could get some schooling and even be ordained. An educated layman's or a priest's orthodoxy could still be called into question, of course; a man could misuse his intelligence and learning, be proud and stubborn, and through vice allow himself to be led astray. And if he were an *espiritual,* a devotee of the affective sort of prayer that gained widespread popularity in Teresa's times, he might be suspect just for espousing that cause.

Still, the culture did not automatically assume of all males what it did of all females, namely that *by nature* they were barred from personal, social, or ecclesiastical authority, that *by nature* they were incapable of certain levels of learning, or that *by nature* they were highly susceptible to delusion by the devil. Given such assumptions, and in view of Teresa's remarkable spiritual and apostolic achievement, it does not seem to me incidental to her story that she was a woman, and I have underscored this conviction wherever appropriate throughout the text.

Although this volume is meant to be an examination of certain aspects of her inner life and growth, and not a *biography* of Teresa, it seemed best to orient the reader at the outset by providing an overview of Teresa's life, context, and the significance of her teaching and projects *(Teresian Chronology,* and Chapter 1). The remaining chapters, however, take their direction from Teresa herself, who in all her writings fashioned what amounts to a multilayered commentary on her own experience. She told the reader her personal story, making general applications of her experience, bringing in other opinions from time to time, engaging in disquisitions and dialogue with real and imagined interlocutors. Her disarming and insightful self-disclosure aimed to edify and teach; she meant her life with God to be used as an example for others.

Therefore, Chapters 2–6 of this volume all begin with a leisurely recounting of an episode from Teresa's life, drawn from her writings. Then, reflecting on the episode, I present a particular aspect of the dynamic, or pattern, of her life with God. Chapter 2 reflects upon her fundamental determination to seek God no matter the consequences. In Chapter 3, we see contemplative prayer as the pathway to encounters with God as loving friend. The refinement of her capacity for human relationships is the topic of Chapter 4. Next we focus upon the contemplative enlargement of vision that engaged Teresa in divine perspectives and concerns (Chapter 5). And finally, in Chapter 6, we confront the unstoppable creativity of the mystic, Teresa's desire for deeds and apostolic service, her embrace of all that is encompassed in the classic Christian phrase, "imitation of Christ." A personal, impressionistic reflection on imagining Teresa (Chapter 7) brings the book to a close.

I hope that this book will serve as an inducement to the reader to go to the sources and enjoy Teresa's own writings. In the meanwhile, if I succeed in bringing alive a sense of Teresa's life with God in the midst of her time and place, I want to share the satisfaction that success would give me with everyone who helped me write this book. I mention only a few here; many more go unnamed but not by any means unthanked.

Thanks to Anne M. Minton, who read every word and in between the lines; to Harvey D. Egan, S.J., whose encouragement began this project and whose critical reading strengthened it; to Dan Novotny, for his astute comments and affectionate comradeship; to Jodi Bilinkoff, for the help of her scholarship and the stimulation of her conversation; to Susan Rosen, Julie Murray, Lisa Schoenwetter, and Cynthia Maybeck for generously giving me their time and good suggestions; and to the entire Andover Newton community, where among the learned saints not a few mystics may be found.

I first read Teresa's *Life* twenty-three years ago in a bowfront house in Boston. I had joined a Roman Catholic lay institute whose members, having Teresa as their patron, chose a book of hers to read aloud together each October, the month in which her feastday falls. I am no longer a member of that group, but I have never stopped reading Teresa. And I am ever deeply grateful for the gift of making her acquaintance in the generous *regazo* of the *Institución Teresiana*.

Feast of St. Teresa of Avila   J. Mary Luti
October 15, 1989

Terms and Abbreviations

I. Terms

Throughout this volume certain terms appear untranslated. I have left them in Spanish because they have no satisfactory English equivalents. In order to give the reader access to these terms, so much a part of the definition of Teresa's world, I offer a glossary in which I also include certain words that, although familiar as English words, seem to me to require some contextualization before the reader encounters them in the chapters of this book. I hope these explanations will be of help in following more closely the story that unfolds as *Teresa of Avila's Way*.

Beatas

This term refers to Spanish women who, in the late fifteenth and early sixteenth centuries, were attracted to a new way of devout life. These women did not wish to follow a formal religious life in a recognized Religious Order, or perhaps they were unable to do so. Generally, *beatas* lived a simpler life than that of the traditional monasteries. Moreover, dedication as a *beata* could be perpetual or temporary (some young women lived the life of a *beata* until marriages could be arranged for them). *Beatas* took private vows of chastity and usually followed a rule of their own devising, or that of an Order. Some lived in communities with a chosen superior. Many could be found, however, living a rule of life singly in their own homes in their own home-sewn habits, a choice made fairly frequently by widowed women. Sometimes widows made their houses available to women who sought community; houses of *beatas* were called *beaterios.*[1] Some *beaterios* were eventually received (if the women so petitioned) or placed (if a bishop or other official thought it wise or necessary) under the jurisdiction of a Religious Order and became regular monasteries of that Order, and the *beatas* became nuns. *Beatas* sometimes performed deeds of charity in the towns they lived in, but most were enclosed and devoted themselves to prayer and penitence.

The increasing popularity of this relatively unregulated style of religious life, the intense atmosphere of spiritual revival, and the apparently large numbers of women of Jewish ancestry who were attracted to the life created, in certain ecclesiastical quarters of Castile, deep reserve with respect to *beatas.* This suspicion increased when some particularly talented women went public with their spiritual experiences and gathered a following that included priests, religious, and uneducated layfolk. While it seems certain that many of these spiritually adept women were genuinely gifted, some probably were deliberately deceptive or deluded. A few spectacular cases cast a pall over the rest. The authorities were always wary too of clerics who, for upright reasons or less noble purposes, encouraged these women, heard confessions, promoted their causes, even lived in their houses. Many *beatas* fell under the Inquisition's hand as false mystics, *incubi,* or allegedly lascivious seducers. Teresa of Avila, who counted a few well-known *beatas* among her friends, was sometimes fearful that her religious experiences would be classed with the experiences of *beatas* that had been denounced as fraudulent.

Conversos

Conversos were "new" Christians, Jews who had accepted Christian baptism under various forms and degrees of coercion,

[1]The *beatas* that eventually became Carmelites and constructed the monastery Teresa of Avila entered in 1536 had first congregated in a house provided by a "widowed" *beata,* a woman who had been the long-time companion of the canon and archdeacon of the cathedral of Avila, Nuño González de Aguila, with whom she had four children. After his death, doña Elvira González de Medina engaged in lengthy lawsuits with her own children to obtain the inheritance her "husband" had meant her to receive, and invested her money in the establishment of a *beaterio.* She became the informal superior of the group. See Jodi Ellen Bilinkoff, "The Avila of St. Teresa; Religious Reform and Urban Development, 1480-1620," (Ph.D. diss., Princeton Univ., 1983), 67–68. Prof. Bilinkoff's book, *The Avila of St. Teresa: Religious Reform in a Sixteenth-Century City* (Ithaca, NY: Cornell University Press, 1989) was unavailable at the time I completed the manuscript of *Teresa of Avila's Way.*

during attempts made in the late fifteenth century to impose religious unity on a Spain that had been for centuries tricultural and trireligious (Christian, Jewish, Muslim).[2] In 1492, all Jews were obliged either to convert to Christianity or be expelled from Spain. Those who remained and accepted baptism, *conversos,* received little acceptance in return. Even though among the masses who converted and their immediate descendents, a great number probably adhered to the new faith loyally,[3] Spain's "old Christian" population treated these "new Christians" with a marginalizing contempt and popularized the notion that *conversos* were, to a person, insincere Christians, secret practitioners of Jewish rites, or "judaizers," and therefore heretics who posed a serious threat to the integrity of Christian faith in Spain. The Spanish Inquisition was created in 1478 largely for the purpose of dealing with judaizing new Christians, gradually expanding its powers over all issues touching on the orthodoxy of Catholic faith in Spain.

By the early sixteenth century, concern about purity of bloodline held a central place in the mentality of all sectors of society. Laws of "pure" or "clean" blood *(pureza* or *limpieza de sangre)*[4] prohibited *conversos* and their descendents, sometimes down to the fifth and sixth generations, sometimes in perpetuity, from occupying certain posts in civil government and universities, and from entering most Religious Orders. Not surprisingly, suppression of information about forebears who had converted to Christianity from Judaism was of great importance. The attempted erasure of one's unclean heritage took a variety of anxious forms, commonly including the purchase of aristocratic status and the

---

[2]Muslims were forcibly converted as well, and eventually, early in the seventeenth century, their descendents were also expelled from Spain. Here we refer primarily to the question of the converted Jew because of its conenction with Teresa's experience.

[3]See Julio Caro Baroja, *Los judíos en la España moderna y contemporánea,* vol. 1 (Madrid: Ediciones ISTMO, 1978), 289-313. *Conversos* adopted many postures: some became virulent apologists for the Catholic faith and attacker of Judaism; some denounced and persecuted "crypto-Jews" either out of authentic zeal or economic interest; others satirized their correligionists; still others became (on the other side of the coin) apologists of Judaism; and some were martyred for their Jewish faith as judaizers; some satirized "new Christians" who were sincere in their faith. Finally, some *conversos* sought forms of religious experience that led to perceived heterodoxy; and some, as a consequence of conflict within themselves between the "Law of Moses and the gospel of Christ," abandoned both in effect by taking refuge in speculative philosophy.

[4]See Albert A. Sicroff, *Los estatutos de limpieza de sangre: Controversias entre los siglos XV y XVII* (Madrid: Taurus, 1979).

accompanying noble genealogies, outright fabrications that "proved" one's pure blood and entitled the purchaser to exemption from certain taxes as well as to affix the titles *don* and *doña* to their given names.

In 1485, Teresa of Avila's paternal grandfather, Juan Sánchez, was punished by the Inquisition as a judaizer in Toledo.[5] At the time a wealthy man, his run-in with the Inquisition probably left his fortune depleted, since penitents were normally required to turn over a large fraction of all they were worth as part of the often-elaborate penance. But it is likely that the public humiliation of his exposure, even more than the partial confiscation of his fortune, caused him to pull up stakes and attempt a new life in Avila. The energetic businessman prospered there anew. Eventually he bought his way out of the penalties imposed on him by his status as a *reconciliado* (or "reconciled" penitent) and into the ranks of the lower nobility *(hidalguía).*[6] Juan Sánchez emulated the lavish life of aristocrats and made good marriages into old Christian families for his children. But it was impossible to hide completely the stain of the *converso.* Lawsuits eventually dredged up the past. Even though the Sánchez family won confirmation of their status as *hidalgos* with a glorious family tree, they never won total acceptance in a town that was not fooled by any of the astute moves made to secure a place of prominence for the family. Nor was Teresa's father able to maintain the family's considerable fortune. He abandoned the family's businesses (the Sánchez were traders in silks and woolens, and financiers) perhaps because such activities were regarded as dishonorable for a true gentleman. A gentleman's honor was said to depend in large measure upon the appearance of genteel indolence and luxury, sustained solely by investment income. Don Alonso was determined to act according to all the expectations associated with his purchased status. His investments in land, however, proved un-

---

[5]Teresa's father was about five years old at the time of Juan Sánchez's disgrace. Witnesses involved in a family lawsuit in Avila claimed that Alonso and the rest of Juan Sánchez's sons were made to walk in the penitential processions with their father. Alonso was fourteen when the family moved to Avila.

[6]Because he was a financier as well as a merchant and often handled ecclesiastical finances, Juan Sánchez needed the false certificate of *hidalguía* as much for securing his livelihood as for securing his social reputation. As a *converso reconciliado* he would have been barred from such dealings.

fortunate. By the end of his life (1543), Alonso was in debt for huge sum, the family fortune sacrificed to the Castilian obsession with reputation.

Honor

In sixteenth-century Spain, one's honor was one's all. Once based on personal qualities like heroism and considered an attribute of the nobility, by Teresa's day honor was firmly attached to more external markers like rank, pedigree, wealth, and, of course, ethnicity or caste. Complex codes governed male and female behavior (not surprisingly, the female code had to do primarily with sexual propriety), and enormous effort and money was expended on maintaining all the trappings of station. Ostentation ruled the lives of the nobility, from lowest ranks to highest. Whether one was truly of noble lineage, authentically old Christian, or as wealthy as one looked was not the question: to *appear* so was enough. Thus, for these classes deception often was, ironically, the key to an honorable existence. Even certain occupations were considered dishonorable, or associated rightly or wrongly with the *converso* class; engaging in financial and commercial pursuits, servile labor, medicine, and even some forms of intellectual endeavor could bring disgrace to oneself and one's family. A careless word about someone's ancestry, if repeated often enough or with sufficient venom by someone envious of another's wealth or position, could bring that person's honor crashing down, never to be repaired. Honor was extensive; it touched everything. Honor was external; it was the opinion *others* held of a person's prestige. Honor was, above all, fragile; old resentments could boomerang as social ostracism or public death.

To decry such a state of affairs was to criticize one of the assumptions on which the world turned. A few voices could be heard in loud protest and scornful satire throughout the era, however, and Teresa of Avila's was among them. Brought up in a household where aristocratic pretensions were upheld energetically and honor was nursed with the kind of high anxiety only a *converso* could bring to the endeavor, Teresa's struggle against honor's tyranny was first of all a struggle against herself. Extricating herself from its assumptions and demands took a good part of the first forty-three years of her life and touched upon the rejection of flattery, learning to suffer insult, eschewing family pride, foregoing conversations with brilliant gentlemen in convent parlors. Eventually she would be able truthfully to write, "I have always esteemed virtue more than lineage"—a bold and unmistakable rejection of her society's values.[7] The frequency of this topic in her writings makes it clear that the mature Teresa was as preoccupied with destroying the illusions created by the doctrine of honor as others in her world were in maintaining them. In the last twenty years of her life, she not only criticized her society's values, but worked also to sublimate and transform them through her reflections upon them in the light of the gospel, her reform of the Carmelite Order, and her mystical encounters with Christ, who invited Christians old and new to become members of his family, share his honor, and enjoy his riches and largesse, without deception or anxiety.

Demons

Teresa, like nearly everyone in sixteenth-century Christian Europe, believed that devils existed and that God permitted them, as a part of the divine plan, to act anywhere in the world, tempting God's children and plotting to thwart all efforts on behalf of God's reign.[8] Moreover, from its beginnings the Christian monastic tradition emphasized the activity of demons in the spiritual journey and underscored the notion that Christian life is spiritual combat with the forces of evil.[9] Teresa inherited this tradition and viewed many of the impediments to her own mystical progress, attempts to suppress the Carmelite reform, and even some of the psycho-spiritual and physical sicknesses that afflicted the reform's nuns and friars as the malicious handiwork of these agents of evil. But she also held that although still very active in

---

[7] *Foundations,* 15:15.

[8] See for example *Life,* 25:19: "the devils are His slaves (and there is no doubt about this because it's a matter of faith) . . . "

[9] See for example the life of one of the most influential of the early desert ascetics, the hermit Antony of Egypt, in which the successful monk is depicted as a combatant who has gained mastery over Satan and all his agents. Athanasius, *The Life of Antony and The Letter to Marcellinus,* tr. and intro., Robert C. Gregg (New York: Paulist, 1980). For the connections and tensions in the monastic tradition between the notion of spiritual combat or asceticism and contemplation, see Andrew Louth, *The Origins of the Christian Mystical Tradition. From Plato to Denys* (New York: Oxford Univ. Press, 1983), 2nd ed., 98–131.

the world and capable of huge damage, Satan and his cohorts were already doomed since God had gained a decisive victory over evil in Jesus Christ. God was on the side of the faithful Christian combatant. The lesson she stressed in her struggles with *all* forms of evil, human as well as demonic, was that God could be counted on to create freedom, bestow strength, and capture the victory. The scrupulous and frightened soul[10] was the soul that had yet to understand the true situation: Satan is wily and dangerous, but God is *God.*

God provided means for defeating the demons: prayer, penance, vigilance, the practice of the basic Christian virtues of charity and humility, and the obedient pursuit of God's will. As a Catholic Teresa also had faith in the use of sacramentals (the crucifix, holy water, making the sign of the cross, and the like) to weaken the devil's power or frighten him away. Wary of other forms of remedies in use in her day, like incantations, foul-smelling concoctions, and amulets, she did make use of a priest-exorcist when cases of what was understood to be possession turned up among nuns in her charge. Fortunately, her collaborator, the mystic, poet, spiritual director and sometime administrator, John of the Cross, was a very successful exorcist.[11]

Teresa also counseled truth; she believed that, as the Father of Lies, Satan was best defended against by a life lived in truth and according to the truth, especially the truths of Scripture, Catholic dogma, and the observance of the Church's traditional rites and ceremonies. She claimed that God once told her that "all the harm that comes to the world comes from not knowing the truths of Scripture,"[12] and she consulted theologians so that

---

[10]Teresa used the term "souls" when referring to persons embarked upon the spiritual journey. She believed that all the person's relations with God were conducted within the human soul, with its structures of intellect, will, memory, and imagination. Thus, it was the soul that experienced God directly. What the soul experienced of God, however, was frequently felt in the body, and although Teresa understood the two as distinct in her anthropology, she knew from experience that they were closely related and that one could be a help or hindrance to the other.

[11]See for example, *Letters* I, 115.

[12]*Life,* 40:1. Given the fact that the reading of Scripture in the vernacular was sharply restricted during the sixteenth century in Spain; and given the impression that many people have that Catholics were not either very familiar with or fond of the Bible, readers of her works are often surprised at how imbued Teresa was with the Scriptures and how highly she esteemed them.

they might help her discover "whether all her experiences were in conformity with Sacred Scripture."[13] Such consultations were necessary, in her view, for any soul who wished to avoid the snares of spiritual deception the devil was so good at devising, for Satan was never so active as when a soul set out earnestly on a search for God; never so active either, she thought, as in her troubled times when he had disrupted the Church's unity, set Christians to warring against Christians, turned the hearts of men and women to unheard-of excess and duplicity, distorted human relations by raising the spectre of impure blood, and cast a spell of lukewarmness, timidity, and intellectual pride over so many of the very men—theologians and preachers—who constituted the frontlines in the battle with the enemies of God.

In Teresa's writings, we encounter demons in many guises, including animal forms. Teresa spoke of snakes, dogs, and toads. But she saw them also as misshapen humans or grotesque little creatures. Some, with bodies aflame, once tried to catch her with their hands; she also smelled their brimstone stench and heard them striking loud blows and shrieking curses as she prepared for prayer. They could live anywhere they chose but had preferred habitats in dank places heavy with shadow, like groves and caverns. Teresa, however, was convinced that in all Spain the place of most likely encounter with the demons was Seville. The hub of the Indies trade and a crossroads for every type of human enterprise and vice, Seville was wealthy, showy, luxurious, immensely busy, and self-important. It was in Andalusia, a region that to the Castilian Teresa seemed exotic, the air full of cloying scents and the barely comprehensible sounds of the southern tongue. Seville was also *hot,* and filled with Andalusians, a people Teresa regarded as a totally untrustworthy lot.[14] The devil gave her as much if not more trouble in that grand city than anywhere else in Teresa's travels, even arranging for her a run-in with the tribunals of the Inquisition over reported scandals in the newly established discalced monastery.[15]

---

[13]*Testimonies,* 58:7.

[14]See *Letters* I, 229, 279, 357.

[15]*Foundations,* 25:1, 14; 27:29. Stephen Clissold, *St. Teresa of Avila* (London: Sheldon Press, 1979), 176–193.

Contemplation

The term contemplation is used in this volume (along with "mental" prayer) to refer to the kind of prayer that is exercised silently and interiorly (different from "vocal" prayer: recited, prescribed, formulaic, liturgical or ritual *prayers),* in search of a loving encounter with a living God. The Christian tradition East and West has spoken through the centuries of various degrees, stages of growth, or steps that adepts in the prayer of contemplation experience. Broadly however, most contemplatives acknowledge a difference between the kind of contemplation that a person can "work at," or a level of closeness to God that one can achieve mainly through personal effort (for example, meditation that employs human reasoning lovingly to reflect upon and consider Scripture passages) and contemplation that is "supernatural" or "infused," degrees of loving union with God that a person can neither cause nor control, in which the person is drawn to God in ineffable ways. The person upon whom infused contemplation is bestowed *normally* experiences unusual phenomena (trance-like states, voices, ecstatic flight or elevations) and *always* undergoes profound transformations of human life and consciouness, becoming more lovingly engaged in the service of others.[16]

That Teresa was a mystic means that she was a contemplative whose life became a mirror of intimacy with God. She answered what she perceived to be a divine invitation to gaze as directly as humans can upon the face of God in love and for the sake of love, in the depths of her own being where God dwelled. At the same time, she saw that face everywhere, for the same God she discovered within was indeed to be found in all creatures and powerfully at work in the events and structures of the world. Mystical or supernatural contemplative prayer trained her inner eye in love and attuned her sensitivity to divine realities incarnated in the real world, and human realities as they truly are, bathed in the light of God.[17]

---

[16]From time to time I also refer to "mystical prayer." I understand the term to be more or less synonymous with infused or supernatural contemplation.

[17]Cf. William Johnston, S.J., *The Inner Eye of Love. Mysticism and Religion* (San Francisco: Harper & Row, 1982), 24–25.

Alumbrados

In the early years of the sixteenth century, especially in the region of Castile, spiritual movements espousing various forms of mental prayer began gaining large numbers of adherents. Members of the Franciscan Order, and particularly friars of *converso* origin, often figured in the formation of groups of devout women and laymen intent upon a life of greater interiority by means of affective prayer. But divergent tendencies among the practitioners of this form of spirituality created tensions among them and eventually led to charges of heresy against certain factions of the *alumbrados,* or "enlightened ones," whose practice of prayer stressed absolute passivity and total abandonment of the soul in all its faculties to God.

In other words, for example, although all the *espirituales* and *experimentados* (the "spiritual" or "experienced" ones, as they were called) believed that the exterior practices of religion were useless without the interior love and conviction that made them meaningful, the *alumbrados* who practiced abandonment were said to have urged the rejection of externals altogether. They were accused of teaching that once illumined through mystical union with God, they would have no need of practices of austerity and penance nor any reason actively to cultivate virtue. In a few cases, such teaching led to the conclusion that the abandoned one was not capable of sin, since his or her only occupation was to remain passively in union with God, turning aside from all distraction, interior and exterior, including the act of moral decision-making. With the will captured by God, no moral consequences accrued to human action. The abandoned one was not capable of *consent* to sin and, therefore, coud not be said to sin. "Abandoned" *alumbrados* shared many assumptions about the spiritual life with other "spirituals," but the exclusivism and exaggeration of their views and practices made the more moderate spirituals (like Francisco de Osuna, Bernardino de Laredo, Teresa of Avila, and John of the Cross) eager to dissociate themselves with what came to be judged an unorthodox spiritual movement.

Monastery and Convent

"Monastery" and "convent" are used regularly and interchangeably in this volume to refer to the dwellings in which Religious Order men and women (in our case, nuns and friars of the Carmelite Order) lived and worked. The Religious were "cloistered" or "enclosed" within them in seclusion from "the world," although the strictness of such enclosure varied widely from house to house (another word commonly in use to speak of monasteries and convents) and was conceived somewhat differently for men than for women.

II. Abbreviations

Unless otherwise noted, throughout this volume quotations from Teresa's writings are taken from the recent three-volume translation of Teresa's collected works (excluding the letters) by Kieran Kavanaugh, O.C.D. and Otilio Rodríguez, O.C.D. [*The Collected Works of St. Teresa of Avila,* 3 vols. (Washington, D.C.: ICS, 1976–85)]. For the sake of simplicity, I cite the title of Teresa's books in an abbreviated form, followed by the chapter and paragraph number as they appear in the Kavanaugh and Rodríguez volumes. (These chapter and paragraph numbers are standard in most editions of Teresa's works.) Thus, *The Book of Her Life = Life; The Book of Her Foundations = Foundations; The Way of Perfection = Way; The Interior Castle = Castle; Spiritual Testimonies = Testimonies,* and so on. For excerpts from Teresa's letters, unless otherwise noted, I cite the two-volume translation by E. Allison Peers [*The Letters of Saint Teresa of Jesus,* 2 vols. (London: Sheed and Ward, 1980)]. Citations will appear as *Letters,* followed by the volume number (I or II) and the page number. All these citations are used with permission of the publishers, for which I express my thanks. I also wish to thank the editor of *Studia Mystica* for permission to make use of a slightly revised version of my article, "A Marriage Well-Arranged: Teresa of Avila and Fray Jerónimo Gracián de la Madre de Dios," *Studia Mystica* vol. XII, n. 1 (Spring, 1989), as part of Chapter 4.

TERESIAN CHRONOLOGY

1486 Teresa's grandfather, the *converso* Juan Sánchez, takes up residence in Avila. Alonso, Teresa's father, was fourteen years old.

1505   Alonso marries doña Catalina del Peso. Two children are born: María and Juan. Catalina dies in September of 1507.

1509   Alonso marries for a second time: doña Beatriz de Ahumada. Hernando is born in 1510; Rodrigo in 1511.

1515   March 28, Teresa de Ahumada born in Avila. Baptized April 4. *The monastery of the Incarnation inaugurated in Avila.*

1517   *Luther's 95 theses.*

1518   Teresa's brother Lorenzo is born. *Magellan begins the circumnavigation of the world. Cortés inaugurates the brutal conquest of Mexico.*

1521   Pedro de Ahumada is born. *Luther, declared a heretic in the previous year, appears before Charles V at the Diet of Worms. Edict branding him an outlaw forces him into hiding at Wartburg. The conquest of Mexico is completed.*

1522   Teresa's brother Jerónimo born. *Zwingli begins reform of the Church in Zurich.*

1527   Augustín de Ahumada born. *The future King of Spain, Philip II, born in Valladolid.*

1528   Juana, Teresa's youngest sibling, is born. In November of the same year, her mother dies.

1531   Teresa's oldest sister, María, is married. Teresa sent to boarding school run by Augustinian nuns. *Zwingli dies. Pizarro begins conquest of Peru. Calvin begins reformist activities in Paris.*

1532–1533   Teresa becomes ill and leaves the convent school. Convalescence in Hortigosa and Castellanos de la Cañada. Teresa decides to enter the convent. In 1534, her brother Hernando leaves for Peru. *Henry VIII declared Head of the Church in England.*

1535   Teresa enters the monastery of the Incarnation in Avila. Her brother Rodrigo leaves for Río de la Plata. *Erasmus of Rotterdam dies the following year. Calvin's* Institutes *(1536) published.*

1537   Teresa makes her religious profession.

1538   Teresa becomes seriously ill and leaves the Incarnation. Reads the *Third Spiritual Alphabet* of Osuna. Begins the practice of the prayer of recollection. Treatments by the *curandera* in Becedas begin in 1539. Returns to the Incarnation in August of that same year. Her resultant paralysis will last three years. Afterwards, her interior life turns lukewarm, and she abandons the practice of mental prayer.

1540   Her brothers Lorenzo and Jerónimo join an expedition to America.

1543   Teresa nurses her father until his death, December 26. The following year she returns to the practice of prayer and begins making rapid, even alarming progress.

1545   *The Council of Trent convenes.*

1546   Two of Teresa's brothers die in battle in Peru. Her brother Augustín sails for America. *Death of Martin Luther.*

1554   Teresa's "conversion" occurs in Lent. Begins to consult Jesuit confessors. *In 1555, Treaty of Augsburg signed, bringing a measure of religious peace to German states.*

1556   Teresa's "spiritual betrothal." *Ignatius Loyola, founder of the Society of Jesus, dies in Rome. Abdication of Charles V in favor of Philip II.*

1557   Teresa resides with doña Guiomar de Ulloa. Consultations about her spiritual experiences with Francis Borgia, S.J. Rodrigo dies in battle in Chile.

1558   Teresa's spiritual experiences attributed to demonic influence. *Elizabeth I ascends throne of England.*

1559   Intellectual visions of Christ *(Life,* 27:2). *Publication in Spain of the Inquisitor Valdés' Index of forbidden reading, and other strict measures aimed at sealing Spain off from Protestant influence.*

1560   Teresa and her counselors continue to struggle over her unusual spiritual experiences. Transverberation (spiritual wounding of the heart). Imaginative visions of Christ. Con-

sultations with Pedro de Alcántara. Vision of hell. First
plans for a reformed convent laid out. First extant version
of an account of her spiritual life written for the Dominican Ibáñez.

1560– Secret preparations under way for first reformed convent,
1562   St. Joseph's in Avila. Teresa meets María de Yepes at the
home of doña Luisa de la Cerda and modifies her plans
for reform. While staying in Toledo, she renews acquaintance with García de Toledo. St. Joseph's is inaugurated
in August of 1562. Lawsuits regarding the new convent
mount. A version of *The Book of Her Life* is completed
in 1562. Teresa enters St. Joseph's in December, 1562. She
begins writing *The Way of Perfection*. In the next year,
John of the Cross receives the Carmelite habit in Medina
del Campo. Teresa writes the *Constitutions* for her reform.
Council of Trent ends, 1563.

1564   First professions of four nuns at St. Joseph's. *Calvin dies
in Geneva.*

1565   Teresa completes the final version of *Life*. Her brother Hernando dies in Colombia.

1566   Teresa composes the first version of *Meditations on the
Song of Songs*. Visit to St. Joseph's by Alonso Maldonado,
Franciscan missionary to Mexico, during which Teresa experiences an increase in apostolic zeal. Sometime during
1562–66, first version (perhaps also the second) of *The Way
of Perfection* also completed. *Reports of French Calvinist
iconoclasm circulate widely in Spain.*

1567   Carmelite General Rubeo visits Avila. Permission to found
other reformed convents granted. In August, Teresa es-
tablishes a discalced monastery in Medina del Campo.
John of the Cross is persuaded to join the reform movement. Perhaps second version of *Way* also completed in
this year.

1568   Foundations in Malagón and Valladolid. *Life* sent to Juan
de Avila for his evaluation. In November, first convent
for friars established in Duruelo. *Moorish uprisings in
Granada.*

1569   Foundation in Toledo. In Pastrana, foundations for women and for men are also made. Teresa composes *Soliloquies.*

1570   Foundation in Salamanca. The discalced friars establish a college at the University of Alcalá de Henares. *Elizabeth I excommunicated by Pius V.*

1571   Foundation in Alba de Tormes. Against her will, Teresa becomes Prioress of the Incarnation. *Defeat of Turkish armada at Lepanto.*

1572   Teresa's "spiritual matrimony" *(Testimonies,* 31). John of the Cross is confessor at the Incarnation. She writes *Response to a Spiritual Challenge.* Jerónimo Gracián receives Carmelite habit in Pastrana. *Revolt against Spanish domination in the Low Countries. St. Bartholomew's Eve Massacre of French Huguenots in Paris.*

1573   Teresa begins recording history of her monasteries in *Foundations.* The discalced friars make foundations in Seville, Granada, and La Peñuela. *Turkish conquest of Cyprus.*

1574   Foundation in Segovia. The second version of *Song* completed. The Teresian friars establish a convent in Almodóvar del Campo. Teresa's term as Prioress of the Incarnation expires.

1575   Foundations in Beas and Seville. In Beas, Teresa meets Gracián for the first time. Teresa authorizes a foundation in Caravaca (completed the following year). In Seville, accusations against her are made to the Inquisition. Opposition to her reform mounts. Teresa is ordered to retire to a convent of her own choosing and desist in the work of the foundations. Her brother Lorenzo returns from America with his children.

1576   Teresa examined by the Inquisition. She composes two depositions in her own defense *(Testimonies,* 58, 59). Adds several chapters to *Foundations.* Teresa's portrait painted in Seville by Fray Juan de la Miseria. Writes *On Making the Visitation.*

1577   She writes *A Satirical Critique* and *The Interior Castle.* John of the Cross taken prisoner by opponents of the reform. With Teresa's remote supervision, Caravaca foundation made by Ana de San Alberto. Arrival in Madrid of a new papal nuncio, Felipe Sega, suspicious of Teresa and her work.

1578   John of the Cross escapes from prison in Toldeo. Although Teresa warns against the move, aware that it will be perceived as defiant, an assembly (Chapter) of the discalced friars held at Almodóvar. The papal nuncio annuls all decisions taken at the Chapter. The Carmelite General Rubeo dies.

1579   Teresa begins travelling again.

1580   Foundation at Villanueva de la Jara. Teresa becomes seriously ill in Toledo. In June, papal permission granted for the discalced to form a Province separate from the calced. Teresa travels to Valladolid where she suffers a relapse. Foundation in Palencia.

1581   First official Chapter of the discalced at Alcalá. Gracián elected first Provincial. Foundation in Soria.

1582   Teresa leaves Avila for the last time. John of the Cross and Ana de Jesús establish a discalced convent in Granada. Teresa founds in Burgos. Travelling through Palencia, Valladolid, and Medina, Teresa arrives in Alba de Tormes in late September. Seriously ill at her arrival, she dies on October 4 (the next day became October 15, owing to the introduction of the Gregorian calendar. Teresa's feastday celebrated on this new date).

1614   Beatification of Teresa of Avila.

1622   Canonization.

1970   Declared a Doctor of the Church by Pope Paul VI.

1

Teresa of Avila[1] in Context

A new monastery and a new life

In the year of our Lord, 1515, the holy sacrifice of the Mass was celebrated for the first time in a newly constructed monastery located outside the walls of Avila on the broad plains of the Ajates Valley. The building, although austere, was spacious, its site and size a welcome change for the Carmelite *beatas* who were to dwell there and adopt the quiet decorum of the regular life. Their former residence had been a cramped house on a busy street with insufficient space for an infirmary, refectory, or proper dormitory. They had had no garden either, and their choir was so exposed to the public thoroughfare that noisy (and nosy) passersby were a constant annoyance. With gratitude and relief, then, the *Te Deum* was intoned at Santa María de la Encarnación on the fourth day of April in the City of the Knights.

On the same day, inside the walls of Avila in the parish church of St. John, the third child and first daughter of don Alonso Sánchez de Cepeda and Beatriz de Ahumada[2] was reborn in the waters

[1]"Teresa of Avila" is the name by which she is best known in the English-speaking world. Her family name was Teresa de Ahumada. As a discalced nun, she took the name Teresa de Jesús, renouncing her family name in the egalitarian spirit which characterized the reform. See Juan Bosco, "A la recuperación de un nombre perdido: Teresa de Jesús," *Monte Carmelo* 90 (1982): 266–304.

[2]Beatriz (1495?–1528?) was Alonso's second wife. Catalina del Peso y Henao was his first. She bore two children and died in 1507. Alonso (1480?–1543) was the son of a wealthy Toledan merchant. Teresa described her parents in *Life*, 1. See José Gómez-Menor Fuentes, *El linaje familiar de Santa Teresa de Jesús y San Juan de la Cruz* (Toledo, 1970); Teófanes Egido, "The Historical Setting of Saint Teresa," *Carmelite Studies* 1 (1980), tr. Steven Payne and Michael Dodd: 122–180 (hereafter, "Historical Setting"); Efrén de la Madre de Dios and Otger Steggink, *Tiempo y vida de Santa Teresa* (Madrid: BAC, 1977), 7–20 (hereafter, *Tiempo y vida*).

33

of baptism and given the name of no known Christian saint, Teresa. Nearly twenty-one years later she would become a nun; the monastery she would enter was the Incarnation.[3]

The state of convent life

The life of the monastery as Teresa de Ahumada found it upon her entry in 1535 was hardly as its first inhabitants had envisioned. They had hoped their new surroundings would permit the serene unfolding of a strict monastic regimen. But they were soon swamped with scores of applicants who swelled the house to capacity, and beyond. The crush of entrants put the convent under severe economic strain, but the house continued to accept practically everyone who came. By the time Teresa arrived, as many as 180 women had crowded in.[4] And although authentic religious aspirations and fidelity to the monastic rule could be found in groups of nuns among the multitude, in general the convent's life of piety and community was in some disarray.

Many young women of Avila's nobility[5] were placed in the Incarnation as a solution to the perennial problem of situating daughters in life. When these young ladies entered the convent, many brought with them and maintained the trappings of their life in the world, including sometimes a small entourage of relatives, friends, maidservants, cooks, and the like. The size and location of their cells often depended on their secular social standing. The distribution of "executive suites" could occasion internal wrangling; nuns did not shrink from loudly defending their injured honor if assigned too small, too drafty, or too unlovely a place to live while they served God.[6] Cells could also be

[3]Nicolás González y González, *El monasterio de la Encarnación de Avila*, 2 vols. (Avila, 1976) (hereafter, *Encarnación); Otger Steggink, *Arraigo e innovación en Teresa de Jesús* (Madrid: BAC Minor, 1976), 51–65 (hereafter, *Arraigo*).

[4]*Arraigo*, 51 and n. 35. Teresa reported the total number of nuns as 180, *Letters* II, 835–36; the *Libro de la Provincia de Castilla* noted that in 1567 there were 144 nuns *de velo* (professed choir nuns), even though the monastery's sustainable capacity was only 60. How many lay sisters also lived there the report does not say.

[5]The report of the Carmelite General Rubeo's official visit to the province of Castile, cited in *Arraigo*, 59–60, reveals the family names of the daughters of nearly every leading family in Avila.

[6]A dispute of this kind was settled by the intervention of one Miguel Torres, S.J., in 1550. See *Encarnación*, vol. 1, 197–98.

bought and sold; thus the wealthiest nuns inhabited the best rooms, and the poorest slept in the common dormitory. Many of the convent's noble ladies could look to well-off relations for gifts of food or money to buy it, warm clothing and other comforts when conditions at the Incarnation grew too difficult to bear. Or they could simply leave, to be taken care of for a time at home, especially when they became infirm.

The nuns could also receive and dispose of revenues from property. Teresa, for example, received an income of this kind and because of it was able to underwrite convent celebrations of the feast of St. Joseph. Nuns regularly left the Incarnation for short or extended periods on missions to seek alms for the common needs of the convent. Some were also summoned, as Teresa habitually was, to spend time with married laywomen of noble houses, acting as companions, confidantes, and showpieces. These visits, along with convent parlor conversations with relatives and friends, were often the source of increased patronage or other forms of generosity, which the convent economy, as well as its social prestige, depended heavily upon. When such comings and goings were denounced and attempts made to regulate them more strictly, nuns who wanted them to continue could have been, and sometimes were, motivated by a concern for the common welfare—fewer visits, fewer alms. Opposing reforms was not always a sign of laxity.[7]

Religious observance at the Incarnation strained under the weight of such inequity. The resentment, bickering, and physical deprivation (some nuns were actually starving) associated with overcrowding, aggravated by the highly stratified social class structure of the "world" transplanted with all its blind, self-preservative instincts into the convent confines, sapped the life of the community. The Castilian obsession with lineage, honor, and wealth complicated the style and quality of religious life, and much of the blame for whatever tepidity was to be found at the Incarnation may be laid at the feet of this preoccupation.

Men also frequented the convent with what some regarded as alarming regularity. These were relatives and friends seeking good counsel, town dandies flirting with attractive nuns under cover

---

[7] *Encarnación*, vol. 1, 201; *Arraigo*, 55–57. For Teresa's opinion of her own frequent good will missions among the nobility, see *Life*, 32:9.

of pious conversation, priests hearing confessions, and religious
superiors carrying out prescribed visitations. Their easy access to
the nuns, even when entirely innocent, caused scandal among the
pious outside the convent walls, needlessly disturbed the devout
within, and encumbered the good governance of an already un-
wieldy house.[8]

The choice of religious life

Such was the convent Teresa entered alone and on the sly early
in the morning of the Feast of All Souls, November 2, 1535. Her
father, a strict man and, in her words, a devout Christian who
fairly adored her and who was much loved by her in return, had
stoutly opposed her entry. It nearly killed her, she said, to defy
him.[9]

Nothing is known for certain of don Alonso's own plans for
his daughter or why he was at first intransigent about Teresa's
vocation to the religious life. Perhaps he felt simply that, twice
a widower with most of his children grown and gone, he could
not do without her. Perhaps he was arranging a good marriage
for her.[10] Or perhaps he shared the view that Teresa herself would
later echo, that even though the vocation to the vowed life was
in principle a safer way to salvation than life in the world, worldly
entanglements, sometimes so necessary for a convent's survival,
could place a devout young woman's virtue, even her salvation,
in mortal jeopardy.[11] And Teresa's virtue was by no means an
indifferent thing to Alonso Sánchez de Cepeda.

Just how zealously he regarded it may be seen from an example
in Teresa's adolescence. In her autobiography she alludes to an
apparently compromising incident with a male cousin some four
years before her clandestine entry into Carmel. Her behavior with
this man, and the general displeasure don Alonso felt toward her

[8]For first-hand reports of these and other complaints by Incarnation nuns, see Otger Steggink, *La reforma del Carmelo español: La visita canónica del general Rubeo y su encuentro
con Santa Teresa (1566–1567)* (Rome: Institutum Carmelitanum, 1965), 289–311 (hereafter,
La reforma).

[9]*Life*, 3:7; 4:1.

[10]Teresa did allude to a possible marriage negotiation when she recounted the tale of her
indiscreet behavior with a relative, *Life*, 2:9.

[11]*Life*, 7:5, for example.

increasing intimacy with a female relative of whose frivolity he disapproved, led him to place Teresa in a convent boarding school and out of harm's way. How serious these incidents were we cannot tell, for Teresa was stingy with the details; but in the context of the rules that governed Teresa's world, it is certain that her family's honor was very much at stake.[12]

Don Alonso dissimulated the reason for packing Teresa off so that the world would not guess at the family's embarrassment.[13] Teresa's mother was dead, her older sister had married, and only males remained in the household. No suitable female supervision was avilable at home. Any good father would have seen to it that a young and very attractive daughter was shielded from the occasions for dishonor such a situation entailed. But whatever lay in fact behind Teresa's near dishonor, the swiftness of her father's reaction may well have shocked her into considering the hard reality that a woman in Castilian society was not a free agent and that every action she took or left undone would be weighed and measured precisely, enhancing or forever tarnishing her name and that of her family. That experience taught her never-to-be-forgotten lessons about parental vigilance, good companionship, and the value of healthy pastimes. It was also her first real and bruising run-in with the tyranny of honor.

From her account of her formative years, it seems that Teresa did not find *romance* distasteful; it was *marriage* she "feared."[14] Perhaps her reluctance was rooted in simple observation: her mother had died at the age of thirty-three after bearing ten children. By the time Teresa was astute enough to notice such things, Beatriz's beauty had faded; she was, in Teresa's description of her, old before her time.[15] She had been a good wife, except, according to Teresa, for having indulged her imagination and desire in the furtive reading of romantic novels and racy poems of chivalry denounced by Catholic preachers and emphatically forbidden by her spouse.

In fact, deceiving don Alonso became a regular activity of both mother and daughter. Teresa later wished they hadn't wasted their

---

[12]*Life*, 2:7.

[13]*Life*, 2:6.

[14]*Life*, 3:2.

[15]*Life*, 1:2; *Tiempo y vida*, 36–41.

time on what she had come to regard as trashy books; yet she excused her mother, pointing out that the practice never interfered with Beatriz' primary obligations. The more mature Teresa was not blind to the stifling effects of an ideology of female behavior that confined women imaginatively and physically to the world of the household and all but encouraged deceit on the part of wives. She once even congratulated the nuns of her first reform convent, St. Joseph, on having been delivered, by virtue of their vocation, from such "subjection."[16]

Sixteenth-century marriage manuals usually described a wife's role in marriage as ideally "separate but equal" to the husband's.[17] But they invariably went on to spell out the duties, attitudes, and virtues proper to the married Christian woman in terms that, in effect, loaded onto her shoulders practically the entire responsibility for the marriage's success. The wife was to oversee the household, raise the children, set good example, convert the husband from evil ways to good if necessary, and remain herself absolutely above reproach in everything touching her own and her husband's honor. At the same time, a wife was considered to be something of a child, always in need of basic instruction. More than any other virtue, what was admired in the perfect wife was silence and submission to her husband. According to moralists, she was not even to have a say in the selection of friends; all socializing was to be regulated by her husband's wishes.

Marriage was surely not always the way books said it should be, and doubtlessly many wives found their way around the countless prohibitions and demands which the ideals of Castilian Christian culture imposed. One notion, however, could not easily be circumvented. Marriage was still generally regarded as a second-class Christian road to salvation. Bringing little Christians into the world was a worthy occupation, but, as sexual intercourse was invariably required, marriage and its debt were generally treated in an ambivalent spirit.[18] Moreover, frequent childbirth, although

---

[16]*Life*, 2:1; *Way*, 26:4.

[17]Among the most widely read manuals were Juan Luis Vives, *Institutio Foeminae Christianae* (1523); Pedro de Luxán, *Coloquios matrimoniales* (1550); and Fray Luis de León, *La perfecta casada* (1583). Innumerable sermons and tracts popularized such teachings.

[18]For example, echoing classical and Christian themes, Juan Luis Vives warned that even licit intercourse is dangerous. In *De officio mariti* (1528), he conceded that it is better to marry than to burn, but that one should take care not to become addicted to the remedy.

greatly benefiting the Christian commonwealth by populating it with new citizens, was exceedingly dangerous to women's health. Perhaps Teresa had seen too much of the ills attendant upon frequent pregnancy and childbirth; perhaps she did not wish to grow old prematurely as her own mother had done; perhaps she did not wish to be confined to the house, forbidden access to her pastimes or to friends of her own choosing. She referred to some of these marital realities in her works but never linked them explicitly to her own reasons for fearing the married state at the time of her life when she was debating the relative merits of the choices available to her.

Thus, it is impossible to say with certainty what lay behind Teresa's terse admission of repugnance in Chapter 3 of her autobiography. We do know, however, that for a long time she was also far from sanguine about the other avenue open to her. Teresa knew that the religious life, even in relatively comfortable houses, still involved hardship. She had seen up close the authentic religious observance of the nuns at the convent school to which her father had bundled her off, the Augustinian house of Our Lady of Grace, and had found the rigors practiced by its inmates altogether excessive. Even though she grew to like those earnest women, admired their virtue, and led a reasonably devout spiritual life, she remained "strongly against" becoming one of them. In fact, she felt such "antagonism" toward religious life that she "asked God not to give [her] this vocation."[19]

An illness (the first of many she suffered in her life) forced her to leave the school. During her recuperation, she stayed for a few days with a pious uncle who asked her to read devotional works aloud to him. She complied even though she didn't find them interesting. The reading sessions, however dull, served to revive memories of her early childhood fervor. She remembered the pious little girl with dreams of adventure who read saints' lives and decided to run away to Moorish territory to obtain a heroic destiny, martyrdom at the hands of the infidel, but who found to her dismay that "having parents" was an obstacle even a future saint could not avoid. (Put off in that ambition, she and her brothers had taken instead to the game of hermits and nuns right

---

[19]*Life,* 2:8; 3:1-2.

in their own back yard.)[20] In the silence of her reclusive uncle's house, Teresa felt drawn again to that childish but generous piety but was repulsed by the thought that religious life would entail relinquishing her "pleasures." For three months, her indecision preoccupied her.

Her resolution to become a nun seems finally to have been motivated by a consideration of the long run—the religious state was held by all to be "the best and safest." To remain as she was, or eventually to marry, carried no certainty of salvation. To become a nun could be a ticket to heaven. The choice may have been repugnant, but its logic was compelling to a young woman raised in a devout household and in a world in which concern for one's salvation was equalled only by concern for one's reputation.[21] Once Teresa decided, nothing stood in her way. Alonso gradually reconciled himself to losing her; a year after her entry, he signed her dowry papers, enabling her to receive the habit of the Order of Our Lady. She was professed the following year, November 3, 1537.

A life of prayer

In her first few months in the Incarnation, Teresa was happier than she had expected to be. The other nuns seemed to like her, and she could not complain about her accommodations. As a daughter of the minor (if feigned) nobility, she received a two-level cell with facilities for cooking, space enough for gatherings of friends and relatives, an oratory, and a view of the valley. She was also able freely to indulge her passion for reading and her delight in parlor conversation. But her contentment had more to do, she insisted, with her discovery that God rewards the soul that strives and struggles and, in the end, forces itself to do God's will.[22] She had made, she knew, the right choice after all. Happy though she was, forcing herself to do God's will exacted a price. In the fall of 1538, her health broke down dramatically. Because the local physicians were at a loss to treat her, don Alonso removed the desperately ill Teresa first to the country village of

---

[20]*Life*, 1:4-6.

[21]According to Teresa, her decision was greatly influenced by her reading of the letters of the biblical scholar and hermit-monk Jerome (c. 342–420).

[22]*Life*, 4:2.

Castellanos de la Cañada, then to mountainous Becedas where she was to undergo a cure at the hands of a famous local *curandera,* or healer.[23]

At Castellanos she rested for a few months and once again had an opportunity to read more of the pious books her devout uncle Pedro gave her. Among them was the *Tercer abecedario espiritual (Third Spiritual Alphabet)* by the Franciscan Francisco de Osuna, a book that was meant to introduce devout souls to the method of prayer known as interior recollection. From Teresa's own testimony we know it was Osuna who, for all practical purposes, taught her how to pray.[24] For the convalescing young nun, her reading of the *Alphabet* was a watershed. Although she had long since abandoned the "servile fear"[25] that once characterized her relations with God, nothing in her convent experience had prepared her for the prayer Osuna endeavored to explain in the fat volume Pedro Sánchez placed in her hands.

Osuna spoke of prayer as intimacy, friendship with God, a relationship closer and more stable than the natural links between a mother and her child. By means of this prayer of friendship, the soul is recreated as it moves by degrees into a total, transforming union with a lover God. Salvation and paradise are not put off until after death but can be had in great measure in this life, in the center of the human soul where God dwells waiting. The Christian need only enter that secret place within, leaving behind all that is not God, "recollecting" the senses and the powers

[23]Often translated into English as "quack," a *curandero* was instead a healer who relied on natural remedies. *Curanderos* often had medical training, especially true of *morisco* (of Moorish descent) healers. Sometimes *curanderos* were the only medical assistance available. See Luis García Ballester, *Los moriscos y la medicina. Un capítulo de la medicina y las ciencias marginadas en la España del siglo XVI* (Barcelona: Editorial Labor, 1984). My thanks to Prof. Ellen G. Friedman of Boston College for this reference. Teresa had a broken arm bone set by another healer in 1578. She complained that the treatment had "cost her a great deal" in both senses of that expression (the bone never healed properly and her arm was, for all practical purposes, useless for the rest of her life). See *Letters* II, 561.

[24]*Life,* 4:7. For Francisco de Osuna, O.F.M. (1497-1540?), see Fidele de Ros, O.F.M., *Un Maître de Sainte Thérèse, le Père François D'Osuna* (Paris, 1936) and *Tiempo y vida,* nn. 320-24, 375-384. A good English translation, with an excellent introduction, is Francisco de Osuna, *The Third Spiritual Alphabet,* tr. Mary E. Giles (New York: Paulist, 1981). Osuna was not the only "book teacher" Teresa had. She also read, among many other works, Catherine of Siena's *Dialogues* and Bernardino de Laredo's *Subida del Monte Sión* (which she used to explain her manner of prayer to her early counselors).

[25]*Life,* 3:6.

of the soul and, above all, focusing the will upon its one desire in a gaze of love. The end result should be nothing less than the transformation of reality, a complete upending of human perspectives and expectations, a new person living on a new plane of existence.[26]

The *Alphabet* describes the early stages of a progressive adventure of the spirit. Teresa discovered that although she had never heard much of what she was reading, not all of it came as a surprise. The volume was, it seems, a book that struck her unmistakably as an echo of her own desire, and she devoured it. The copy she used is so heavily marked up with arrows, little pointing hands, and repeated underscorings that entire passages are difficult to make out today.[27] Teresa soon began repeating its teaching to her friends; later in her spiritual journey, she would adapt and transcend its wisdom as she formulated her own teachings on prayer and the Christian life.

Meanwhile, the cure at Becedas had not gone well. Indeed, everyone mistook the frightening cataleptic condition into which she had fallen for death; when she regained consciousness, she found burial wax on her eyelids. At the Incarnation, a freshly dug grave awaited. She was returned to her monastery a paralyzed invalid, a bag of skin and bones.[28] As she slowly recovered in the convent infirmary, she continued to "experience prayer" and acquire a measure of virtue such that, according to her account in *Life,* others were continually edified by her attitudes and conduct, often setting out on a more virtuous path as a result of Teresa's example and exhortations. But once back on her feet and fully reintegrated into the monastic routine (her rehabilitation took a full three years), Teresa let her hold on mental prayer relax.[29]

Others benefited by her reading and her former dedication to recollection; her own father learned from her to pray that way, quickly becoming not merely devout but truly holy. Teresa, however, recited only vocal prayers, observed religious rituals, and

---

[26]For the many varieties and practitioners of this important form of prayer in sixteenth- and seventeenth-century Spain, see Melquidiades Andrés Martín, *Los recogidos: nueva visión de la mística española (1500–1700)* (Madrid: FUE, 1976).

[27]The volume may be seen today at the Incarnation in Avila.

[28]*Tiempo y vida,* 78–81.

[29]*Life,* 5:7; 6:2; 7:13.

performed her monastic duties well, neglecting the prayer of recollection. To her little group of disciples she made convincing excuses for the failure to practice what she so successfully preached, but when she wrote *Life,* she was candid about her facility for deceiving others so as not to lose their esteem. She also made no excuses for herself; her tepidity was the direct result of a false humility about her unworthiness for lofty graces and of her participation in the "open" style of life at the Incarnation, characterized by frivolous conversation, "friendships and attachments," and frequent visits from outsiders.

The gregarious young Teresa knew early on that her personality was a captivating one, and she always relished the rewards of popularity and natural leadership. As a result, she admitted, she was unable to resist for long the allure of the "freedoms" available in the Incarnation. She also reported that in the process of justifying to herself her own bad inclinations, she talked a number of other nuns into believing that in such pastimes no real harm was done.[30]

In fact, the Incarnation was not yet under strict enclosure. Technically, the comings and goings of the nuns and their friends did not constitute a sinful infraction of the rule.[31] But Teresa's conscience was not numb. Gradually, she came to experience herself as a battlefield upon which a great campaign was under way. In *Life* she recorded that Christ appeared to her to express his displeasure with the mediocre turn her religious life was taking.[32] The devil, she said, fought back hard, using all his wiles to persuade her that the vision of Christ had been an illusion and that her honor was in no way compromised by the less than serious path she had taken.[33] An older nun (one of several relatives in the Incaration) tried to counsel her about her mediocrity, but Ter-

[30]*Life,* 7:1-7; 10-13.

[31]*Arraigo,* 56–58. All female religious houses were eventually required, per order of the Council of Trent and, later, Pope Pius V, to enact rigorous enclosure, regardless of whether the women who lived in them felt called to such a cloistered vocation. Even before the promulgation of these decrees, however, Teresa had already enjoined a strict cloister upon the discalced nuns as a measure to ensure the solitude and silence she believed necessary for contemplation and to protect their spiritual liberty from the often-intrusive demands of entangling family obligations and dynastic concerns.

[32]*Life,* 7:6.

[33]*Life,* 7:7.

esa, annoyed with what she considered scandalized overreaction on her benefactor's part, brushed her off.[34] But when one day, as if from nowhere, a "nasty" toad darted across her path, an unnerved Teresa took it as a warning.[35] Meanwhile, lenient confessors told her she was just being scrupulous, that everything was fine.[36]

Thus, Teresa continued to drift until shortly after her father's death late in 1543. She had been making her confessions to Alonso's Dominican priest, "a very learned man."[37] And although she did not break off her flirtation with the "occasions of sin," Teresa did begin again, at his suggestion, to pray. She would vacillate for twenty years more, following what she perceived to be an interior call to contemplation on the one hand and "the world" on the other. During this time, the practice of prayer was hard, almost impossible; her life, she confessed, was an enormous burden. But she did not abandon prayer altogether ever again, and she experienced God's favor in spite of her irresolution.[38]

Although often cited as the great turning point of Teresa's contemplative career, the "conversion" Teresa experienced during the Lenten observance of 1554 was in fact only one of a series of emotional episodes that seemed to signal the fruition of a twenty-year period of uneven but steady conversion and spiritual maturation.[39] Entering the Incarnation's oratory one day, she was brought up short by an image of a "much wounded Christ" that the nuns had borrowed for the observance of the festival. The sight of it "utterly distressed" Teresa. Newly and sharply aware of the benefit of Christ and her own off-again, on-again response to divine love, her "heart broke." She threw herself down before the image, begging that "once and for all" Christ strengthen

[34]*Life*, 7:9.

[35]*Life*, 7:8.

[36]Teresa's life-long preoccupation with the harm lenient or ignorant confessors do to the spiritual lives and psyches of their penitents began at this time. She learned only slowly and through painful experience about the "occasions of sin" and how necessary it is to avoid them in order to progress in virtue. See for example *Life*, 6:4; 7:6-9.

[37]Vincente Barrón, O.P. *Life*, 7:16-17; 19:12.

[38]*Life*, 7:17.

[39]*Life*, 9:1-3. The other memorable events were a powerful reading of a passage from Augustine's *Confessions*, *Life*, 9:7-8; and, somewhat later, a terrifying vision of herself and other souls in hell, *Life*, 32:1-5.

her resolve, and she told him she would not rise from the spot until he heard her. Teresa believed her prayers had been heard; from that day forward, she said, she "went on improving."

Unusual mystical phenomena, such as intellectual visions of Christ, began to punctuate her periods of devotion, causing her confessors and counselors no small concern. Some harbored doubts about their authenticity; others rejected them outright as the doings of Satan. Teresa suffered mightily as a result, torn between trusting her own strong inclination to believe that the phenomena were of God and the unnerving insistence of her confessors that she was the devil's dupe.[40] The help of certain spiritually adept Jesuits from the new college of San Gil in Avila; a favorable verdict on her mystical experiences from the famed Franciscan holy man, Pedro de Alcántara; the prudent counsel of theologians like the Dominicans Báñez and Ibáñez, and the Jesuit Francis Borgia; and Teresa's own growing capacity for spiritual discernment, coupled with her faith that God would not permit her to be deceived, all helped eventually to set her inner life on a freer and more fruitful course.[41]

Still, as was the case with numerous holy women and men of the period, accusations of self-delusion and demonic influence would accompany Teresa throughout her subsequent career as mystic, reformer, teacher, and founder.[42] Time and again she would have to seek out influential, experienced, and educated men to testify to the authenticity of her experiences and to the orthodoxy of the truth she learned from them and which she taught in her books. She would need their expertise to help her formulate the content of her experiences in acceptable terms; and she would need the seal of their authoritative approval because "the times were rough ones" for all devout persons—and for women visionaries and activists, they were rougher still.[43]

[40]For Teresa's account of her troubles with skeptical confessors, see *Life*, 23–26, and Chapter 2 of this volume.

[41]See *Life*, 24:3; 27:16-20; 30:1-7. Pedro de Alcántara's influence on Teresa with respect to the poverty of the first discalced foundation was decisive. See his stern letter to Teresa, 14 April, 1562, cited in A. Barrado, *Estudios sobre San Pedro de Alcántara* (Madrid, 1962), 191–93. In *Life*, 35:4, Teresa summarized her own defiant formulation of the matter.

[42]For inquisitorial interest in the nun of Avila, see Enrique Llamas Martínez, *Santa Teresa de Jesús y la Inquisición española* (Madrid: CSIC, 1972); hereafter, *La Inquisición española*.

[43]*Life*, 33:5, my translation. In the original: *"andavan los tiempos recios"* (these were difficult days, a dangerous period, a bad time). The context is a threat Teresa received about

Reformer of Carmel

As intent as she was upon the interior life, Teresa was by no means isolated from the turbulent events of her day. Seven of her brothers were in America, warring and dying with the *conquistadores* and making their fortunes.[44] She followed the political scene with a keen eye and showed herself a pacifist.[45] She knew about the French Calvinist "Lutherans" (her word for all Protestants) and about the military efforts, which she considered wrong-headed and futile, to reverse the "scourge of heresy" they represented.[46] At home, she felt keenly the sweeping prohibitions of an Index of forbidden books, prepared and promulgated in 1559 under the supervision of the Inquisitor Valdés, and chafed under the limitations it placed on her habit of self-education through voracious reading.[47] At the same time, she was wary of *alumbrados,* and crypto-Protestants; circumspect too about the claims of some *beatas,* since they could, as public opinion and certain inquisitorial processes had it, mislead even the learned, opening the door to the devil and damnation to anyone who ventured near.[48]

Distinguishing the heterodox from the orthodox among the proliferating prayer cells and new spiritual reform movements in sixteenth-century Castile was no easy task. It was complicated all the more by the hostility and suspicion shown by the general populace and the authorities toward the participation of so many *conversos* and women in them.[49] Teresa was a woman, the granddaughter of a Toledan merchant who had judaized and been reconciled by the Inquisition. The utmost discernment and pru-

---

trouble with the Inquisition over revelations and the founding of the first reformed convent. Kavanaugh and Rodríguez translate the phrase to refer not to the atmosphere or times but to Teresa and her companions: "Some persons came to me with great fear to tell me *we were in trouble . . .* " (my emphasis).

[44]Only two returned. See Manuel Polit, *La familia de Santa Teresa en América* (Freiburg, 1905).

[45]*Letters* II, 595–98; 676–78.

[46]*Way,* 1:1-3; 3:1-2.

[47]*Life,* 26:5. Teresa was one of a tiny percentage of Spanish women who could read.

[48]*Life,* 23:2; 26:5; 28:14.

[49]It should be noted, however, that no documentary evidence exists that the Inquisition ever took special note of Teresa's *converso* background in its deliberations about her writings, her behavior, and the goings-on in her foundations.

dence were needed if she wished to proceed untouched. For beginning around 1560, her aim was no longer confined to praying in a particular way herself, plumbing the depths of the mystical realm alone, or with a prayer group, in the confines of her Incarnation cell. She wished to establish a new, small house where other nuns could be taught to do the same, where they could, by their lives of prayer, contribute positively not only to the vigor of the Order but also to the health of the Christian Church.

Reformist ideas were probably on Teresa's mind earlier, but the plan to found a convent was hatched, albeit tentatively, during an afternoon of earnest conversation among a few nuns and laywomen who had been meeting periodically in Teresa's cell to discuss prayer and the religious life.[50] Although these reform-minded women recognized that there was great virtue to be found among nuns in the overcrowded Incarnation, they yearned for a more propitious environment in which to carry on an experiment in prayer and communal living, patterned to some extent upon other discalced ("shoe-less") movements they had notice of, and influenced as well by the general reform enthusiasm which had found a home in the city of Avila.[51]

Fortified by Christ's command to carry out the group's ideas in spite of the serious objections of some of her superiors and confessors, Teresa assumed leadership of the project. By 1562, she had managed to maneuver her way through the vacillations of her superiors in the Order, the outraged opposition of town officials, the threat of withheld absolution, the red tape of Rome, and the timidity of a few of her supporters to open a small house in the city of Avila named for her favorite, St. Joseph.[52]

By the end of her days, she would establish directly or indirectly seventeen such religious houses for women. She would write her spiritual autobiography *(The Book of Her Life);* compile a num-

[50]*Life,* 32:10; *Tiempo y vida,* 134–35. Several of Teresa's kinswomen were involved in the initial discussions, and some eventually joined St. Joseph's.

[51]The group probably had Franciscan discalced nuns in mind. Significantly, in the midst of the difficulties of her own foundation, Teresa has a vision of St. Clare, who encouraged her to carry on. *Life,* 33:13. Teresa was especially devoted to this early Franciscan as a model of poverty and female spirituality. See *Way* 2:8; *Life,* 33:13. Teresa's followers were to wear *alparagatos,* or hemp sandals, instead of leather shoes. She discouraged them from actually going barefoot.

[52]*Life,* 6:6, 8. Teresa believed that this saint had cured her of the serious illness she contracted after entering the Incarnation. Several discalced monasteries were given his name.

ber of revealing personal notes and prayers *(Spiritual Testimonies* and *Soliloquies); * redact legislation for the discalced movement *(Constitutions* and *On Making the Visitation);* and author several books aimed at educating her followers about the meaning of their form of religious life and the way to achieve perfection within it *(The Way of Perfection),* the kind of prayer they were expected to practice and the various moments of the life of contemplation *(The Interior Castle, Meditations on the Song of Songs),* and the history of the foundations in which she had had a hand *(The Book of Her Foundations).* Day-to-day convent life prompted the writing of numerous poems and song lyrics and other pieces for entertainment and edification *(Poetry, A Satirical Critique, Response to a Spiritual Challenge).*[53]

She wrote hundreds of letters, to the king, the pope, bishops, businessmen, religious superiors and confessors, other nuns, noblemen and women, family members, and friends.[54] During the last twenty years of her life, she also travelled constantly to establish new convents, consult with collaborators, and beg for financial assistance; she visited the houses to supervise their progress and to encourage, teach, and discipline the sisters and daughters who were working with her in the effort to restructure Carmelite religious life.[55] Along the way, she was hailed as a saint and miracle worker. With equal enthusiasm, she was denigrated as a fraud: contumacious, disobedient, and self-deluded, a silly and presumptuous woman who wanted to teach men when it was her place to be taught by them. Her writings and her behavior were delated to the Inquisiton (she was eventually exonerated) and denounced at the prestigious University of Salamanca by a theologian angry that so many were being duped because of her.

[53]For a thorough introduction to all Teresa's works, see A. Barrientos, ed., *Introducción a la lectura de Santa Teresa* (Madrid: Editorial de Espiritualidad, 1978) (hereafter, *Introducción a la lectura).* See also the introductions by Kieran Kavanaugh to the three-volume *Collected Works.*

[54]Teresa may have written as many as 20,000 letters, only a small fraction of which are extant. See the introduction to Teresa's letters by Luis Rodríguez Martínez and Teófanes Egido in *Introducción a la lectura,* 427–472. See also their introduction to Santa Teresa de Jesús, *Epistolario* (Madrid: Editorial de Espiritualidad, 1984), 2nd ed., 10–15.

[55]Teresa was reportedly referred to with angry displeasure as a *"monja andariaga,"* a wandering nun, by the papal nuncio to the Spanish court, Felipe Sega, who in the same breath labelled her *"contumaz y desobediente,"* stubborn and disobedient. He accused her also of teaching like a man, against the orders of St. Paul. Teresa herself seems to have heard reports of what Sega had said. See *Letters* II, 610–14.

Yet, many of her closest friends and advisors were eminent theologians and holy persons,[56] a prestigious and protective circle which would also come to include the angry doctor who had excoriated her.[57] Teresa also moved easily among *converso* merchants, many of whom were active in financially supporting the reform, much more at ease perhaps with these men of her own class who shared with her the secret of tainted blood than with the famous noblemen and women with whom she also kept company and did business throughout the years of the foundations.[58] Teresa's reform demanded her tireless devotion; whatever else might happen, whoever might be offended or helped, and despite the risk to her reputation, the reform became the driving motivation for the rest of her life.

The reform and its social meaning[59]

The establishment of the little house of St. Joseph was a break with numerous religious and economic conventions. Despite powerful pressure to do otherwise, for example, Teresa insisted that it was to be established in "absolute poverty." The number of women who could profess there would be limited to thirteen. The nuns would leave their family names at the doorstep. Teresa would teach them to pray contemplatively. And they would understand their role in the Christian Church in terms of what we

[56]See *Testimonies,* 58, a memo Teresa wrote for the Inquisition in Seville in 1576 listing all her consultants over a lengthy period of her life. The list reads like a sixteenth-century Spanish *Who's Who* of theologians and charismatic holy persons. For a study of this memo and its significance, see Tomás (Alvarez) de la Cruz, " 'Esta monja.' Carisma y obediencia en uno Relación de Santa Teresa," in *El Monte Carmelo* 78 (1970): 143–162.

[57]Bartolomé de Medina. Subsequently, Teresa made a point of meeting him to discuss her manner of prayer and her undertakings. It is reported that the force of her personality made of him a Teresian devotee. He retracted his condemnation of her as publicly as he had issued it. Testimony at the beatification hearings of Avila (1610), cited in *Tiempo y vida,* 484–85. Teresa refers to her winning of Medina in *Testimonies,* 58, 8.

[58]For astute observations on Teresa's social relations and attitudes, see "Historical Setting," 158–168. See also Francisco Márquez Villanueva, "Santa Teresa y el linaje" in *Espiritualidad y literatura en el siglo XVI* (Madrid: Alfaguara, 1968), 141–205 (hereafter, "Linaje").

[59]The following discussion relies upon Jodi Bilinkoff, "The Social Meaning of Religious Reform: The Case of St. Teresa and Avila," *Archiv für Reformationgeschichte* 79 (1988): 340–356.

would call apostolate, making an active and positive contribution to the Church's reform and well-being.[60]

Insistence upon strict poverty and limited enrollment was in some measure a reaction against the inequity and chaotic overcrowding Teresa and her earliest companions had experienced at the Incarnation. It was as well an attempt to return to what they envisioned the primitive style of Carmelite life to have been like. More strikingly still, however, it seemed designed to upset the well-entrenched system whereby monasteries were endowed by members of the local nobility to ensure perpetual prayers for their souls, provide placement for unmarried or widowed clan members, and show off the family's resources and generosity, thereby enhancing dynastic prestige and linking monastic institutions and the nobility in a symbiotic relationship of privilege and mutual obligation.

The establishment of a tiny, apparently harmless community of austerity-minded Carmelite nuns caused a frightful upheaval in the city of Avila. The townspeople's objections stemmed ostensibly from the inability of the city to provide alms to yet another religious institution. They centered, too, upon whether the nuns would build a convent wall around a public fountain (water was a scant and valuable resource in Castile) and on whether they would default on annuities owed the city. But the city's elites could not have failed to discern as well the deeper significance of Teresa's little foundation. If it were founded with no endowment or other certain income as Teresa insisted it should, this new religious house would break the hallowed link of lineage by eliminating the need for noble patronage. Moreover, women admitted to the house would really want to be nuns; unmarriageable noble girls would find no haven in St. Joseph's. An upper-class woman who felt a true attraction to austere religious life would be required to live poorly and strictly enclosed, severing economic and affective ties with her kin, turning her back on the code by which they lived.

Not surprisingly, these nobles and principal citizens of Avila were among the most vocal and angry opponents of the project.

---

[60]The number of nuns would later increase to 15 and has never exceeded 21. *Constitutions,* 224–25. The house was to be egalitarian, refusing no one on account of low birth or meager means. See for example *Foundations,* 27:12. The nuns addressed each other only as Sister or Mother.

They were, after all, the ones with the most to lose if the system they had always relied on for spiritual security and for prestige and dominance in the aristocratic circles of Avila were now to be challenged by Teresa and her collaborators. Furthermore, the nobles may have recognized that Teresa's preference for mental rather than vocal prayer also undermined the traditional system. Patrons counted (literally!) on vocal prayers to verify the terms of their endowments. How could they be sure that the Religious had chanted the correct number of prayers for the souls of the nobles and their relatives if they could not measure, that is, hear and count, the prayers they paid for?

The reform as a defense of women and their capacity to pray

But the nobility of Avila were not the only ones to sense a danger in Teresa's plan to enclose within the new house women who would learn to pray contemplatively. During the period of Teresa's initiation into the work of monastic reform, all Europe was caught up in the ecclesiastical crisis we now refer to as the Protestant Reformation, and its outcome in some territories was still not settled. From about mid-century, Spanish civil and ecclesiastical authorities had taken definite, sometimes drastic steps to close Spain off from foreign influences. Their determination to protect the purity of Catholic faith in Spain was strengthened considerably when groups of Protestants were ferreted out in Seville, Vallodolid, and Murcia in 1559. Banning books and strictly controlling Spanish presses occupied a good part of the energies of Inquisition officials in that year. The only books which escaped prohibition were mainly technical works in Latin which no one but the university-trained theologian could read.[61] Church officials stressed outward compliance with ecclesiastical ceremonies and rites, since it was presumed that among the heretic's hallmarks

---

[61] Valdés' 1559 Index was one of a series published in Spain from 1502 onwards. Behind its prohibitions lay the intransigent attitude toward affective mental prayer of the theologian Melchor Cano. For other measures taken during this period, see Henry Kamen, *Inquisition and Society in Spain in the Sixteenth and Seventeenth Centuries* (Bloomington: Indiana Univ. Press, 1985), 65–100. Also José Ignacio Gutiérrez Nieto, "La discriminación de los conversos y la tibetización de Castilla por Felipe II," offprint of the *Revista de la Universidad de Madrid* IV (1973).

was disdain for the Mass, the sacraments, relics, sacramentals and other externals of Catholic faith. Genuflections, crossing oneself, keeping one's eyes wide open and moving the lips while praying acquired immense significance in the scrutinies conducted by the examiners of orthodoxy. No wonder, then, that the practitioners of mental prayer, in which no lips moved and eyes stayed shut, were regarded with increasing suspicion.[62]

Two parties gradually formed. There were those who favored and practiced mental prayer, trusting the knowledge of the divine derived from it, or *espirituales*. And there were those who opposed it, insisting that it was neither mandated by the gospel nor necessary for salvation, that it was the first step to heterodoxy, not subject to the control of the Church hierarchy nor grounded in sound theological science. Surely it would lead the simple (women and the uneducated laity) astray.[63] The major spokesmen for the forces opposed to affective mental prayer were university theologians, particularly the Dominicans of Salamanca. Thus, this group is often referred to as the "learned" or *letrado* faction. The name also underscores the opinion held by most *espirituales* that *letrado* knowledge of the spiritual life was sterile, confined to book learning at best. In the main, the *espirituales* were convinced that no one who had not experienced prayer could understand or pass definitive judgment upon it or upon its devotees.

In this discussion about the merits of mental prayer, Teresa stood with the *espirituales,* repeatedly chiding *letrados* for judging things they had no experiential knowledge of and ridiculing them for being afraid.[64] Some of her most artful ironic rhetoric is reserved for academic theologians. She encircled herself with the protection of their status and credentials; she engaged them

---

[62]See for example the 1525 Edict of Toledo in which several *alumbrado* propositions dealing with outward forms are condemned. Antonio Márquez, *Los Alumbrados. Orígenes y filosofía, 1525-1559* (Madrid: Taurus, 1972), 273–283.

[63]*Letrados* objected to the tendency of *espirituales* to extend the practice of mental prayer to the uneducated laity because such "democratization" was an open invitation to Protestant infections such as non-ecclesiastically mediated experiences of grace and private judgment on Scripture.

[64]In many passages in *Way* Teresa exhorted the nuns to pray in spite of what "they" say about the dangers of mental prayer. See especially *Way* 21, 2-10; a ringing defense of contemplation and a scathing attack on those who oppose it.

to assist in her own formation; she genuinely admired their learning when it was accompanied by humility and devotion; she regarded the theologian's ecclesial role as an indispensable and arduous one in need of support from the faithful's prayers and sacrifices. But she never conceded the possibility that the *letrados'* timidity about mental prayer and their scorn for its practitioners could reflect the purposes of God.

Teresa's movement was a defense of mental prayer in general. In particular, it was also an assertion that *women* were apt subjects for this kind of prayer. Teresa taught women to have confidence in their capacity for direct relationship with God. By means of the contemplative adventure she invited them to embark upon, traditional confinement and cloister could become rich opportunities for the development of freedom of conscience and spiritual liberty. Teresa's movement gave many women a way to participate in the century's turbulent search for right relationship with God, to experience in a new way the mystery of transforming grace, to become, in short, important interlocutors in discussion of the fundamental questions of the age.

If Teresa's communities amounted to a counteroffensive against those who derided or feared the capacity of women for authentic religious experience, they also gave those women a role in repairing what Teresa and her Catholic contemporaries regarded as the demonic damage of Protestantism. As we have already noted, throughout the period in which the idea for the first discalced foundation was forming in the minds of Teresa and her collaborators, Spain was in the throes of a Protestant scare. The discovery of suspect groups in the heart of Castile in 1558 and the Inquisition's imprisonment the following year of the progressive Primate of Spain, Archbishop Bartolemé de Carranza, set off shock waves throughout the country. *Autos de fe,* public spectacles in which large numbers of women and men were executed or otherwise castigated for crimes against the faith in the midst of terrifying and pointed pageantry, deepened the populace's fears that without constant watchfulness the purity of Spain's Catholic religion could easily be sullied from within. The Monarch himself fanned the flames.

As the historian J. H. Elliott has so trenchantly expressed it, Philip II thought religion far "too serious a matter to be left in the hands of the pope.''[65] Personally repulsed by heresy, anxious to extend his control over the Church in his dominions and assume undisputed leadership of the Catholic counteroffensive against the heretic to the north, the King embarked upon a propaganda campaign, fine-tuning the sense of imminent threat. Spain was rife with horror stories about Protestant violence and iconoclasm. Philip wrote urgent directives to the heads of the kingdom's Religious Orders exhorting them to vigilance and to do their part in the struggle.

Deeply affected by the circulating stories of church desecrations, defections of priests and nuns, and the general "havoc the Lutherans had caused" in France and elsewhere, Teresa was moved to add another layer of meaning to her reform project. It would be an apostolic venture, a means of engaging in the defense and reform of the Catholic Church. In *The Way of Perfection,* a book written to set out the rationale and methods of the discalced reform to the nuns of St. Joseph's, she reflected upon this apostolic ideal and insisted that the nuns make it their own, in spite of their being women and, therefore, in the world's eye, of little use in so great a matter. She had, she wrote, "resolved to do the little that was in [her] power," and to strive so that the few sisters who shared that austere life with her should do the same: live their vows with the utmost perfection and make of their prayer an underground spring to refresh and animate "the defenders of the Church," the "preachers and [the] learned men who protect her from attack." Thus would they all be apostles too, committed to "help as much as possible this Lord of mine who is so roughly treated by those for whom He has done so much good . . . "[66]

It was Teresa's intention that the women of the reform be engaged in the defense of Christ's Church and in the salvation of souls. Their prayer was too important, she insisted, to waste on the trivial petitions that were placed before them by men and women of the world. Their vocation, the "business" they were to conduct, was to "discuss with God" things of utmost impor-

[65]J. H. Elliott, *Imperial Spain, 1469–1716* (New York: New American Library, 1963), 227. Not all Spaniards regarded the crackdown on dissent and the drive towards rigid orthodoxy embodied in the Inquisition and royal policy as wise or necessary, however. See Henry Kamen, "Toleration and Dissent in Sixteenth-Century Spain: The Alternative Tradition," *Sixteenth Century Journal* XIX, n. 1 (1988): 3–23.

[66]*Way,* 1:2.

tance: the health of the Church, the salvation of souls, the formation of preachers and theologians, and the restoration of the primacy of God in the world.[67] For Teresa, this pitched battle between God and Satan (as she understood the events of her day) should be waged by the "ecclesiastical arm," preachers and teachers, and men and women of holy and exemplary lives. Military coercion would never succeed in resolving the issues dividing Christians. But she and her nuns, by returning to the Carmelite ideal, could make a positive contribution to that effort.[68]

The urgency with which she commended the mission to her sisters and the confidence she had in their ability to carry it out are expressed in some of Teresa's most memorable and daring rhetoric. She wished women could engage even more directly in the work of recovering souls to the bosom of Christ, and she was aghast that there were some men who would deny to women, on the basis of their sex alone, even the little they were permitted to do. She warned in clear terms against wasting the resources available to the Church in the freely tendered services of women of character and devotion.[69]

Final years

The implications of St. Joseph's and the subsequent foundations were not lost on Teresa, and she felt both the exhilaration and the terror of success. She soon knew also the weariness of compromise. Years of making foundations, organizing and governing them, and solving their practical problems also matured and altered Teresa's ideas about what was pleasing to God and conducive to perfection. Eventually, even her cherished commitment to absolute poverty would go by the boards when necessity mandated flexibility. Often, everything came down to what was possible.

Teresa and her companions were faced as well with the task of securing the future of the movement against those Carmelites who wished to halt it and who, at times, did not stop short of

---

[67] *Way*, 1:5.

[68] *Way*, 3:1-2.

[69] *Way*, 3:7. For a brief discussion of this passage see Chapter 6 of this volume.

coercion and character defamation to achieve their ends. Toward the end of her life, her party's efforts were rewarded with the creation of a separate province for the discalced, but Teresa was scandalized by the behavior of the calced friars in the battle for jurisdiction over the reform, and the entire affair left her jaded.[70]

Teresa of Jesus was renowned for her captivating affability and a sense of humor rich in irony and exquisite sallies. She was blessed too with an enviable gift for friendship with women and men alike. But Teresa's very strength of character and the sharp definition of her personality sometimes made for clashes in which she was not inclined to be flexible. Moreover, she was never an infallible judge of people. Toward the end of her life she found herself at odds with several of the women she had handpicked to run the discalced houses. The cavalier disdain with which they treated her at times is instructive to the modern devotee accustomed to reading Teresa's canonization back into the events of her life. Apparently, even some of the women who worked most closely with her were not overawed.[71]

The last year of her life was embittered by a pathetic family argument over money, precisely the sort of grubbing she had long regarded as futile and demeaning.[72] Moreover, her health was almost entirely broken and was not improved by the hardships of the Burgos foundation (her last) which dragged on for months

[70]See for example her letters concerning the fate of John of the Cross, who had been abducted, and her perceptive remarks about the dangers awaiting discalced emissaries among their calced brethren in Rome. *Letters* I, 495–98; 503–06; II, 511–18; 537–440; 603–05; 614–17. For Teresa's reaction to the suppression of the discalced decreed by the Chapter of Piacenza in 1575, see her energetic letters to the General Rubeo and to Philip II, *Letters* I, 178–184; 187–88; 220–26. Her relief at the news that a separate province was to be created is apparent in *Foundations*, 29:30-31. The Brief granting the separation was bestowed June 22, 1580. Eventually (1583) the discalced became a Religious Order in their own right, although Teresa did not live to see it.

[71]See for example her letter to Ana de Jesús, the Prioress of Granada, *Letters* II, 935–942. There were troubles also with the Prioress of Valladolid, who was engaged in a devious game of playing one superior off another in what amounted to an obsessive drive to acquire a new house; when Teresa left Valledolid for Alba, M. María Bautista's farewell was glacial. At Alba, too, trouble awaited. Teresa de Layz, the convent's founder and benefactor had been interfering in the internal affairs of the convent; as a result, the atmosphere surrounding the election of a new prioress had been poisoned. The victorious candidate did not afford Teresa a cordial welcome nor visit her during her final illness. See *Letters* II, 955–57; 957–59 and Rosa Rossi, *Teresa de Avila. Biografía de una escritora*, tr. Marieta Gargatagli (Barcelona: Icaria, 1983), 286–87 (hereafter, *Biografía*).

[72]See for example *Letters* II, 964–971.

amidst terrible weather, jealous disputes, ecclesiastical resistance, and plain bad luck.[73] Nor were her final months made lighter by the behavior of her friend and collaborator, Jerónimo Gracián. She had singled him out years before as her helpmate, confessor, and confidant. He had also come to be appointed her Carmelite superior. To him she had daringly vowed, fully aware that her regard for him would be interpreted in the worst light, to reverence him in the place of God and obey him in all things. She had even dreamed of a wedding scene in which the Lord "betrothed" them in this holy association.[74]

Jerónimo Gracián de la Madre de Dios was a well-educated, highly polished man, a good deal younger than Teresa, well-known for his intelligence, eloquence, and charm. He, together with John of the Cross, Nicolás Doria and others, were Teresa's picked men in the work of reform. Although earnest and often successful in his multiple endeavors on behalf of the masculine and feminine discalced movements, Gracián had, apparently, no talent for prudence or sustained good judgment. Teresa often overlooked his blunders; she regularly made excuses for him when others pointed out the danger of his erratic approach to his duties and impulsive decision-making in times which demanded level heads and calculating shrewdness. Yet in the final months of her life, the negative information that reached her about Gracián's behavior was too compelling to explain away. Personally hurt by his neglect of her, and alarmed by reports of his autocratic governance and his capacity to be swayed by flattery, Teresa's last extant letter to him, although replete with news and plans, is filled also with reproof, a weary and complaining witness to her deep disappointment.[75]

After Teresa's death, Gracián fell into disfavor with the new authorities of the Order over questions of interpretation of Teresa's vision and spirit. He vigorously defended what he believed to be her authentic design for discalced life and remonstrated vehemently with those who were denying her the title of founder of the discalced friars. For his pains, he was expelled from the Order. Gracián spent the rest of his troubled life in a series of

[73] *Foundations,* 31.

[74] Teresa's friendship with Gracián is discussed in more detail in Chapter 4.

[75] *Letters* II, 964–971.

adventures worthy of a feature film (even getting kidnapped and held for ransom by the Turks), always seeking ways to restore his name and vindicate the interpretation of the reform that he and several of Teresa's closest male and female companions had championed. He wrote several books and treatises on mystical theology and ended his days in Brussels as, ironically, a friar of the Carmelite Observance.[76]

At the time she wrote Gracián that final letter, Teresa's health was on the verge of collapse. She was old and completely worn out, yet still nursing her one remaining and much-desired project, a foundation in Madrid. Once that goal was achieved, she believed she would retire contentedly to Avila and wait for death. It was not to be. Nor would she get to Avila in time to preside at the profession of her niece Teresita as a discalced nun. Instead, her superior ordered her to Alba de Tormes to assist the new Duchess who was about to give birth and required the presence of the nun with the fame of a saint, almost as a talisman. Such service to the Spanish grandees was not new to Teresa, but she never liked it. It was with nothing short of repugnance that she turned toward Alba.[77] A scant two weeks after her arrival, on the feast of Francis Assisi, October 4, 1582, she died at the discalced convent of Alba. Witnesses to her agony later testified that

---

[76]The former Genoese banker Nicolás Doria replaced Gracián as superior of the discalced after Teresa's death. His sympathies leaned in the direction of the extreme ascetical austerity that Philip II preferred Religious Orders to exhibit. Doria also severely curtailed the ministry of the friars in the name of eremeticism and contemplation, something that seemed to John of the Cross (also demoted and castigated by the new authorities) and Gracián to contradict Teresa's desire that the friars also missionize. Nuns (Ana de Jesús, María de San José) who had worked shoulder-to-shoulder with Teresa also experienced ostracism, deposition from office, imprisonment, and even a form of exile as a result of their defense of their view of Teresa's charism. Gracián's sometimes self-serving version of these events can be found in his *Peregrinación de Anastasio,* in *Biblioteca Mística Carmelitana (BMC),* 17 (hereafter *Peregrinación)* and in his "Historia Fundationum," *Momumenta Historica Carmel Teresiani,* ed., Institutum Historicum Teresianum (Rome: Teresianum, 1973–), 3. See also Idelfonso Moriones, *El Carmelo Teresiano,* (Vitoria: Ediciones El Carmen, 1978), and his provocative *Ana de Jesús y la herencia teresiana. ¿Humanismo cristiano o rigor primitivo?* (Rome, 1968). A popularized Spanish version of this work is available in English as *The Teresian Charism: A Study of the Origins,* tr. Christopher O'Mahoney, O.C.D. (Rome: Teresianum, 1972).

[77]Gracián reported Teresa's displeasure, José Gómez Centurión, *Relaciones biográficas inéditas de Santa Teresa de Jesús* (Madrid, 1916), p. 81. See also the testimony of Ana de San Bartolomé, Teresa's secretary and confidante, on the subject of Teresa's last days, Julián Urkiza, " ' Con el mal de la muerte' y 'la hora del dichosos tránsito.' Manifestaciones de un testigo de excepción," *Revista de Espiritualidad* 40 (1981): 311–330.

she repeatedly sighed the now-famous phrase, *En fin, Señor, muero hija de la Iglesia:* At last, Lord, I die a daughter of the Church.

Teresa left the phrase behind unglossed. Perhaps it was a simple statement of a consoling fact: dying "in the Church" meant that she was saved and would soon see God face to face. Perhaps, too, she was referring to the mission she had embraced in the Church all her adult life: she had been the *"nursing* daughter" who had "devoted her mature years to supporting and healing an ailing Mother."[78] But its meaning must at least in part also be rooted in relief at having stayed clear of disaster as far as ecclesiastical officialdom was concerned. In sixteenth-century Spain, it was no easy feat to have remained, in good standing, a daughter of the Church who was also a proponent of contemplative prayer for women, a writer of mystical theology, a travelling founder with close ties to *conversos,* and a renowned mystic whose visions, levitations, healings, and power to spring souls from purgatory were the talk of city, court, and countryside.[79] In fact, all the things a woman like Teresa ought not to have done in the rough times she lived in she managed to do and still come out unscathed. She had, she was certain, been loyal and loving in the cause of Christ. Nothing else mattered.

With the exception of the views of a few persistent detractors who complained to the Inquisition for years after her death that her works contained pernicious errors, lingering skepticism about the authenticity of her sanctity seemed to evaporate overnight. In fact, the apotheosis of Teresa began the instant she died. The nuns of Alba whisked her remains to a gravesite which they heaped with dirt and stones to ward off attempts to steal the treasure for the glory of some other convent or town. When Teresa's remains were disinterred nine months later to be moved to Avila in secret,[80] stories that her body was intact and sweet-smelling circu-

---

[78] This lovely suggestion has been put forward by Jodi Bilinkoff in "Private Prayer, Public Apostolate: The Mission of Teresa of Avila," Paper read at the Seventh Berkshire Conference on the History of Women, Wellesley College, June 20, 1987 (hereafter "Private Prayer").

[79] See a discussion of Teresa's wonder-working in Chapter 6 of this volume.

[80] Discalced factions quarreled for years over where Teresa's remains properly belonged. Her body was removed from Alba on July 4, 1583, and transferred to Avila. By papal decree, it was returned to Alba on August 23, 1586, where it lies today. For Teresa's funeral at Alba, held in an atmosphere of "nervous precipitation," see *Tiempo y vida,* 768-772.

lated widely and became one of the strongest arguments for her rapid elevation to the altars. Miracles and sightings of the glorious virgin were reported in great numbers. Philip II ordered her works collected, and he proudly displayed the manuscript of *Life* in the magnificent library of the Escorial next to manuscripts reputed to be by Chrysostom and Jerome. Biographers scrambled to the task of recording her life according to the canons of heroic virtue of the age. Her relics became objects of intense devotion as well as of unseemly greed.[81]

From her death in 1582, only forty years would have to pass before she was proclaimed officially a Saint of the Church. In 1970, Teresa's exaltation was complete when she became the first of her sex to be given the title "Doctor" in an official act of the Roman Catholic Church.[82]

[81] The modern reader, generally unfamiliar with the powerful socioreligious significance of relics in general and "holy flesh" in particular for Christians in Late Antiquity, the Middle Ages and in some places, into the Early Modern period, will surely find deeply disturbing the account of the gradual dismemberment of Teresa's body with which Stephen Clissold concludes his biography of the saint. Clissold's recitation of atrocities strikes me, unfortunately, as pruriently lurid; he captures the strange and greedy pride associated with the cult of relics but provides only a hint of context in which the reader might gain some perspective on the admittedly repugnant but socially significant practices he catalogues with such relish. Forewarned, see *St. Teresa of Avila,* 254–261.

[82] Paul VI was the pontiff who bestowed the title on Teresa. A few weeks later, he would do the same for Catherine of Siena.

2

A Very Determined Determination

Teresa of Avila was not always a "capital-S saint." As with most human beings, her life was often an enigma even to herself, a puzzle of contradictions and fears, aspirations and joys. The sanctity that many of her contemporaries and the Catholic Church eventually came to ascribe to her was lofty indeed, but it began in a crucible of doubt and pain. Even saints begin at the beginning. In Teresa's case, that beginning meant an extraordinary struggle to gain a foothold on the rock of God, to be hoisted up to see God face to face. That struggle was a painful, protracted one, but Teresa was determined.

"They were all against me"[1]

In Chapter 25 of *Life*, Teresa set out to explain the nature of divine locutions, a phenomenon she experienced frequently, and to illustrate the ways in which "words coming from God" can be distinguished from illusory words of diabolical origin.[2] Toward the end of the chapter, the discussion turns to the important role of spiritual direction in the discernment of benign spirit from bad.

---

[1] *Life*, 25:15.

[2] *Life*, 25:6. Locutions are words from God which the mystic may hear with his or her bodily ears, or perceive interiorly, in the imagination or with the intellect. These words need not be "human" words or messages; some mystics have perceived the sounds of music; some were induced to write "automatically" in a rhythmic manner. In many cases, such as in Teresa's, certain kinds of locutions immediately accomplish what they command, promise, or reveal.

Since the devil is so inventive, she wrote, a person experiencing locutions should seek counsel, "have a master who is a learned man, and hide nothing from him." "In this way," she continued, "no harm can come."[3]

As she wrote that confident assertion, however, the words triggered a rush of memory, and she quickly qualified her conclusion: " . . . no harm can come—*although a lot of harm was done to me through the excessive fears some persons have.*"[4] The subsequent narrative bristles with pained amazement as Teresa describes the manner in which inept spiritual directors had once succeeded in twisting her normal apprehension about locutions into a debilitating terror of demonic delusion.[5]

In the telling, Teresa depicted herself as nearly destroyed by an interior conflict that pitted her belief in the divine origin of her experiences against her counselors' sometimes derisive, sometimes threatening, and ever-fearful dismissal of them. They questioned her humility, and their logic seemed compelling; she was, after all, only one against many who judged her wrong and "were all against [her]."[6] Moreover, "they all led a good life." She, on the other hand, was not given to extreme asceticism; her candor and easy laughter were a far cry from the more sober marks of a sanctity that, according to much contemporary thought on the spiritual life, prepared one to receive mystical graces.[7] Finally, her confessors were "learned men." Their opinion carried an authority that her own could not, for she was a woman, theologically untrained.[8] In such a bind of authorities and expectations, Teresa felt "the greatest scrupulosity" about clinging to the assurance she invariably received while at prayer: the certainty that "the devil will not deceive—nor will God permit this—a soul that does not trust itself in anything and is fortified in the faith . . ."[9]

[3]*Life*, 25:14.

[4]*Life*, 25:14, emphasis added.

[5]These events took place in the years 1559-60.

[6]*Life*, 25:15.

[7]See for example her pointed criticism of such a view and of confessors who frightened souls with it, *Castle* VI, 1:8.

[8]*Life*, 25:14. Teresa's candid, direct way of expressing herself also prompted the serious charge that she was trying to "teach" men, thinking herself, an untrained woman, "wise." *Life*, 28:17.

[9]*Life*, 25:12.

Disconsolate and emotionally exhausted, Teresa came to a crossroads. She could give in to fear and adopt the safe way urged by her confessors or persist in the way she believed God had chosen for her, no matter the consequences for her sanity or reputation. Teresa chose to believe that God would never abandon her, even if all human support should fail. Her narrative describes the moment when, in the depths of her spirit, the voice she claimed to recognize as that of God, whose "words are works,"[10] spoke to her again. "Do not fear, daughter," it said, "for I am, and I will not abandon you . . ." Teresa reported that those words, whose authenticity she was prepared to defend before the "entire world," calmed her instantly. They gave her peace, "together with fortitude, courage, security . . . , and light."[11]

For Teresa, center stage was now occupied by the power of God and Christ. She recalled that in Scripture Christ commanded sea and wind and made them obey.[12] She declared her faith in the God who makes stone hearts pliant and was strengthened by the knowledge that "the King" gives the faithful servant strength to vanquish demons, demons who are after all, she reasoned with increasing rhetorical excitement, nothing but God's slaves.[13] If God were for her, who could be against?

To recount her victory over fear, Teresa constructed a scene redolent with the spiritual athleticism and boldness of the saints whose *Vitae* had since childhood and throughout her monastic life fueled her religious imagination. Flush with sudden certainty that God was on her side, she brandished the cross she had clasped in her hands and invited the onslaught of hell: "Come now all of you," she taunted, "for, being a servant of God, I want to see what you can do to me."[14]

There was nothing they could do to her. Teresa's fear left her the moment she saw that the devils themselves were afraid, especially of souls that "try truly to serve God" and, having lost all concern for their honor, see through the lies of the world.[15] That

---

[10]*Castle* VII, 2:7.

[11]*Life,* 25:18.

[12]Cf. Mk. 4:35-41.

[13]*Life,* 25:19.

[14]*Life,* 25:19.

[15]*Life,* 25:21.

revelation also put her confessors' exaggerated prudence in a new and unflattering light. Spiritually timid, unable to concede that God might not be bound by their own spiritual principles, and cowed by the real and imagined dangers of the times, they feared for their own reputations as much as they wished for her salvation,[16] and would not budge from the tried and true. But for Teresa, anyone who failed to trust God more than his own prudence was a potential enemy of the truth of experience, namely, *God's unfailing trustworthiness,* confirmed by Scripture time and again. "Let all learned men rise up against me . . . , let the devils torment me; . . . for I have experience of the gain that comes from the way You rescue the one who trusts in *You alone.*"[17]

"May it please the Lord," she concluded,

> that I not be one of these but that His Majesty favor me so that I may understand by repose what repose is, by honor what honor is, and by delight what delight is—not the reverse; and a fig for all the devils, because they shall fear me. I don't understand these fears, "The devil! The devil!," when we can say "God! God!," and make the devil tremble . . . What is this? Without doubt, I fear those who have such great fear of the devil more than I do the devil himself, for he can't do anything to me. Whereas these others, especially if they are confessors, cause severe disturbance; I have undergone some years of such great trial that I am amazed now at how I was able to suffer it. Blessed by the Lord who has so truly helped me![18]

According to Teresa, this dramatic episode confirmed and strengthened her intuition that God was able and willing to sustain what was begun in her. She had summoned every reserve of courage and determination to overcome one of the most formidable obstacles blocking her path toward God, namely *fear:* fear of losing her reputation, fear of abandonment by people who counted, fear of the demons inside and out, fear of trusting her own experience in the face of contradiction by persons authorized to judge that experience.

---

[16]Her confessors were, she wrote, "very fond" of her. *Life,* 25:14; *Castle* VI, 1:8-9.

[17]*Life,* 25:17, emphasis added.

[18]*Life,* 25:22. This encounter was by no means the last one Teresa had with demons. See for example, *Life,* 31.

Teresa would not have been true to the religious worldview of her time (in which every good thing came from God, and the evils caused by "the world, the flesh, and the devil" existed by God's sovereign permission) had she not also viewed her early confessors as "great servants of God" whose "tyranny" and "persecution" were trials God permitted for her greater good.[19] Still, as a result at least in part of that bitter experience of "the opposition of good men to a little woman,"[20] she formed a vivid picture of the pursuit of holiness in her day as an embrace of martyrdom for which "great courage is necessary."[21] Thus the anchor of her own spiritual life attached ever more firmly upon the rock of a *muy determinada determinación:* a very determined determination.[22] Tenacious, fearless determination was, Teresa was certain, a working key to the door of God, a door that was opening ever more widely for her, and a door she meant to open for others.

"[I]n this matter of desires,
I have always had great ones . . . "[23]

During her frightful difficulties with uncomprehending spiritual directors, Teresa ascribed the courageous determination she drew upon solely to special divine assistance.[24] But she was also by her own description a naturally stubborn person, often getting her way by sheer force of will. Possessed of leadership and vision, she was not one to give up a fight easily, even if she also sometimes gave in to others in order to please. That natural single-mindedness made all the more congenial to her the ideals of the

---

[19]*Life,* 28:17.

[20]*Life,* 28:18; 30:6. One of the greatest torments she endured had to do with the threat of withheld absolution. For a woman seeking counsel and comfort in the arduous process of spiritual discernment and who relied on confession for sacramental assurance, that there would be "no one to hear my confessions" was a severe trial. See for example *Life,* 24:14-15.

[21]*Life,* 31:17. Of course, as observed in the Note at the beginning of this volume, the notion of the Chrisitan life as spiritual combat has a venerable pedigree in the history of Christian spirituality, and particularly in the monastic tradition.

[22]*Way,* 21:2.

[23]*Life,* 13:6.

[24]Teresa reported that the confessors who favored her also suffered calumny and were likewise in need of special divine assistance. See for example *Life,* 28:15-16.

religious culture in which she was nurtured, especially the notion that heroism can catch God's eye, that hard things bravely suffered merited divine reward.

That notion was embedded even in play. As a child she and her siblings pretended to be martyrs; in games they lost their heads to Moorish steel and gained thereby eternal glory. They built backyard hermitages in which to undertake imaginary penance for terrible sins whose names they probably could not pronounce. They frightened themselves with the awesomeness of the word "forever," with its potential pains eternal as well as joys complete. They resolved to seek heaven, no matter the cost.[25]

The interior vacillations that ended with the adolescent Teresa's rejection of makeup, gossip, flirting, romance novels, and marriage in favor of convent life reflects, as Teresa told it, the same ideal: better to set one's face bravely to the suffering of the sure way than to place one's soul in danger by exposing it to the snares of the world.[26] Teresa reported in *Life* that God did indeed reward her somewhat grim determination to "use force with [herself] to please Him."[27] She found the "courage against [herself]" necessary to act on the decision to leave her father's house without his knowledge or permission, courage she claimed not previously to have possessed.[28]

Later, she made up her mind to practice the prayer of recollection but, because she had no experienced spiritual guide, only slowly realized that she would get nowhere if she continued to dance on the edge of "occasions of sin."[29] She made plenty of

---

[25]In Teresian hagiography, much is always made of these childhood activities as the signs of a precocious religiosity, the harbingers of future sainthood. Certainly they denote a kind of piety, but reflect also, if not more, the typical imaginative resources available to children in a culture imbued with Christian assumptions and dominated by Christian institutions. It should be noted that Teresa's childhood contemporaries also played "Christians and Moors" (in the same way, perhaps, as American children used to play "cowboys and Indians"), and even "Inquisition and accused." See América Castro, *La realidad histórica de España* (Mexico: Porrua, 1971), 4th ed., 320, n. 16.

[26]Teresa did not renounce her good taste and appreciation for beautiful things, however, even if she gave up coveting them. See for example *Letters* I, 34; 458.

[27]*Life*, 4:2.

[28]*Life*, 4:1.

[29]See for example *Life*, 8:10. In the classical vocabulary of Catholic spirituality, "occasions of sin" refer to those circumstances, persons, or actions which, while not necessarily sinful in themselves, are seen to provide the opportunity, or "occasion," for committing sin and should, therefore, be avoided by anyone seeking to lead a life of perfection.

resolutions to avoid them, but her resolutions "profited little."[30] Nonetheless, because her desires were fervent and ambitious, she marvelled to "[see] clearly that [God] does not fail to repay, even in this life, every good desire." As "miserable and imperfect as my deeds were," she wrote, "this Lord of mine improved and perfected them and gave them value, and the evils and sins He then hid."[31]

During the twenty-year period in which Teresa attempted to maintain a life of serious prayer while failing to foster the conditions that favored contemplation, her courage and determination stood her in good stead. On one level, as Teresa noted in a self-deprecating passage of *Life,* her determination to practice prayer was pure *chutzpah:*

> . . . I see clearly the great mercy the Lord bestowed on me; for though I continued to associate with the world, I had the courage to practice prayer. I say courage, for I do not know what would require greater courage among all the things there are in the world than to betray the king and know that he knows it and yet never leave his presence [since I am practicing prayer].[32]

But beneath the cheeky sort of courage involved in playing both ends against the middle, Teresa recognized in herself the mettle of authentic determination; it may have been imperfect prayer she practiced, but she practiced it, and God again rose to the occasion:

> . . . for some years I was more anxious that the hour I had determined to spend in prayer be over than I was to remain there, and more anxious to listen for the striking of the clock than to attend to other good things. And I don't know what heavy penance could have come to mind that frequently I would not have gladly undertaken rather than recollect myself in the

[30]*Life,* 4:9.

[31]*Life,* 4:10. In *Life,* 13:6, Teresa also blamed "excessively discreet" confessors for holding beginners back. Neophytes were better off with a director of vision and *authentic* prudence, "someone to make [them] fly." With such a master, they were sure to advance more rapidly and turn their great "desires into deeds." Timid directors, on the other hand, would "teach them to be toads."

[32]*Life,* 8:2.

> practice of prayer . . . I had to muster up all my courage . . .
> in order to force myself; and in the end the Lord helped me.
> After I had made this effort, I found myself left with greater
> quiet and delight than sometimes when I had the desire to pray.[33]

Because of her own experience, Teresa believed that God is drawn to the seeker who is not content with little. In her view, God can be counted on to respond to human determination, bestowing ever greater courage on the soul that aims high; more than meeting the expectations, sooner or later, of the soul that dares entertain lofty desires; "paying" with success the person who, laying aside fears of failure, seeking nothing but the glory of God, and trusting in God's "power to accomplish all," decides to "put a good inspiration into practice," no matter how impossible the project might appear.[34] Indeed, no matter how imperfectly that soul desires, how haltingly it follows through, how short it may fall in the end, what counted for Teresa was determination to set out, determination to persevere, determination to begin all over again. She stressed, then, a doctrine of spiritual ambition and repeatedly underscored the necessity of "holy daring."[35]

Teresa's God was emphatically "a friend of courageous souls," a God who truly "wants this determination."[36] Limitless and incredibly generous, even while sending trials and permitting the soul to experience suffering, this God valued and rewarded even flawed effort and desire. "My God is not the least bit touchy," Teresa once declared to her sisters in an effort to head off their discouragement over daily backsliding, "He does not stoop to trifles."[37] The important thing was to desire as much as one could desire, for with this God there was no telling what could happen. Teresa spoke from her own experience when, at the height of her powers, she taught that "one must not put limits on God; . . . His Majesty has the power to do whatever He wants and is eager

[33] *Life*, 8:7.
[34] *Life*, 4:2.
[35] *Way*, 16:12.
[36] *Life*, 13:2.
[37] *Way*, 23:3; my translation. See also *Way*, 20:3.

to do many things for us."[38] "God does not," she insisted, "deny Himself to anyone who perseveres."[39]

Such human effort sustained in the face of trial and personal inadequacy was necessary in the spiritual life because, at root, it signified for Teresa the desire of the soul to be conformed entirely to God's will.[40] Indeed, it demonstrated that a soul was truly in love with God. For in Teresa's experience, although God often enticed the soul and cemented its love with ineffable celestial delights, love of God was not a simple matter of feelings and heavenly favors; rather, it was fundamentally a matter of the will, a "strong determination to please God in everything"; a generous disposition even to "swallow death"; to work, to serve, and to suffer; to want what God wants; to see the world and humankind from God's point of view; to claim and proclaim the upside-down values of God's kingdom in a world, her world, characterized by ostentatious pretension, deceit, and the pitiful waste of energy in blind attachment to empty honor.[41]

A Christian's courageous determination, heroic desires, and bottomless confidence could not, however, ever be considered measures of personal worth. They were not achievement badges worn on the sleeve and could not be credited as one's own accomplishments. *Determinación determinada* was not, for Teresa, a pious cover for human self-sufficiency, nor did it signal the kind of individual autonomy that later thinkers would trumpet as the sign of humanity's coming of age. Rather, she believed that a person's capacity to set the search for God at the center of life and sustain it courageously until the end was itself a grace of inestimable worth.[42] If a person's efforts proved successful in laying the foundations for subsequent spiritual growth and mystical union with God, the glory was all God's.

Now, Teresa certainly knew that she was a remarkable person. She conducted herself as a spiritual teacher, monastic reformer,

[38]*Castle* VI, 11:1.

[39]*Life,* 11:4.

[40]For example, *Castle* II, 1:8; *Foundations,* 5.

[41]See for example *Way,* 11:4; *Foundations,* 5:10; *Castle* III, 1:7; 2:10; IV, 1:7; *Life,* 11:13.

[42]*Life,* 11:9. See also *Life,* 39:9-16 where Teresa is careful to point out that just because we have been faithful to the effort to pray, and have done so even with true humility, we still do not *deserve* special graces and delights.

and self-conscious author with a kind of straightforward assurance that at times scandalized even her friends. She defended her ideas, fought to correct what she considered slanderous interpretations of her motives, and insisted on her rights as a founder and reformer when challenges to her way of doings things were raised within the discalced movement. She thought of herself as important, perhaps crucial, to God's plan for the reform of the Church in Spain. But in explaining her survival, her successes, her mystical prowess, her obvious impact on people and institutions, in justifying her incursions into masculine realms, when suffering insult or absorbing praise, for Teresa, only one thing was certain: her God was the origin and grantor of all the good she possessed, including the determination with which she believed she had attracted God and in return for which she was showered with greater courage and untold spiritual gifts.

Another was equally certain: she was a sinner, never completely safe from her own perversity. As a sinner, however, she understood herself also to be undeniably the object and recipient of the imponderable mercy of God in Christ. When Teresa counseled humility, one of her favorite counsels, she was doing no more than insisting that Christian lives be built on a firm foundation whose basic material is the embrace of what is real and true. In Teresa's spiritual lexicon, humility meant truth. Teresa got the definition directly from God, who told her: "This is true humility: to know what you can do and what I can do."[43] The human soul, when rooted in this authentic humility, recognizes its gloomy prospects if God does not aid it; but more importantly, it learns also to rejoice in and build upon its capacity for great blessings. It does not defile its dignity (after all, it is *God's dwelling!)* with timid or impoverished desires, nor is it intimidated in the face of opposition.[44]

It is not unusual, Teresa knew from experience, for a soul that begins receiving extraordinary favors from God to be frightened by fears of vainglory. It seems to that person, as it had once seemed to her, "that it is humility not to acknowledge that God

[43]*Testimonies,* 24.

[44]*Life,* 10:4; *Letters* I, 75. See also *Testimonies,* 49, in which Teresa recorded God's response to her wonderment that "such majesty [Godself]" resided "in something so lowly as [the] soul." "It is not lowly, daughter," God replied, "for it is made in My image."

is giving them gifts." But it is not so. "Let us," she continued, "understand clearly the real fact: God gives them to us without any merit on our part." They inspire gratitude, which in turn awakens love. "And it is very certain," she concluded,

> that while we see more clearly that we are rich, *over and above knowing that we are poor,* more benefit comes to us, and even more authentic humility. Anything else would amount to intimidating the spirit, making it believe that it isn't capable of great blessings . . . [45]

For Teresa, the authentically determined and courageous soul, the soul that dares to stare down devils, stand up to *letrados,* and dream heroic dreams of service to the King is the soul that knows its true condition and accepts that reality humbly, that is, in truth. Such acceptance was the starting point for gratitude, peace, and an enviable interior freedom. A Christian could be daring, sure of her cause, and absolutely confident of victory because and only if she lived in and by such a truth: the human person is a sinner and alone can do nothing. God, who is and can do everything, in the mystery of mercy and grace, wants to do—is even now doing—amazing things with, through, and for us all.[46]

That a Christian, then, should desire the face of this immensely merciful and gift-giving God and be unconditionally determined to settle for nothing less was, for Teresa, the very will of God. These were the truths Teresa claimed to have learned by experience in prayer. On them she took her stand, learning gradually to fear nothing, expect everything, and live a life of desires and deeds hidden and public, breathtaking in their audacity.

"It is not for women"[47]

The female stereotype of Teresa's day included the conviction that women were by nature weak and vacillating creatures, unable

---

[45] *Life,* 10:4, emphasis added.

[46] For Teresa's teachings on authentic humility, its relation to self-knowledge and knowledge of God, its foundational role in the spiritual life and its relation to confidence, daring, and freedom of spirit, see among other places, *Life,* 10:4-6; 13:1-4; *Castle* I, 2:8-13; *Way,* 41:4.

[47] *Way,* 21:2.

except by extraordinary infusions of divine grace to be resolute. Indeed it was, liturgically at least, considered a measure of the infinite power and condescension of God that the Christian martyrology included the names of women at all.[48] When the world's attention was drawn to a woman of courage or strength, it was usually taken as a sign that God was up to something serious, so unusual and miraculous was it, according to the ideology of gender, to find such virtue in women.

That flesh and blood women *could* and actually *did* on occasion exhibit determination and courage was not discounted; in the period's debates over the comparative merits of women and men, for example, male profeminist authors brought to public attention and conveyed deep admiration for the numerous determined and daring women they found in history, classical literature, and on the contemporary scene.[49] But since the virtues in question were invariably associated with masculinity and spoken of as *manly,* the possibility of *women's* courage, by being thus subsumed, was always thus denied. Given the way gender was constructed in Teresa's day, it was difficult, if not impossible, for both women and men to talk in any other way about courage, strength of character, and determination demonstrated by women.

Throughout her writings, Teresa seems to take for granted much of the ideology that, in praising women, dissociated them from their sex. In one instance, she emphatically reminded her sisters

[48]Until recently, for example, the Roman liturgy of a female virgin and martyr included an admiring collect lauding God for miraculously granting even to the weak sex the victory of martyrdom: *"Deus, qui inter cetera potentiae tuae miracula, etiam in sexu fragili victoriam martyrii contulisti . . . "*

[49]The practice of adducing the example of female worthies for the purpose of defending their cause in debates concerning their moral nature, equality, or superiority *vis-à-vis* men, capacity for education, fitness for public roles, and other issues is as old as Plutarch who, in his moral essay *Mulierum virtutes,* argued that male and female virtue are identical. The use of catalogues of holy, virtuous, or civic-minded women increased in the early modern period, as profeminist men and women attempted to reformulate received notions about women in the face of a new wave of antifemale polemic and the tightening of some social, religious, and economic controls on women. For a caveat with respect to the conclusion that such catalogues reveal feminist sentiment in the twentieth-century sense, see the comments of Hilda Smith in *Reason's Disciples: Seventeenth-Century English Feminists* (Urbana: Univ. of Illinois Press, 1982), 27. In 1627, an anonymous panegyric on poetry appeared at Seville. It concluded its praise of the genre with a list of women worthies, all poets, that included Deborah, Judith, the Virgin Mary, the Sibyls, Proba—and St. Teresa of Jesus. See Ernest Robert Curtius, *European Literature and the Latin Middle Ages* (New York: Harper and Row, 1952), tr. Willard R. Trask, 557.

that they were to avoid the simpering, vacuous rhetoric of affection apparently in use among the nuns of convents like the Incarnation, where the rules of worldly manners were practiced along with the religious rule.[50] Inevitably, among those women, favorites were played, cliques were formed, and little dramas of jealous pique were acted out. Among the nuns of the reform, Teresa proscribed the use of frivolous endearments, for such words were often used as territorial markers, to proclaim allegiances, to wound or arouse; they could also be signs of what she understood to be morally dangerous friendships, a perilous lack of attention to the true Beloved. If one wished to show genuine affection for one's sisters, Teresa taught, one should go beyond words and seek to relieve them of their burdens, pray for them, rejoice in their progress in virtue and practice authentic charity. No distinctions were to be made among persons, no attention paid to rank, family honor, and points of pride.[51]

Undoubtedly it was frequently the case (not only in Teresa's era, but also throughout the history of female monasticism) that a woman responding to a strong religious calling might elect the vowed life in part to secure time, space, and permission for contemplation, reading, scholarly reflection, the exercise of leadership, and other activities not easily procured as a married woman in the world. But it was also true that many women, socialized into an insubstantial image of self and having entered the convent as a recourse rather than a vocation, fashioned within the convents a life familiar to them in which they engaged in stereotypical behaviors engendered by the systematic deprivation of their sex: childish affectations, gossip, exaggerated timidity, and the like. It was this "very womanish" behavior that Teresa hated. She declared that she did not want her sisters "to be womanish in anything." Indeed, she did not want them "to be like women" at all, *"but like strong men."*[52]

Teresa thus invited the nuns to eschew a femaleness associated with pusillanimity and changeability and to claim for themselves a "virile" character. She urged them to believe that God could, with their cooperation, overcome in them the deprivation of their

[50] *Way,* 7:8.

[51] *Way,* 7:5-10.

[52] *Way,* 7:8, emphasis added.

condition: "If you do what lies in your power," she assured them, "the Lord will make you so strong that you will astonish men."[53] If they were to give in to their "natural weakness," however, they would lose the "great crown" God has in store for them. But trusting that "God can do all," and "fighting with faith," they would certainly overcome, for God has throughout history already given "fortitude to many saintly girls . . . , since they were determined to suffer for Him." The virtues God had already bestowed upon them would help them "act with determination and forget the reasons the intellect presents[,] and your own weakness." Indeed, God "enjoys having His works shine forth in weak people." In weakness there is room for God to manifest power.[54]

Imbued with such traditional convictions about the weak shaming the strong, she praised the pioneers of the discalced reform, holding up the first nuns' courage as a harbinger of miracles: "[C]onsidering . . . the courage God gave them to serve and to suffer for Him, certainly not a characteristic of women, I often thought that the riches God placed in them were meant for some great purpose."[55] God showed his greatness in "weak little women" who were, however, "strong in their desires . . . "[56] In *Foundations,* she created something of a gallery of courageous females, handing on to Carmelite posterity vivid portraits of the likes of doña Casilda de Padilla,[57] Catalina de Cardona,[58] Ana de la Madre de Dios,[59] Catalina Sandoval y Godínez,[60] and Beatriz de la Madre de Dios.[61]

Although in most of her rhetoric about the nature of women and men, Teresa, like all her contemporaries, seems to have accepted the ideology that "the masculine" was the standard by which to measure and describe all fortitude and determination,[62]

---

[53]*Way,* 7:9.

[54]*Song,* 3:5.

[55]*Foundations,* 1:6.

[56]*Foundations,* 4:5.

[57]*Foundations,* 10–11.

[58]*Foundations,* 28.

[59]*Foundations,* 16.

[60]*Foundations,* 22.

[61]*Foundations,* 26.

[62]See for example *Foundations,* 8:6; *Castle* IV, 3:11; VI, 6:4; *Way,* Prologue, 3.

she understood through experience that not all men were resolute, just as she knew by experience that not all women were fainthearted.[63] Her own determination in the face of male timidity was one source of that knowledge. She was deeply concerned, for example, that the masculine branch of the Order in Castile was dwindling in numbers and in need of revitalization; concerned, too, that the women of the discalced movement would have no like-minded Carmelite friars to attend to their spiritual needs. Thus, she determined to persuade the Father General of the Carmelite Order to reconsider his initial decision not to allow the establishment of convents of friars who wished, like Teresa's nuns, to follow the primitive rule.

Rubeo, although a partisan of reform, apparently did not relish the idea of stirring up a province already divided in its opinion concerning the pace and style of change in the Order. He had, therefore, bowed to the dictates of "human prudence." Teresa claimed that the bold, persuasive letter she wrote him (after having "prayed to the Lord over the matter very much") prevailed over his hesitation, and resulted in his granting her patent letters for the new foundations. Even so, he attached difficult conditions to the authorization. To make matters worse, Teresa had not yet secured the male collaboration she would need in order to get the project off the ground.

When the permissions arrived, then, Teresa admitted both to great consolation and a sudden sinking feeling. But having previously declared to Rubeo that "the difficulties that could arise were not sufficient to set aside so good a work," she practiced what she was preaching and put aside her own misgivings. True to expectations, she reported, "[n]either courage nor hope failed, for since the Lord had given the one thing, He would give the other. Everything now seemed very possible, and so I set to work."[64] In an exclamation aimed primarily at herself but that, in the context of her determined approach to a reluctant superior, might apply equally to the General, she summed up the lesson in this way:

[63]See her self-characterization as one possessed of *recio corazón* (a robust spirit, or strong-hearted) and "not like a woman at all" in *Testimonies,* 3:6; a similar allusion in *Life, 8:7.*

[64]*Foundations,* 2:6.

> O greatness of God! How You manifest Your power in giving courage to an ant! How true, my Lord, that it is not because of You that those who love You fail to do great works but because of our own cowardice and pusillanimity. Since we are never determined, but full of human prudence and a thousand fears, You, consequently, my God, do not do Your marvellous and great works. Who is more fond than You of giving, or of serving, even at a cost to Yourself, when there is someone open to receive?[65]

Teresa stood up to provincials and governors, bishops and benefactors, whenever the stakes involved what she perceived to be the work ordained by God. As she worked to establish the first foundation for friars at Duruelo, for example, she found it necessary to remind the provincial, Fray Alonso González, "of the account he would have to give if he hindered a work as good as this when asked by God to carry it out."[66] She cut through the troublesome foot-dragging of civil and ecclesiastical officials during the difficult Toledan foundation by requesting an audience with the governor. Shaming him with reference to his wealth, comfort, and status, she "told him that it was hard to accept the fact that there were *women* who wanted to live with . . . austerity, perfection, and withdrawal from the world" while male officials who themselves were willing to "bear nothing of this but lived in comfort" stood presumptuously in the way of "these works that were of such service to the Lord." The governor, "deeply moved" by her spirited sermon, quickly acquiesced.[67] Even so, Teresa continued to encounter difficulty in Toledo, and her scorn for those who opposed her determined efforts can be felt in the pointed irony with which she reported their "astonish[ment] at such boldness that a *useless little woman* should found a monastery against their will."[68]

[65]*Foundations,* 2:7.

[66]*Foundations,* 13:6. See also the pair of bold, direct, and canny letters Teresa wrote to the General Rubeo in 1575–76 during a period of great crisis for the reform. In one, Teresa menacingly reminded the General of Gracián's connections with the Court and the King's likely intervention on her behalf *(Letters* I, 180); in another, she announced: "When we both stand before [the] judgment seat, your Reverence will see what you owe . . . Teresa of Jesus" *(Letters* I, 221).

[67]*Foundations,* 15:5.

[68]*Foundations,* 15:11, emphasis added. See also *Testimonies,* 30, for Teresa's summation

She was also annoyed by "men of prominence, learning, and high intelligence" who made a great deal of fuss because they were not gifted with feelings of devotion and consolation in prayer; their complaining inability to suffer dryness and wait resolutely for God to act seemed to her to denote a lack of "freedom of spirit and the courage to accomplish something."[69] Often she found men as fickle and indecisive as women were purported to be, and even her most cherished male friend and collaborator, Jerónimo Gracián, was on numerous occasions the object of her criticism for, among other things, his lack of backbone and his tendency to whine at hardship. Her male supporters were like twigs, she said, easily broken and scattered by unexpected winds.[70]

In the end, however, Teresa was pursuaded that neither men nor women could ever hope to be determined and strong in the face of the challenges presented by the world, the flesh, and the devil without engaging in *prayer.* Prayer was, for her, the very source and instrument of courage, daring, and desire. Unless one prayed, that is, cultivated a deep and lasting friendship with God, one could not know and savor the substantial realities upon which authentic courage had to be constructed. In and through prayer, self-knowledge and knowledge of God issued in liberating contempt for the world's values and fearlessness in the face of its ensnaring deceptions—praise, blame, honor, reputation, wealth, status, prideful learning, and the rest. Prayer made the soul bold beyond imagining; the saints' heroic achievements, their near-foolhardy and "crazy deeds" were explicable for Teresa only because those women and men were persons enveloped in God through prayer.[71]

But prayer itself required determination, as we have seen, not only in order to persevere in the beginning when all seems so arduous but also and perhaps especially in the later, deeper, more mysterious encounters in which the soul is both buffeted and becalmed by unheard of delights whose psychosomatic effects leave the soul

---

of the reason for her persistence in the work of the foundations: "I grew certain the work was God's, and so I threw myself into difficult tasks . . . "

[69]*Life,* 11:14.

[70]*Testimonies,* 3:1.

[71]Teresa often complained that the courageous zeal of times past was difficult to find among Christians of her day, even among those vowed to the religious life. See for example *Life,* 7:5.

bewildered, exhausted, and afraid.[72] The very experience of
prayer, as Teresa taught her disciples to practice it, assumed on
the part of the initiate a certain level of courage and persevering
determination, precisely the virtues women were presumed not
to possess. Moreover, since women were held to be more susceptible than men to the snares of demonic delusion in the spiritual
life on account of their sensuality, many of her sisters had been
schooled to believe that for women, even the attempts to practice contemplation was sheer temerity, a reckless flirtation with
disaster: *it is not for women.*

It was also widely held that a degree of theological sophistica-
tion was necessary to practice contemplation; and if some learning were necessary ordinarily, it was considered all the more vital
in a time when, in the view of many of Teresa's Catholic contemporaries, the true Church was being threatened by the forces
of subversive private judgment and disregard for the externals of
Christian faith and worship. As already noted, some Spanish theologians were teaching that the exercise of mental prayer, especially by groups of the illiterate and unschooled, contained within
itself the seeds of bitter fruit: rejection of the authority of Church
teaching and practice in favor of some subjective version of truth,
unauthorized and inevitably unorthodox scriptural interpretation,
rebellion, licentiousness, iconoclasm, and all the rest that had
come popularly to be associated with the Protestantism Spain so
deeply feared.

Thus, it was a foregone conclusion that the evident ignorance
of women, their natural "poverty of reason and softness of
mind,"[73] would have harmful consequences if they practiced
prayer other than that prescribed as the broad path for all the
laity. Having been systematically hindered from access to formal
knowledge on the basis of this assumption about their incapacity
for the hard work of the mind, most women were indeed ignorant
of the theological and psycho-spiritual doctrines that might have
supported and facilitated their interior lives. Teresa admitted frequently, for example, that she lacked the technical terminology
to explain her experience in the clear formulas of mystical theology; although it is also true that as an *espiritual,* she claimed that

---

[72]*Life,* 13:2; 20:4; 39:21; *Testimonies,* 59:9; *Way,* 18; *Castle* VI, 5:1-12.

[73]The opinion of Domingo de Soto (1494–1560), a leading Spanish Dominican theologian.

the simple language of direct experience was always to be preferred to the pride-prone rhetoric of speculative theologians. *Espirituales* had, in their view, no ultimate need for academic theology, although they all admitted its ancillary usefulness.

Thus, theology without experience held no fascination for Teresa, but learning that grew out of and helped illumine the soul's journey to union with God was something she envied. Her regard for theologians who were themselves men of prayer was as deep as the scorn she expressed for the academics and preachers who presumed to teach about God without firsthand knowledge of their subject. Still, she bemoaned the limitations *imposed upon her sex* because of their ignorance, and with authentic anguish, took note of the chains that bound her and her kind to self-defeat:

> O Lord, take into account the many things we suffer on this path for lack of knowledge! The trouble is that since we do not think there is anything to know other than that we must think of You we do not even know how to ask those who know, nor do we understand what there is to ask. Terrible trials are suffered because we don't understand ourselves, and that which isn't bad at all we think is a serious fault. This lack of knowledge causes the afflictions of many who practice prayer; complaints about interior trials, at least to a great extent, by people who have no learning; melancholy and loss of health; and even the complete abandonment of prayer.[74]

In addition to its inherent rigors and the dangers it was assumed to pose for women in particular, the life of prayer that Teresa advocated sparked fear because it seemed to deviate from the popular notion of the goal of religious life, namely, the salvation of one's own soul and intercession on behalf of benefactors. Teresa believed that the rigorous observance of the austere rule of Carmel, including its injunction to pray without ceasing, was to be, among other goals, the nuns' way of helping to contain and repair the damage of schism. But when she explained that they were continually to turn over in their hearts the state of the Church

---

[74]*Castle* IV, 1:9. For other references to the disadvantages suffered by women and others because they are *idiotas* (illiterate) and *sin letras* (lacking studies, or formal higher education), see *Castle* I, 2:6; IV, 1:14; V, 3:10; VI, 7:5; *Life,* 11:6; 13:19; 26:3; 40:8; *Way,* 28:10; 41:6; *Foundations, 5:2; Song,* 1:8; *Life,* 27:3; 28:6.

and its need for holiness, she was apparently met by fears that by so doing, the nuns would be distracted from the business of securing their own salvation. In Chapter 3 of *Way,* she urged them to put aside fear and self-concern and adopt a posture of apostolic heroism through prayer:

> If you are uneasy because you think your sufferings in purgatory will not be shortened, know that by this prayer they will be; and if you must still pay some debts, so be it. What would it matter were I to remain in purgatory until judgment day if through my prayer I could save even one soul? How much less would it matter if my prayer is to the advantage of many and for the honor of the Lord. Pay no attention to sufferings that come to an end if through them some greater service is rendered to Him who endured so many for us.[75]

As for those persons who would frighten them by parading before their eyes examples of women who had been led astray by toying with mental prayer, Teresa was emphatic about what her sisters' attitude should be: "Should anyone tell you that prayer is dangerous, consider him the real danger and run from him . . . There will be danger in not having humility and the other virtues. But that the way of prayer be a way of danger—God would never will that."[76] Indeed, Teresa added, such is the shortsightedness of the "world" that the critics of those who practice prayer completely forget that *not* to pray is far more dangerous than its opposite. "[M]any thousands," she wrote, " . . . have fallen into heresies and great evils because they didn't practice prayer, but engaged in distractions."[77] Teresa saw the mark of the devil in antiprayer propaganda; trotting out the fate of a handful of lost souls among the "multitude" who practiced prayer profitably was his way of preventing Christians from seeking God in the first place. Terrified of damning their souls, they "[run] away from good to free themselves from evil." In Teresa's judgment, those who thus frightened potential persons of prayer "under the guise of zeal"[78] were guilty of "a wicked contrivance." In such perni-

[75]*Way,* 3:6.
[76]*Way,* 21:7.
[77]*Way,* 21:8.
[78]*Way,* 21:9.

cious reversals of truth Teresa saw an attack on God; thus, she begged, "O my Lord, defend Yourself!"[79]

For Teresa, the treasure to be gained by travelling the "royal road" of contemplation was so great, everything else "so trifling," and the prize in fact accessible, that no warnings, no bad apples, no demons were sufficient to persuade her not to try.[80] She knew from experience how crippling fear is, how swiftly it can snuff out freedom and make one acquiesce to mediocrity. As one who had stood her ground and exorcized the spectres of imposed self-doubt, as the longtime beginner who finally waved a cross at fear and saw it fade away before her very eyes, Teresa shared her wisdom with her sisters in a passage that reveals how acutely aware she was of the denial of female capacity for authentic interiority that lay at the base of the authorities' cautions about the practice of prayer:

> [T]hose who want to journey on this road . . . must have a great and very resolute determination to persevere until reaching the end, come what may, happen what may, whatever work is involved, whatever criticism arises, whether they arrive or whether they die on the road, or even if the whole world collapes. You will hear some people frequently making objections: "there are dangers"; "this one was deceived"; "another who prayed a great deal fell away"; "it is harmful to virtue"; "it is not for women, for they will be susceptible to illusions"; "it is better they stick to their sewing"; "they don't need these delicacies"; "the Our Father and the Hail Mary are sufficient."
> . . . [D]on't pay any attention to the fears they raise or to the picture of the dangers they paint for you . . . Sisters, give up these fears; never pay attention in like matters to the opinion of the crowd. Behold these are not the times to believe everyone; believe only those who you see are walking in conformity with Christ's life.[81]

[79] *Way,* 21:8.
[80] *Way,* 21:1.
[81] *Way,* 21:2-10.

3

To Be with Someone Who Loves Us

Several tensions in the religious life of her time and place reverberate in Teresa's counsel to "believe only those who you see walking in conformity with the life of Christ." One involved the quietist excesses of "enlightened ones," or *alumbrados,* and false mystics; another the large number of priests, theologians, and Religious whose lives were, in her opinion, mired in mediocrity; and a third had to do, as we have already seen, with those theologians upon whom she heaped her irony in *Way,* the *letrados,* who opposed the practice of contemplation outright.

Teresa eschewed the quietism of the *alumbrados,* and she believed that the pseudomystics placed too much emphasis on extraordinary spiritual experiences, or on extravagant penance. Such ill-formed souls lacked convincing signs of seriousness about the life of the spirit; they were not ready to be obedient when obedience was called for, shouldered crosses (like illness and contradiction) complainingly, and failed in basic charity toward their neighbors. The problem of mediocrity lay in not praying enough, or not praying at all. The *letrados* condemned what they knew nothing about and were too wrapped up in their sterile learning to try.

It was widely believed that pseudomystics laid out a slick path to heresy and damnation for their followers. Teresa believed, moreover, that unspiritual priests and theologians who would not pray placed their own souls in peril and made themselves incapable of efficacious cure and salutary instruction of the many souls entrusted to them by virtue of their office and vocation. Thus, countless unfortunate Christians were slipping into the devil's grasp.

"Believe only those who you see walking in conformity with the life of Christ," Teresa admonished her sisters, only those who *pray,* and only those whose prayer is authenticated by evidence of detachment, humility, charity, and an embrace of the cross. Teresa understood the needs of souls, the state of the Church, and the condition of the world to be such that no time remained any longer for anything except the ultimate business of God. And to be about that business one also had to be about the business of prayer.[1] If indeed "the one who knows God well does God's work better," as she had once asserted,[2] then it was crucial for the success of God's work to waste no time in entering into the dialogue of knowledge and love, the dialogue of prayer.

Conversation with the angels

In 1555, Teresa met doña Guiomar de Ulloa, a well-to-do noble widow of twenty-eight. Yomar, as Teresa called her, was famous for her beauty and had earned during her youth and brief marriage a reputation for extravagant ostentation. But she renounced her days of high living upon the death of her husband, three years before her meeting with Teresa. When she turned her energies to prayer and mortification instead of arranging another marriage, she also turned her palace into a monastery of sorts and herself into something of a sign of contradiction. Teresa liked her (she said the two of them were "like sisters") and insisted on the genuineness of Yomar's piety: "she is more of a saint than people realize." But not everyone agreed. The lady continued to be the subject of a good deal of unfavorable comment and censure, but Teresa was always quick to defend her.[3] Yomar had a sister and two daughters in the Incarnation, and it was probably during visits there that she heard of Teresa, whose spiritual struggles and supernatural experiences were by this time the talk of the cloister and even of the town.[4] Drawn to persons who practiced their pi-

[1] Cf. *Testimonies*, 3:7.

[2] *Foundations*, 3:5; see also *Way*, 3:5.

[3] *Life*, 24:6; 30:3; *Letters* I, 30; 142.

[4] For example *Life*, 28:12; 29:14; 33:5; 40:21; *Testimonies*, 9.

ety with deliberate dedication, Yomar decided to take Teresa under her wing.

Doña Guiomar entered the scene at an important moment for Teresa. Her spiritual guide, the Jesuit Diego de Cetina, had been unexpectedly transferred out of Avila. Cetina had directed Teresa no more than two months,[5] but his "common sense and sincere piety"[6] had been a relief in the wake of the somewhat rigid treatment she had experienced at the hands of her previous counselors, Gaspar Daza and the pious layman Francisco de Salcedo. Cetina was not perfect; he too could be rigid and impatient, but at least he understood her, for like Teresa he actually practiced mental prayer.

Teresa was deeply depressed by his abrupt departure. As at other crisis points in her development, she fell seriously ill. She left the Incarnation to spend time at the house of a relative, determined all the while to find herself another confessor from the Society of Jesus, since the Jesuits seemed well-equipped to help her.[7] It was at this point that "The Lord was pleased that [she] become friendly with a widow of high nobility who practiced prayer and was a very close friend of members of the Society." Yomar took Teresa to her palace, and there she began making her confession to Yomar's priest, a young Jesuit named Juan de Prádanos, recently assigned to the College of San Gil.[8]

The association was fruitful beyond calculation. In matters of mortification and "detachment from creatures," for example, Teresa's former counselors had pushed her faster than she had been ready to go. As she put it, her spirit had been "not at all strong but very fragile,"[9] and the stress caused by asking too much of herself all at once had been a torment. Prádanos took the pressure off. He knew that she had made persistent and sincere attempts to gain a certain freedom with respect to her human relationships, all to no avail. Teresa herself had learned through these failed efforts just how caught she was in the need for human approval and attention. Feeling too daunted to keep up the

[5]*Life,* 24:1.

[6]*Tiempo y vida,* 107: *sentido común y sincera piedad.* My translation.

[7]*Life,* 24:4.

[8]Teresa remained with doña Guiomar for nearly three years.

[9]*Life,* 24:5.

struggle, she had begun to rationalize her captivity as not offensive to God. Rather than mortify her or forbid her to spend time in the convent parlor, Prádanos patiently heard her out and asked her only to turn the matter over in prayer: sincerely to "commend the matter to God for some days and recite the hymn *Veni Creator* so that God might give [her] light about the better course of action."[10]

The young Jesuit knew that in order "to please God completely," Teresa would eventually have "to leave nothing undone." Yet he also knew that conversion could not be commanded and that, although not negligible in the life of a disciplined spirit, no directorial insistence, penance, technique, or strategy could succeed altogether in *forcing* the requisite reordering of her relational and affective life. In prayer, however, anything could happen, and Prádanos helped Teresa trust in its grace.[11]

Teresa took his request seriously and set out on a course of prayer, "begging the Lord," as she put it, "to help me please Him in all things." One day, while engaged in this prayer, she began the hymn to the creative Spirit that Prádanos had asked her to recite. Before she could finish it, she was completely overwhelmed:

> . . . a rapture came upon me so suddenly that it almost carried me out of myself. It was something I could not doubt, because it was very obvious. It was the first time the Lord granted me this favor of rapture. I heard these words: *"No longer do I want you to converse with [human beings] but with angels."*[12]

The words so profoundly impressed Teresa that, in her estimation, they accomplished within her what years of effort on her own had been unable to achieve with any permanence or consistency. "I [did not] think I could succeed in the matter," she wrote,

---

[10]*Life*, 24:5.

[11]*Life*, 24:5, 7.

[12]*Life*, 24:5, emphasis added. Rapture is "irresistible contemplation" in which the soul experiences union with God so close that it can even *seem* as if the two are one without difference. Rapture bestows important spiritual strengths upon the soul such as courage, discernment, and an increased desire for God. Raptures may be partial or full, absorbing body and spirit in varying degrees. Teresa discussed raptures in the sixth mansions of *The Interior Castle*. See also *Christian Mysticism*, 136–37.

"I had already tried it . . . Now in this rapture the Lord gave me the freedom and strength to perform the task . . . May God be blessed forever because in an instant He gave me the freedom that I with all the efforts of many years could not attain by myself."[13]

She had sought not the abandonment of human relationships, friendship, and intimacy but the ability to embrace them for the right reasons and without self-seeking; not the cold cutting of ties but the establishment of bonds on a new footing; not withdrawal from human discourse but the transformation of discourse and friendship. The efforts she had made had been worth making, to be sure, but when the victory came, she experienced it as a work of grace, communicated efficaciously in the midst of loving conversation.

From that time on, every conversation with human beings would also be in fact a conversation with "angels"—an authentic outgrowth and reflection of the primary conversation of prayer and friendship with God, as well as an unerring path to take her back again to prayer more rooted than before in the loving God. Human conversation and friendship would be a distraction, or a danger posed to the spirit, only if the habitual conversation partner were not a God-seeker, not a friend of the Friend. As Teresa put it:

> These words have been fulfilled for I have never again been able to tie myself to any friendship or to find consolation in or bear any particular love for any other persons than those I understand love Him and strive to serve Him; nor is it in my power to do so. . . . If I'm not aware that the person seeks to love God or to speak about prayer, it is a painful cross . . . to deal with him.[14]

Prayer as friendship with God

Prayer became the axis of Teresa's life. But what is meant by the term prayer, as it was so frequently employed by Teresa and

[13]*Life*, 24:7, 8.
[14]*Life*, 24:6.

the *espirituales,* is not always susceptible to neat exposition since, as Teresa repeatedly asserted, in order to understand what prayer is, prayer must be *experienced.* Teresa's writings (all of them in one way or another about her own practice of prayer, and doctrine based on that practice) record a great variety of spiritual experiences grouped under the rubric of prayer, the fruits of a woman's search for direct, interior connection with God: from the thoughtful recitation of the Creed or The Lord's Prayer, to the simplest exercise of meditation, to the most complex and sublime encounter of mystical union.

What lends unity to the multiplicity of experiences recorded in her books is Teresa's characterization of that connection: it is all about *friendship.* If prayer is any one thing, she explained to her sisters, it is "an intimate sharing between friends" for which one must frequently take time in order "to be alone with Him who we know loves us."[15] Even the Christian whose prayer life consists mainly of simple recitation of established prayers is, in Teresa's view, well-positioned for intimate friendship with God, for when one recites vocal prayers "with an understanding of whom we are speaking to," God listens and "speaks well to the heart when we beseech Him from the heart."[16] When a soul says "Our Father" and understands "who this Father of ours is and who the Master is who taught us this prayer," it is nothing less than an authentic "act of love."[17]

At its best, vocal prayer is attentive conversation with God (or Mary or the saints). The one with whom the soul speaks is ever near, and the soul makes an effort to be increasingly aware of that presence and "remain with that friend" as long as she can. Throughout the day, she "acquire[s] the habit" of similar communication with God even (if the soul finds the practice helpful) by carrying an icon of the Lord in order to look at the image of the friend from time to time and speak to him. Teresa encouraged these and other simple, even "silly"[18] practices as aids to vocal

---

[15]*Life,* 8:5; see also 7:1; 8:3.

[16]*Way,* 24:5.

[17]*Way,* 24:2. Teresa stands in a long line of Christian writers who treat the Lord's Prayer mystically, including such Patristic authors as Tertullian *(De Oratione),* Cyprian *(De Dominica Oratione),* and Origen *(Perieuches).* Her commentary occupies Chapters 27–32 of *Way.*

[18]*Life,* 9:3; 34:8; *Way,* 14:12.

prayer and beginners' meditation, because she believed that all prayer is at bottom friendship, and that friendship demands care, attention, and communication. "[T]he failure [frequently] to communicate with a person, she taught, "causes both estrangement and a failure to know how to speak with him. For it seems that we don't know him, even if he may be a relative; family ties and kinship are lost through a lack of communication."[19]

At first, such communication is somewhat external, an exercise of imagining or representing to oneself, as Teresa used to do, Christ as our loving companion. The person doing the imagining, however, finds she must expend effort to maintain that presence and "water the soul," like a gardener lugging buckets when no other irrigation is available and the skies have not yet provided rain.[20] Eventually, however, as the communication becomes more and more interior, the person develops a greater awareness of and sensitivity to a reality that always elicited great wonder and gratitude from Teresa: *that we are not empty or hollow inside.*[21] The God of love dwells at the very center of the human soul, an extremely rich palace.[22] We are invited to seek within the companionship of God and Christ, to glimpse within the beauty and worth of our humanness, to cherish within the dignity of our having been created in God's image and redeemed by Christ's love, and to experience at every turn the invitation to ever-increasing intimacy.

At this stage, the soul learns through practice to establish a habit of turning inward "to enter [the] paradise within itself to be with its God and close the door to all the world."[23] Inside the "little palace of the soul" where God is "seated upon a very valuable throne, which is your heart,"[24] it is not necessary "to shout in order to speak to Him," for God lets the soul know "that He

[19] *Way,* 26:9.

[20] *Life,* 11. See the remainder of Teresa's famous consideration of the four ways of watering a garden, an allegory about "degrees" of prayer, in *Life,* 11–22.

[21] *Way,* 28:9-11. The overarching metaphor of Teresa's finest treatise on the spiritual life, *The Interior Castle,* is precisely that of the castle-soul, into which each person enters to seek God at the center of what it is to be human. Many rooms, or "mansions," must be explored along the way.

[22] *Way,* 28:9.

[23] *Way,* 29:4.

[24] *Way,* 28:9, 11.

is present.''[25] This gathering of the self for an inward gaze is recollection, a form of prayer that although achieved by practice and human effort, is nonetheless contemplative in its dynamic; it seeks a real meeting with the divine and often becomes the threshhold for the prayer of quiet, in which little human effort is required. Instead, God now "gives this prayer," and it is the beginning of "pure" or infused contemplation.[26]

In her most mature work on the life of the spirit, *The Interior Castle,* Teresa described in great detail and with remarkable psychological insight all these and many further degrees of friendship and conversation with God, including the most intimate form of communication the soul is privileged to experience—union, or spiritual matrimony. In that experience, the communication that occurs is as silent, in Teresa's words, as "the building of Solomon's temple where no sound was heard." At the center of the human being, "in this temple of God, in this His dwelling place," God alone and the soul "rejoice together in the deepest silence."[27]

In the pages of Teresa's writings we get a sense of the kind of communication with God at which she became adept. Regardless of the topic she was at any point addressing, and no matter the intended audience or addressee, *God* is always and everywhere her primary interlocutor. God's communicative presence is felt everywhere: intercessions, praises, exclamations, and complaints rise constantly to the surface of her prose. The reader becomes an eavesdropper on a running, rich, free, and open-ended conversation of a soul with God.[28] Teresa believed that one can and must talk with God about anything: everyday concerns and long-range hopes, people, things, and events; nothing lies out of bounds. Conversation, even union with God could take place any-

---

[25] *Way,* 29:5.

[26] *Way,* 30:7; 31:2. *Christian Mysticism,* 127. The prayer of quiet is discussed in the fourth mansions of *Castle.* It is, as its name implies, a state of deep interior peace and quiet in which a person's will is captivated in love by God. God's presence permeates the recesses of the will, spreading joy and increasing the soul's capacity for giving and receiving love. This state, in which the will is absorbed in God and the other faculties (imagination, memory, etc.) are going about their everyday business, can last only a few moments, or it can go on for days.

[27] *Castle* VII, 3:11.

[28] She was aware of her tendency to interrupt her narrative with prayer and asked her addressees to pardon her, for "in speaking about myself I am dealing with my feelings, and therefore it is often very difficult to resist continuing to proclaim the praises of God as I put down in writing the many things I owe Him." *Life,* 14:12.

where, anytime, during the most ordinary activities or in the silence and solitude of a stay in a hermitage.[29] Teresa hoped that many people would begin the conversation and make friends with God, persevering through the stuttering early meetings to the time when it need no longer be carried on exclusively by means of words but take instead the other forms which all good friends and lovers know: the gaze, the silent sharing, the gesture of wordless embrace.[30]

Discovering the friend

Teresa's mature friendship with God was founded upon simple, affective exercises that tended toward greater and greater personalization of prayer. Early in her development, as we have already seen, she relied upon the method of recollection taught in *The Third Spiritual Alphabet*. That teaching gave Teresa a framework in which to understand and appreciate some of the supernatural experiences she was already beginning to have as a result of her habit of reflection upon scenes from the gospels, especially those related to the Passion of Christ.[31] And, more important perhaps, it filled her with the determination to persist in prayer. Initially, the results were more wonderful than she could have hoped for: "At the end of this time that I remained [in Hortigosa], the Lord . . . began to favor me by means of this path [of recollection]; so much so that he granted me the prayer of quiet. And sometimes I arrived at union, although I did not understand what one was or the other . . . "[32] Teresa had little insight into her prayer early on; all she knew was that it seemed easy, spontaneous, and wonderful.

Before long, however, she entered an extended period during which she engaged in an authentic struggle to unleash her capacity to speak to God directly, to speak with God as a friend. This was the period in which Teresa's "determined determination" led her

[29]Reportedly, Teresa once went into an ecstatic suspension in the convent kitchen, causing excited comment: the holy Mother in rapture with a frying pan clutched in her hand. See *Tiempo y vida*, 194–95.

[30]The prayer of "simple gaze." *Castle* VI, 7:11. See also *Life*, 27:10.

[31]For example, the gift of tears. See *Life*, 4:7.

[32]*Life*, 4:7.

to create for herself what the Carmelite rule of the Incarnation at that time did not require or provide: daily periods of solitary, personal prayer, clung to faithfully no matter how she felt, no matter how well or badly her prayer was going. Moreover, for much of this nearly twenty-year period, Teresa was without a spiritual director, a circumstance she later lamented and which certainly contributed to her somewhat erratic progress.

During this time, for example, she experienced some remarkable mystical favors; but equally or more often, she found herself tied to meditation books in order merely to concentrate.[33] She quickly discovered how useless she was for the kind of prayer that required reasoning. For Teresa, this *discursive* prayer seemed impossible because, among other things, she could not tame her unruly, wandering imagination. Like bothersome, "restless moths" at night who never light, her imagination fluttered through her mental disquisitions, disturbing her concentration; like a "raving lunatic who no one can subdue," it gave her no rest.[34] Without a spiritual book of some kind, even if it were just to leave it lying open and unread upon her lap, Teresa's prayer drifted away unanchored.[35]

Teresa taught from her own experience, then, an important and freeing lesson to her sisters: one should not force oneself to pray using a method uncongenial to temperament or talent. "[I]t must be understood," she wrote, "that not all imaginations are by their nature capable of this meditating, *but all souls are capable of loving.*"[36] The point of prayer is love and not technique. Teresa therefore followed paths that helped her and learned, sometimes painfully, to discard those that did not, making use of whatever was at hand to aid her in cultivating her friendship with God. As far as she was concerned, "the important thing is not to think

---

[33]*Life,* 4:9.

[34]See *Life,* 9:4-5; 15:6; 17:6; 30:16; *Way,* 19:2; 26:2; *Castle* IV, 1:6, 13. Discursive prayer means meditation in which the understanding, or reason, and the imagination are actively engaged in some form of consideration (for example, of a biblical passage, the content of a vocal prayer, the meaning of a scene from Christ's passion, etc.). Discursive prayer is the source of many fruitful religious emotions, and often leads the person to make resolutions about amending his or her way of life. The danger of discursive prayer is that it can tire the mind; it can also lead persons not well-grounded in humility to prefer their own mental compositions to the restful, quieter prayer that God might be trying to bestow upon them.

[35]Except after receiving holy communion. See for example *Life,* 4:9. Many of Teresa's most profound mystical intuitions and visions occurred after receiving holy communion.

[36]*Foundations,* 5:2.

much but to love much; and so do that which best stirs you to love."[37]

During this same period, friendship with God was also demanding of her a new level of personal integrity. She was being called to stop wasting time on matters that did not lead to her goal, to curb her self-confessed vanity, and radically to reorder her relational priorities. Teresa did not fail to guess at the nature of these demands as essential to the quality of her relationship with God; but she had failed to be consistent about them. Although she continued faithful to her meeting times with God, she knew she was not bringing a true self to the meeting. An agonizing experience of inner contradiction, of a self divided, was the result. Eventually, Teresa lost hope in her ability to make her life cohere with what she experienced of God's mercy in prayer and grew certain that the difference in the condition of the friends was too great an obstacle to continuing the relationship. She believed herself unworthy of God's friendship, and for about a year[38] abandoned entirely the effort to pray, taking it up again only after her father's death.

The next ten years[39] constituted a long, gradual conversion during which prayer continued to be a very troublesome way to make friends with God, but one which Teresa was convinced as never before was the only way. Toward the end of those years, under the direction of Cetina and Prádanos, her struggle for a more authentic self also shifted ground. She began to experience real compunction about her sins and failings, rather than the narrow self-concern that had generated her earlier, paralyzing fears about

---

[37]*Castle* IV, 1:7. For example, even though expensive images of Christ, the Virgin Mary, and the saints were to be avoided, Teresa believed that paintings and statues were licit "means for enkindling love." Thus the reported iconoclasm of the Protestants struck her as dangerous for souls seeking to love God in as many ways as possible. See her conversation with God about this "error of the Lutherans," *Testimonies,* 26; also *Life,* 9:6. Note too that Teresa's first intellectual vision was of the "form" of the risen Christ "as it is in paintings," *Life,* 28:3. Teresa is best understood as a "kataphatic" mystic, proceeding primarily by the way of affirmation and images; she experienced God as more immanent and personal than other and unknowable. John of the Cross, the author of *The Cloud of Unknowing,* and others whose mysticism is primarily negative, imageless, "empty" and "dark," represent the "apophatic" tradition, in which God's transcendence and the mystic's inability to comprehend anything about God with the intellect predominate. For a good discussion of these two classical emphases in contemplation, see Harvey D. Egan S.J., "Christian Apophatic and Kataphatic Mysticisms," *Theological Studies* (September, 1978) 399–426.

[38]Probably 1543–44, halfway through the twenty-year period reviewed here.

[39]Until 1554–55.

unworthiness. She learned to regard the confession of her sinful-
ness not only as an opportunity to acknowledge her helplessness
and fundamental unworthiness in God's sight but also and more
importantly as an occasion to sing *the mercies of God.*[40]
Her scathingly negative self-assessments did not change, for in
her eyes, they said who she truly was; but they no longer led her
to withdraw or hide from God. Overcome with gratitude, amazed
by grace and the relentlessness of God's goodness, her sinful reality began rather to draw her closer to her friend; what she
thought of as her creaturely nothingness became one of the tightest
bonds forged between them.[41]
She still wished, however, not to offend through even the most
venial of sins or imperfections; only ingrates slighted their benefactors, and Teresa knew how much she owed God. Because her love
for God was growing deeper and wider, she continued to discipline
and examine her life in the hope of acquiring "detachment from
all created things": the radical interior freedom that stems from
ultimate dependence upon God; the capacity to *renounce* if need
be even what is good; but even more profoundly, the capacity
to *embrace* everything in God's good creation without possessive-
ness toward it nor enslavement of self by it. All Teresa's words
about the necessity of practicing the virtues of poverty, obedience,
humility, and self-discipline can be understood in this light; for
her, they are both means to and effects of authentic interior liberty. For her, they are aids in the reordering of priorities that arises
as an urgent necessity out of the prayerful encounter with God.
Unhappily, in her view she seemed always to be taking one
step forward and two steps back. Yet all these efforts and experiences were not in vain. Her emotional encounter with the image of Christ during Lent of 1554, her profound identification
with the repentant and converted Augustine shortly thereafter,
and the spiritual betrothal she experienced under the direction of
Fr. Prádanos in 1556, described above, mark their culmination.[42]

[40]Although Teresa acknowledged a correlation between ascetical preparation and mystical
progress, she always insisted also on God's freedom to give "favors" to anyone at anytime,
even if the person were in mortal sin, for God's own glory and for God's own reasons. See
for example *Way,* 16:6-8; *Castle* I, 1:3; IV, 2:9-10; V, 1:12; V, 4:12, 7:9; 8:5.

[41]See for example *Life,* 15:14; *Castle* VI, 7:3.

[42]*Life,* 9:1-2; 7-8.

Somehow, the mysterious interweaving of human determination and divine and graceful mercy (characteristic of middle stages of prayer in Teresa's schema) created a turning point, a moment of truth that opened the way for doña Teresa de Ahumada to become, by God's grace alone, the mystic, Teresa of Jesus.

The stamina of Teresa's unfolding mystical life was tested immediately by the group of confessors and friends that began scrutinizing her soul after Prádanos fell ill in the winter of 1557 and then left Avila.[43] In Chapter 2 of this volume, we witnessed her victory over their fears and the demons that tried to rob her of interior freedom. She had also to cope with those who, far from decrying her increasing and uncontrollable visions, voices, and raptures as the illusions of a fraud, hailed her eagerly and uncritically as a saint.[44] Teresa eventually emerged from the ensuing bouts of scruples and human respect with her serenity intact, thanks in part to the encouragement of respected experts like the Franciscan Pedro de Alcántara and the Jesuit Francis Borgia, and, in part, thanks to a remarkable vision of hell that seems to have wrenched her attention away from the ins and outs of her own soul's troubles and fixed it decisively upon the needs of others. Teresa understood her friendship with God to have reached a point of identification and exchange; giving over self-concern to God, God's concerns became her only care. There were souls to win and save, persons to be converted into friends of God. Teresa was in her forties now; the work of the reform was just over the horizon.

Christ, the friend par excellence

Teresa's understanding of prayer as friendship with God was typical of the teaching of the *espirituales*. Their great achievement was the rekindling of the affections in the practice of prayer, but

[43]Teresa and Yomar lived with him and nursed him in his illness, causing scandalized comment.

[44]Writing many years later to M. María Bautista, Teresa recalled her experiences in Castile: "And one of the things that makes me happy here, and will make me increasingly so, is that there is no suggestion of that nonsense about my supposed sanctity which people talked of in Castile. That allows me to live and go about without fear that the tower of their imagination would be falling down on me." *Letters* I, 195.

their insistence on God's accessibility as friend and companion
exposed them to criticism as cheapeners of the divine mystery.
Critics bore down heavily on the dangers of excessive familiarity
with God, and one prominent theologian characterized Archbishop Carranza's views on mental prayer (which were nearly identical to Teresa's) as "heretical, contrary to the definition of the
Council of Trent, and smacking of *alumbrado* heresy."[45]

The overreaction of many Spanish theologians to what they perceived as the dangers of the kind of affective prayer that placed
God at the center of the soul as friend was in turn attacked by
other prominent scholars and preachers. These persons could
agree with the critics that *some* caution was called for. For example, like Teresa, they did not wish to encourage neglect of basic
duties or charity toward one's neighbor in the rush to devote oneself to the delights of prayer. They warned against faddish excitement about techniques and were wary of many unprepared
people becoming involved too far and too fast with the new spirituality. Yet they refused to damn affective contemplation as the
espirituales were teaching it; the alternative was submersion in
dry intellectual speculation, leaving "nothing for devotion, nothing for the spirit, nothing for the spiritual senses."[46]

Although Teresa's stance in this debate is abundantly clear, it
is important to note that for her, friendship with God even at its
most intimate never meant complete erasure of the vast chasm
she understood always to exist between Creator and creature. God
was, after all, "His Majesty," the "King" and "Emperor," the
"more and more," the all-powerful one whose glory was, in her
own words, "frightening."[47] In contrast with the writings of the
more reserved John of the Cross, she even habitually addressed
God with the formal *Vos* rather than the more familiar *tú*. And
Teresa taught emphatically that all the more advanced forms of
contemplation could be experienced only if and when God chose
to lead the soul to them; no human effort could *determine* the

[45]Mancio de Corpus Christi, cited V. Baltrán Heredia, O.P., "El Maestro Mancio de Corpus Christi," *Ciencia Tomista*, 51 (1935): 42. My translation.

[46]This was the view of the Jesuit General Jerónimo Nadal, cited in M. Nocolau, "Espiritualidad de la Compañía en la España del XVI," *Corrientes espirituales en la España del siglo
XVI* (Barcelona: Juan Flors, 1963), 354.

[47]For example, *Castle* V, 1:8; VII, 1:2; *Life*, 18:3; 22:11; 37:6; 38:17-19; 40:3.

distribution of God's favors. Why God chose to give to this person and not that was beyond human knowing.

Nonetheless, perhaps precisely because she was so conscious of the awesome distance that lay between herself and God, she was all the more taken with the other side of the mystery of God as she understood it, the *divine condescension*. Hers was a God who could not only tolerate the presence of creatures but who actually longed to draw near to them. From the creature's point of view (fully realizing that he or she is less than nothing in comparison to God), God appears as greatly humbled, even humiliated, in the act of being so present to souls, and the soul who experiences that loving condescension is struck "silly with grateful amazement."[48]

Teresa was attracted powerfully to the mystery of divine condescension particularly as it was manifested in the person of Jesus Christ. This self-emptying of God profoundly moved her, especially when she dwelled upon the common faith that the incarnation had been undertaken for *her* sake, for the sake of miserable sinners. His having assumed human reality, becoming a "slave" and a "servant" for the sake of women and men, made Christ our "very good friend," since we are able to see and identify with him in his own "weakness and trials." Likewise, he makes "good company" for us, for he understands the human situation and knows of what stuff we are made.[49]

Teresa's Christ is the Christ she found in the gospel stories, the man of poverty, humility, compassion, miracle, suffering, forgiveness, and love. In all the scenes and mysteries of his earthly life, she contemplated him, immersed herself in his example and sacrifice, cultivated her gratitude and compunction by comparing her own life to his, and consciously sought to live his experiences and walk in his way. She frequently cited her sense of identification with Mary Magdalene, the Samaritan woman at the well, and other biblical characters in whose intimate dialogues with Jesus she longed to participate.[50]

---

[48]*Life*, 15:8, *boba* (dumb, or ignorant). This praise for God's humility is preceded by a swipe at the learned who, in Teresa's opinion, could stand a little more "study of humility" and less reasoning; her remark about God's humbling of self was censored.

[49]*Life*, 22:10; 37:5.

[50]*Song*, 6; *Way*, 15:7; 17:5; 26:8; 19:2; 34:7; 40:3; *Castle* VI, 7:4.

Christ was also her risen and eternally glorified Lord and King
whose presence indwelled her own interior castle and whom she
experienced in vision and voice, in companionship of every sort,
in the Church, and in particular in the Eucharist, where Christ
was humbled and glorified, accessible and powerful, and above
all *tangible,* all at once.[51] The "most Sacred Humanity" (her most
typical expression) was clearly and wonderfully displayed to the
eyes of her spirit even in the very bosom of the ineffable Trinity.[52]
In vision after searing vision of the triune God, later recalled for
her confessors in her personal notes, Teresa noted the enflesh-
ment of the Son; and when the voice of the divine reached her
spiritual senses, it was the risen Christ "in his Humanity" who
spoke to her.[53]

The humanity of Christ was absolutely central to Teresa's developing relationship with God in prayer. Indeed, the only time
she tried to do without the doorway of Christ's incarnate reality
and engage in a more severely apophatic prayer, her soul eventually experienced a suffocating constriction and her spiritual progress nearly came to a halt. Eventually coming to her senses, she
believed that she had acted "like a traitor."[54] Later, she conceded
that God can call some persons to a state of prayer in which the
intellect becomes incapable of meditation on the life and passion
of Christ, and everything creaturely, including Christ's humanity,
is placed in a cloud of unknowing; but she insisted that such a
suspension must be God's doing alone. The soul should not

[51]See especially Teresa's meditation on the words, "Give us this day our daily bread,"
Way, 33–35. Teresa felt bodily health increase with the reception of communion, *Testimonies,* 1:23; Jesus tells her that he is always with her and shows her his wounds after communion, *Testimonies,* 12:6; she has an intellectual vision of the Trinity after communion, and
a vision of Christ glorified in the host, *Testimonies,* 13; the host turns to blood in her mouth;
Christ's blood is experienced as a "reward" for being faithful and delicate in the preparation of a holy day, *Testimonies,* 22:1; her spiritual matrimony is accomplished in the moment of holy communion, *Testimonies,* 31; she has visions of the Trinity after communion
on St. Lawrence Day, *Testimonies,* 42:52; she recorded an appearance of Christ and union
with his Body in the Eucharist in *Testimonies,* 44. Teresa's Eucharistic piety and communion-
related mystical experiences have yet to receive the kind of deep and attentive exploration
that, for example, Carolyn Walker Bynum has made of medieval female mystics in *Holy
Feast and Holy Fast. The Religious Significance of Food to Medieval Women* (Berkeley: University of California Press, 1987).

[52]*Testimonies,* 65:3; also 51.

[53]*Testimonies,* 59:23.

[54]*Life,* 22; *Castle* VI, 7:15.

deliberately attempt to induce it in an effort to reach "higher" stages of prayer.

More importantly, in Teresa's opinion, even souls led in the way of negation and suspension of the intellect must continue somehow to walk with the indispensable companion, Jesus Christ. "Perfect contemplation" is a passing state; sooner or later, because we are not cherubim permanently enkindled in love, our human wills require stoking. Dwelling on the simple mysteries of Christ ignites the soul in love. Thus, even the most proficient must not, in Teresa's view, neglect or despise the mysteries of the life of Christ, as if to dwell on him (or even make use of images) somehow denoted spiritual imperfection or an inferior form of spirituality. Neither were souls inclined to apophatic prayer to devalue the celebrations and commemorations the Church proposes to the faithful as a corporate way of living with and meditating upon the Savior. Perhaps with *alumbrado* passivity and quietism in mind, Teresa was concerned that too much stress on the totally interior delight of the state of imageless suspension and absorption in God could loosen a person's hold on a truly *sacramental* and *incarnational* understanding of Christian life. Thus, she could even suggest that persons intent on bypassing all concepts, images, and things corporeal in their prayer might end up as heretics, with no appreciation for the Eucharist and a disdain for the externals of worship.[55] In her opinion, such souls must also take care not to become so absorbed in the experience of the prayer of quiet that they end up doing harm to their mental or emotional equilibrium.[56]

That perfect prayer consists in the bypassing of everything corporeal, including the sacred humanity of Christ, and that the soul by its efforts should strive to enter such a state, was a view taught by some contemporary *espirituales*. But in her own mature teaching on prayer, Teresa clung to her opinion that their doctrine was a serious mistake, open to dangerous misinterpretation:

> To be always withdrawn from corporeal things and enkindled in love is a trait of angelic spirits not of those who live in mortal bodies. It's necessary that we speak to, think about, and

[55]*Castle* VI, 7:11, 14.
[56]*Castle* VI, 7:13.

become the companions of those who having had a mortal body accomplished . . . great feats for God. How much more is it necessary not to withdraw through one's own efforts from all our good and help which is the most sacred humanity of our Lord Jesus Christ.[57]

Contemplation of the sacred humanity fosters gratitude; it provides "living sparks" that enkindle even more love for the Lord in the soul.[58] Neglect of the humanity exposes the soul to the risk of losing the only "Guide" capable of leading it into the deepest mansions, the center where the King awaits, because, Teresa believed, only Christ is the way, only Christ is the light, and no one goes to God except through him.[59] If in the most profound reaches of the journey inward some souls *can* do without occasional meditation on Christ, it is only because it is characteristic of the prayer of such souls that they are already continually in the presence of the incarnate one.[60] No matter what the other teachers of prayer might say on the matter, Teresa concluded, no one, "no matter how spiritual he may be," could persuade her that her objections were rooted in ignorance (some colleagues had apparently been disputing with her over this point, saying that "she did not understand" apophatic prayer), or that a soul can make true and lasting progress in the mystical way by trying to dispense with the humanity of Christ.[61]

A living book

Teresa's experience of the closeness and condescension of the divine man Christ placed him squarely at the heart of her spiritual growth in a strikingly concrete way when, probably in 1559,

[57]*Castle* VI, 7:6. Many commentators point out that Teresa broke with Osuna's teaching on the matter of Christ's humanity and its role in mystical progress.

[58]*Castle* VI, 7:11.

[59]*Castle* VI, 7:6. Note that Teresa is very aware that she is engaging in New Testament exegesis, and that "they" might not like what she says. See also *Castle* VI, 7:14.

[60]*Castle* VI, 7:9.

[61]*Castle* VI, 7:5-15. Note that in VI, 7:14, Teresa criticized ("I can't bear this") the exegesis of the scriptural passages used by her opponents to justify their position, adducing the example of the Virgin Mary to defend hers.

she and many others like her found themselves suddenly bereft of much treasured reading material. Most of the spiritual books and theological treatises, biblical expositions, and vernacular Scriptures pored over by *espirituales* were included on the list of forbidden matter prepared by the Inquisitor Valdés. "Only the Latin editions were allowed," Teresa noted with chagrin, for she did not normally understand Latin, except for the familiar passages of her Breviary.[62] Wherever the Index was strictly enforced, even the small number of women and other laypersons who *could* read, but who read only Spanish, were denied a valuable source of nourishment for their devotion and instruction for their spiritual formation. Having always enjoyed and greatly profited from reading such books, Teresa experienced a keen sense of sad disappointment at the turn of events. True to her experience of him as friend, she portrayed Christ as responding to her care: "Don't be sad," she heard him say, "I shall give you *a living book.*"[63]

Shortly after receiving this locution, Teresa experienced the presence of Christ as teacher in ways that gave her "so much to think about and such recollection," that "I had very little or almost no need for books. His Majesty had become the true book in which I saw the truths. Blessed be such a book that leaves what must be read and done so impressed that you cannot forget!"[64] Although she would continue to cherish books and recommend good reading for her sisters of the reform, Teresa believed also, along with many of the *espirituales,* that in the end books were at best substitutes for the living book, helps for reaching finally the living pages of Christ wherein true spiritual doctrine and truths of the most lofty sort were imbibed simply and directly from the source of truth itself.

The *espirituales* shared a conviction that the life of the spirit could be grasped and taught correctly ultimately only through *experience*. Although most were not anti-intellectuals, strictly speaking, they often adopted a tone of scorn for dogmatic theology, so estranged then from the mystical apprehensions of God from which it had sprung. In their view, the dry speculation of academic theology was no match for the direct, experiential knowl-

[62]*Life,* 26:5. Teresa reported a *mystical* understanding of Latin from time to time, however.

[63]*Life,* 26:5, emphasis added.

[64]*Life,* 26:5.

edge gained through contemplation. In that conviction, they viewed theology and theologians (unless these were also spiritual persons) not as *useless,* by any means, but as *ancillary* in the search for God.[65] Thus, even though spiritual books were excellent aids (the *espirituales* produced scores of them), they could never supply what one could learn in the book of Christ himself. "His Majesty was always my Teacher," Teresa said.[66] And when she began writing her own spiritual books, very soon after "they" forbade the reading of "many [spiritual] books in the vernacular,"[67] she claimed to teach nothing that was not among the lessons she had learned first by experience from Christ, the living book.

The "truths" she learned in prayerful encounter with God were, in her words, "more than if many learned men had taught me." "[E]xtraordinary truths about this Truth" were "impressed" upon her during periods of "very loving communication" with God, and Teresa *understood* with her whole being the doctrines she believed.[68] She was directed to the very core of the mysteries of Christian faith, and she grasped wholly and directly what was presented to her, in a way that mocked the artificial divorce between affect and intellect, heart and head. Contemplation became for Teresa a way of loving-knowledge, a way of knowing-being, a way of understanding-living.

Teresa wanted her own prayer and the prayer of her sisters to be rooted in Scripture, tradition, and the liturgical rhythms of the Church's corporate worship. She desired that they consult the learned (as she did throughout her life) especially those whose specialty was Scripture, so that their prayer would be informed from

[65]See for example Teresa's sometimes contradictory statements about the sort of spiritual director (learned only? spiritual and "experienced" only? both learned and experienced?) she thought best for persons who wanted to pray seriously. *Life,* 13. She also believed that theological learning could, in some cases, actually be *detrimental* in the search for God.

[66]*Life,* 12:6.

[67]*Life,* 26:5.

[68]*Life,* 40:4. The repetition throughout this passage (40:1-4 especially) of forms of the word *truth* is another of the hebraisms that Teresa employed from time to time in her writings (an echo of sixteenth-century vernacular speech), and brings to mind the solemn rabbinic saying with which the historian Peter Brown concludes the introduction to his book on early Christian asceticism, a declaration with which Teresa would have profoundly concurred: "Every judge who judges a judgement of truth, true to the truth of the matter, causes the glory of God to dwell in Israel." See *The Body and Society. Men, Women, and Sexual Renunciation in Early Christianity* (New York: Columbia Univ. Press, 1988), xx.

the beginning with good and approved doctrine, and so that the experiences they had could be plumbed for authenticity with the line of God's Word and the collective wisdom of the Christian community. She once prayed to be delivered from "foolish devotions," the sort of interior life that was constructed on ignorance and led, in her view, to error and self-delusion.[69] Yet she also believed that all the reading, studying, theologizing, consultation, and judgment that humans engaged in could never teach as clearly, as unforgettably, as efficaciously, and as *wholly* the truth which the "divine Truth" taught by experience, the loving-knowledge displayed in the pages of Christ, the living book.

Bride of Christ

The notion of friendship with Christ in and through the loving conversation of prayer devolved quite naturally for Teresa in the traditional imagery of nuptial love inherited from a variety of patristic and monastic sources, and nourished always by the richly explicit erotic material of the biblical *Song of Songs*.[70] In the Christian mystical interpretation of this Hebrew scripture, Christ is the pursuer, the bridegroom, the lover, the husband; the soul is the pursued, the espoused, the beloved, the bride. The spiritual life is a passionate courtship, and the experience of love fraught with both excruciating pain and exquisite delights: kiss and caress, longing, seduction, union, desolation, fulfillment, abiding presence, and sudden explosions of sensation, somatically-experienced aching loneliness in the loved-one's absence. But even though the erotic language of the tradition was fully sanctioned, its explicitness was usually diffused with spiritualizations and allegory so as not to scandalize, or worse, overfeed the fervid imagination of more sensual souls and induce them to dwell more on the human referents than the spiritual signs.

Teresa did not shy away from reporting her mystical experience in such frankly sexual terms, and although she accepted the spiritual allegories of the tradition,[71] she did not think it proper to

---

[69]*Life*, 13:16.

[70]For Teresa's own brief commentary on selected verses, see *Song, 215-260*.

[71]*Castle* V, 4:3.

explain away altogether the shock value of sensual imagery. She believed that the words could not be dispensed with since they were meant to enkindle a "mad" love. Moreover, she asserted that since the source of such a way of imagining and talking about one's experience of God lay in Scripture, God had surely authorized it; thus, it had to be good.

Teresa observed as well that some people have small and dirty minds; they would have preferred that the inspired writer choose "another style" to make the point, and they prudishly "avoid listening" to the erotic passages. Like "poisonous creatures [that] turn everything they eat into poison," such people "create fears" and snicker at the language devised by the Holy Spirit to show the soul how much God really loves it.[72] What scandalized Teresa was not that the language of divine love appropriates the terms used for the experiences of human love and sexual union, but that Christian people who are the objects of such intensely passionate and personal love are embarrassed or horrified by such words. "Indeed," she remarked:

> I recall hearing a priest . . . preach a very admirable sermon, most of which was an explanation of those loving delights with which the bride communed with God. And there was so much laughter, and what he said was so poorly taken, that I was shocked. He was speakng about love since the sermon was on Maundy Thursday when one shouldn't be speaking about anything else.[73]

Moreover, in Teresa's view, divine *deeds* aplenty bear out the descriptions: God's friendship with humanity to the point of assuming its flesh, the invitation to unite with Christ's body in the Eucharist, the kiss of peace and friendship in prayer.[74] Teresa taught her sisters, then, that no one should be surprised when souls are invited to say of the divine bridegroom, "Let him kiss me with the kiss of his mouth."[75]

[72]*Song,* 1:3-4.
[73]*Song,* 1:5.
[74]*Song,* 1:12.
[75]*Song,* 1:2.

Traditional bridal allegory with its erotic language is not the only source from which Teresa drew in order to express her experience of love, betrothal, and marriage with Christ. She freely used comparisons from actual human marriage, as it was both preached and practiced in her own culture. For example, we catch a glimpse of the customs surrounding arranged marriages when she described the prayer of union as comparable to the short period during which, after betrothal discussions have been held, a meeting between the engaged couple is permitted so that they might "become more satisfied with each other."[76] She scolded those who opposed the kind of affective prayer she experienced and taught for denying to God what they would never deny to humans—loving attention. She wrote:

> Oh God help me, here below before getting married a person will know the other partner, who he is and what he possesses. We are already betrothed and before the wedding must be brought to His house. Here below they don't try to make those who are betrothed renounce such thoughts. Why should they try to prevent us from thinking about who this man is, who His Father is, what country He is going to bring me to, what good things He promises to give me, what His status is, how I can make Him happy, and in what ways I can please Him . . . ?[77]

Moreover, her observation of ordinary human marriage provided her with a point of comparison for another crucial aspect of mystical spousal relations: "here below" (in the culture of sixteenth-century Castile), a wife shared not only the good times with her husband but also the bad. If his honor belongs to her, so also will she have to suffer his dishonor.[78] If Christ is "His Majesty" with endless gifts and riches to bestow, giving the beloved a spiritual liberty that entails dominion over the world with him,[79] he is also the crucified one, poor, despised, and trodden upon. Teresa often expressed immense desires to identify with

[76] *Castle* V, 4:4.
[77] *Way*, 22:7.
[78] *Way*, 13:2-3.
[79] *Way*, 19:4-5.

Christ in suffering and sacrifice and thought of herself and her sisters as *esposas del Crucificado*—brides of the Crucified.[80] "I desire to suffer, Lord," she wrote, "all the trials that come to me and esteem them as a great good enabling me to imitate You in something. Let us walk together, Lord. Wherever you go I will go; whatever You suffer, I will suffer."[81] Brides of Christ were not to turn their backs on him when he turned his face to Jerusalem: "Take up that cross, daughters . . . In stumbling, in falling with your Spouse, do not withdraw from the cross or abandon it."[82]

But if in many ways the life of divine intimacy bore comparison to human unions, Teresa was also well aware of the limits of the metaphor. For her, marriage to Christ was by far a better option than marriage to a man. She had seen marriages like that of her younger sister become dreadful, dragging punishments because of sour, mean, and disappointed husbands. Teresa seems to have known something about the physical cruelties many women endured in marriage; she seems struck also by the psychological hardships imposed on wives as a result of a marriage ethic that demanded, among other things, constant accommodation of the woman's mood to the man's.[83] Teresa believed in the long-held and widely accepted notion that marriage as a state of life is inferior to the state of consecrated virginity, and held it all the more firmly, perhaps, because in her era consecrated virginity and the vows of monastic life were being questioned and discarded by some humanists and all Protestants in favor of a more dignified theology of the Christian vocation of marriage. For Teresa, virginity's superiority lay not only in its spiritual worth, but also in the real freedom it afforded. With an eye to actual experience, she observed that marriage frequently came down to "being subject to a man who is often the death of [women] and who could also be, God forbid, the death of their

---

[80]*Letters* II, 939.

[81]*Way,* 26:6. Cf. Ruth, 1;15.

[82]*Way,* 26:7.

[83]See for example *Way,* 11:3, where, by way of shaming the nuns for having complained about "women's little sicknesses," Teresa invoked the forebearance of some married women who suffer "heavy trials and serious illnesses but for fear of annoying their husbands dare not complain."

souls.''[84] From this, God had freed them, Teresa told the nuns, by marrying them to Christ.

Her own parents' union seems to have been strained by her father's rigidity and the weight of impending financial ruin. Her mother's recourse to deception in the matter of reading books of chivalry was duly noted by Teresa, and, as we have seen, although she later judged the books to have been a waste of time, she never condemned her mother for sneaking them, since she only did so once all her other obligations were fulfilled. This little escape from constant vigilance may not have been a particularly noble or elevated one, but Teresa seems to have understood why it occurred. She cannot have failed to notice that in her mother's deception lay an act of ever-so-timid rebellion deeply rooted in the woman's need to carve out, amidst the demands placed on her to be entirely for her husband, even in her moods, an imaginative moment solely her own.

Later, when drawing on her knowledge of the standards expected of wives as expressed in popular marriage manuals of the day, Teresa may well have had her mother's actions in mind. If so, that memory adds great strength and poignancy to her depiction of the superiority of the divine spouse over the human and her congratulations to her sisters that it is into his hands they had had the good fortune to fall. In this striking reversal, Jesus takes the woman's role. Perhaps, given the assumptions of Teresa's times about female subordination, this christic self-emptying is the ultimate of divine condescensions:

> They say that for a woman to be a good wife to her husband, she must be sad when he is sad, and joyful when he is joyful, *although she never is.* (See what subjection you have been freed from, Sisters!) The Lord, *without deception,* truly acts in such a way with us. *He* is the one who submits, and He wants *you* to be the lady with authority to rule.[85]

[84]*Foundations,* 31:46. Physical violence in marriage was not unknown to Teresa, and she clearly disapproved of it. She disapproved as well of violence in the religious life, especially the sadism that passed for ascetical heroism in some convents. She was shocked by reports that the discalced nuns in Malagón were being taught to practice mortifications that included administering beatings to one another. To the Prioress of Seville she wrote: "It looks as if the devil is teaching them to do these things . . . On no account must you ever order, or allow, any nun to strike another—and that applies to pinching too—or bring up your nuns with the severity you saw practiced at Malagón; for they are not slaves . . . " *Letters* I, 340.
[85]*Way,* 26:4, emphasis added.

Teresa's own mystical marriage with Christ took place, according to her account, in Avila in the difficult year of 1572, after she had been ordered back to the Incarnation to be its prioress. Arriving in Avila to assume the office, she was greeted by rioting nuns, many angry not so much that *she* was to be their prioress, but that a leader not of their free election was being imposed upon them by their provincial authorities. Teresa, who had never wanted the office in the first place, gradually gained their respect. After a very trying first few months, she observed with satisfaction that the convent had settled into a more orderly regimen under her reforming hand.[86] Shrewdly, she managed to convince her superiors to permit John of the Cross to abandon his work training Carmelite students at Alcalá and become the confessor to the nuns of the Incarnation. Between the two of them, a remarkable change was wrought in the life of all at the venerable monastery.

Temperamentally, John and Teresa were poles apart. She was expansive, expressive, affectionate, ready to open her heart and soul to anyone with and in whom she felt that unmistakable tug toward God. John, although gentle and, reportedly, rather sweet, was a man under strict control, reserved, travelling a road to God named *nada,*[87] who shaped in secret his enormous artistic sensitivities and spiritual flights into masterfully crafted sensual poetry of classic stature. In public, John was all business, with only occasional bursts of cheerful humor displayed usually for the benefit of the young nuns and friars of the reform, so often in need of encouragement. As confessor of the Incarnation, he was Teresa's confessor too, and he saw it as his duty to include her in his efforts to bring all the souls of that house to the utmost perfection. True to the theory and practice of spiritual direction of the times, he often mortified as well as encouraged her. Her admiration and affection for him, as well as her obligation to be responsive to her spiritual director's advice, caused her not to balk at his sometimes severe directives.[88] On occasion, however, his actions toward her seemed at best arbitrary. Yet it was on just

---

[86]*Letters* I, 93–95; 99–101; 113–15.

[87]"Nothing." John is a representative of the apophatic tradition of mysticism, characterized by negation and "unknowing."

[88]John was, however, by no means among the most severe spiritual directors of his day. On the whole, he was considered quite gentle and patient.

such a mortifying occasion that Teresa's union with her divine spouse was consummated. She told it this way:

> [W]hen I was receiving Communion, Father John of the Cross who was giving me the Blessed Sacrament broke the host to provide for another sister. I thought there was no lack of hosts but that he wanted to mortify me because I had told him it pleased me very much when the hosts were large . . . His Majesty said to me: "Don't fear, daughter, for no one will be a party to separating you from Me," making me thereby to understand that what just happened didn't matter. Then He appeared to me in an imaginative vision . . . and He gave me His right hand and said: "Behold this nail; it is a sign that you will be My bride from today on . . . [F]rom now on not only will you look after My honor as being the honor of your Creator, King, and God, but you will look after it as My true bride. My honor is yours, and yours Mine."[89]

Teresa had received the richest of all mystical gifts. Unlike other times, when her experience of loving union with her friend and spouse had been of shorter duration, this experience was permanent, the seal placed upon her mature spiritual life. A profound interior peace seemed to settle into the very atoms of her body and spirit, and in spite of the tremendous challenges and upheavals that still lay ahead in her active life, she henceforth remained steady. Teresa could not describe the moment except to say that "the Lord wishes to reveal for that moment . . . the glory of heaven. One can say no more than that the . . . soul is made one with God."[90] Her soul, she later recalled, experienced what Paul meant when he wrote, "For me to live is Christ, and to die is gain."[91]

When she described the gift of spiritual matrimony in *Castle,* she noted also that the peaceful, powerful effects of such a union are even beneficial for others, "streams of milk" from "those divine breasts" with which God is always sustaining the soul.[92]

[89]*Testimonies,* 31.
[90]*Castle* VII, 2:3.
[91]*Castle* VII, 2:5; cf. Phil., 1:21.
[92]*Castle* VII, 2:6.

The soul's desire to serve God and to serve others increases, fear and anxiety is removed, and death would be no more at this stage than "a gentle rapture."[93] These effects, Teresa wrote from experience:

> . . . are given by God when He brings the soul to Himself with the kiss sought by the bride . . . Here an abundance of water is given to this deer that was wounded. Here one delights in God's tabernacle. Here the dove Noah sent out to see if the storm was over finds the olive branch as a sign of firm ground discovered amid the floods and tempests of this world.[94]

The person married this way to God is not by any means perfect with the perfection of the plaster saint, Teresa was quick to point out, nor is she completely immune from suffering various forms of pain and torment, especially when she sees a soul go astray. Nor is the person thus married to God in any sort of privileged position. On the contrary, Teresa asserted that God grants such favors to "fortify our weakness," because the real measure of the soul married to God is not sweetness, but the ability "to imitate Him in His great sufferings."[95]

Even at the center of the castle, where all is calm and suffused with the light of God, and where the soul possesses at last the object of its desire, Teresa insisted on *obras:* works of love, service to neighbor, the virtues necessary to a life for others.[96] To be truly spiritual, then, is not merely to exist in delightful and profound peace at one with God but also to suffer generously, to commit oneself unreservedly to others' good, to cross into the territory of truth and humility, to look reality in the face and know its worth from God's point of view, serenely embracing without counting the cost whatever befalls in the day-to-day walk with the loving companion. The beginning is also the end: to be and to do, in love and suffering, with the one whom we know loves us.

[93]*Castle* VII, 2:7.

[94]*Castle* VII, 3:13.

[95]*Castle* VII, 4:4-5, 8.

[96]*Castle* VII, 4:8-9; 14-15.

4

We Who Love Each Other in Christ

Teresa of Avila believed that complete reorientation of the affective life toward God alone did not demand rejection of human love nor evasion of the commitment required by authentic human friendship. Rather, that experience seems to have had the effect of making her freer to enter into remarkably intimate friendships with both men and women. Her early attempts at friendship had been governed by the tremendous pressures involved in maintaining the honor, esteem, and prestige demanded by the codes of social conduct she had imbibed in her youth and which throughout early adulthood she had found exceedingly difficult to challenge. Her gradual conversion away from those values involved new friendships that grew beyond a primary need for love and approval and put aside the worried counting up of honor gained or lost in order to create partnerships for the hot pursuit of God. These new friendships aimed to emulate the love shown forth in the flesh of Christ, fully human because completely joined to God.

Certainly Teresa taught that the spiritual journey requires single-heartedness and a measure of silence and solitude. As the inheritor of a splendid monastic tradition, she envisioned the reform of her order in part as a restoration of the original Carmelites' desert and mountaintop eremeticism.[1] But solitude, silence, and well-guarded cloister never meant estrangement from others who were also seeking God.[2] On the contrary, in Teresa's view, cultivating a lasting friendship with God in this life is possible *only*

---

[1] See for example, *Way*, 11:4; 13:6.

[2] Although cloister did afford protection from entanglements with kin and a consequent loss of spiritual freedom. See "Social Meaning," 350–51. See also *Way*, 8:3-4; 9.

when accompanied and supported by the friendship of like-minded people. *Solo Dios basta,* she had written: only God suffices; but she believed at the same time that one never goes to God alone.[3] Teresa believed that when God is the unfailing bond between friends, naked self-interest, characteristic of the deceptive friendships of "the world,"[4] could be unmasked as an evanescent, meaningless, and pitiable basis for human relationships. The lasting basis of worthy relationships was grace; the object, to assist the friend in the common quest, a quest not only for personal intimacy with God but also for ways to slake the "thirst for souls" such intimacy always inflicted.

In Teresa's experience, too, friendship in God and toward God was not some palid, super-spiritualized relationship devoid of real human feeling. On the contrary, such friendship always plunged her into the full range of joy and suffering associated with the formation and growth of all human relationships. "It is," she affirmed from experience, "love that costs dearly."[5] For Teresa, this form of friendship was the only sort that merited the noble name.

"This man is fit to be our friend"[6]

During the winter of 1561 Teresa and her collaborators were hard at work in Avila preparing the house that was to become the first convent of the reform, St. Joseph. She was anxious that the news of the foundation's progress not reach her provincial's ear, since earlier he had abruptly withdrawn his sanction, refusing to receive the house under his jurisdiction. Presumably, he was satisfied that a compliant Teresa had resigned from the enterprise. She was, then, rightly fearful of the consequences were he to get wind of her continued involvement.

Teresa had been circumspect enough to do nothing in her own name; doña Guiomar, her own sister Juana, and her sister's hus-

[3]See for example her assertion about the powerful attraction exercised by the saints upon other souls, such that if the devil were to gain one of these holy souls for himself, he would thereby be gaining a multitude. *Castle* V, 4:6.

[4]Cf. *Life,* 21:1; *Way,* 6:6.

[5]*Way,* 6:9.

[6]*Life,* 34:8.

band, Juan de Ovalle, were the fronts for all the necessary oper-
ations. Still, the project was Teresa's, as she herself recognized
with an air of harried desperation still vivid in the retelling many
months later:

> In procuring the money, acquiring the house, signing the con-
> tract for it, and fixing it up, I went through so many trials of
> so many kinds that I'm now amazed I was able to suffer them.
> In some of them I was completely alone; although my compan-
> ion did what she could. But she could do little and so little that
> it almost amounted to nothing more than to have everything
> done in her name and as her gift and all the rest of the trouble
> was mine.[7]

Now, with renovations in full swing, it was more and more difficult to keep what was supposed to be a secret project under
wraps. Just *how* difficult became apparent when, spying Teresa
and her sister in the congregation, a local preacher reportedly began railing against the foolish presumption of nuns "who were
leaving their convents to found new Orders" out of intemperate
desires for "freedoms" not proper to their sex or state. Mortified by the public denunciation, Juana is said to have laid into
Teresa, demanding that she pull out and go back to being an ordinary nun.[8] Teresa was undeterred, but she knew better than anyone else that "the whole thing would have to stop" if the uproar
continued and the provincial found out.[9]

As it turned out, the provincial (who was not in Avila at the
time) had other things on his mind. For one, there was the matter of servicing the great families of Castile whose favor was crucial to religious houses—in this case, the widow of the "very
prominent gentleman" Arias Pardon, doña Luisa de la Cerda.
Teresa reported that this lady was so grieved by her husband's
death "that they feared for her life."[10] Casting about for spiritual companionship with which to soothe her sorrow and provide diversion for her court, she settled on Teresa, whose

[7]*Life,* 33:11.
[8]*Tiempo y vida,* 150, and n. 59.
[9]*Life,* 34:1.
[10]*Life,* 34:1.

reputation as a mystic had spread in part because of careless discussion of her spiritual situation by the priests who counseled her. Teresa was not only apt, she was also available, since she belonged to "a monastery where the nuns were allowed to go out." The provincial thus acquiesced to "the strong, irresistible desire" to see Teresa that doña Luisa had capriciously conceived. On Christmas eve, Teresa learned she had been ordered to Toledo to console the widow.[11]

At first, Teresa was upset by her superior's command because of her distaste for being put on display. She always claimed not to regard herself as particularly saintly, nor did she approve of piety that demanded performances. More immediately, she wondered whether some sort of demonic plot might be afoot and feared that her absence would mean the end of St. Joseph's. Some of her associates were certain they smelled a rat and argued that she should write to the provincial and beg off. But Teresa gradually sensed that it would not hurt to leave Avila; with the most controversial figure out of the stirred-up scene for a while, the gossip would fizzle for want of fuel.

Moreover, in prayer she discovered that *God*, not the devil, was behind this unexpected development. God "would be greatly served" by her going, and that "for the business concerning the monastery it was fitting" she be absent until the papal document she had solicited should arrive with all the requisite permissions and protections for the venture.[12] Her stay in Toledo turned out to be not merely fruitful but frankly revolutionary with respect to her notion of convent reform. For it was at doña Luisa's palace that she met the odd, compelling "*beata* of our order," María de Jesús Yepes, whose passionate dedication to the ideals of the earliest Carmelites had led her on a strange quest that would (shortly after their encounter) culminate in the foundation of an austere reformed convent in Alcalá. From María de Jesús, Teresa heard, apparently for the first time in all her years as a Carmelite, that the rule under which Carmelites were living in their day was a mitigated one, and that the ancient Carmelites had lived not on regular income, but owning nothing, in the absolute poverty that alone guaranteed spiritual liberty.[13]

[11]*Life*, 34:1.
[12]*Life*, 34:2.
[13]*Life*, 35:1-2.

St. Joseph's had not been planned according to such a radical vision. According to Teresa's account, however, she was so taken with the challenge to abide by the evangelical counsel of poverty in letter and spirit that she determined to proceed with St. Joseph's *only* on that basis. Backed up by the fervent encouragement of Pedro de Alcántara, a vision of Clare of Assisi, and other assurances human and divine, she held fast to that determination, fending off the serious theological and pastoral objections raised by some of her advisors, most notably, the Dominican theologian Ibáñez.[14] In prayer, Christ confirmed the route of absolute poverty, and Teresa happily reported the pledge of divine assistance: "He would help me," she wrote, since it was "the will of His Father and His own" to found the monastery in poverty.[15]

Her enthusiasm for absolute poverty as a way of liberation was strengthened by firsthand observations of the way the wealthy and high-born actually lived. Teresa was immensely ill at ease in doña Luisa's palace. Everything was "a cross" for her; "comforts caused [her] great torment," and she strained not to grow negligent in the midst of the "big fuss" that was made over her.[16] She also realized that some persons had grown jealous of her intimacy with the *Señora;* to safeguard their own status, they tried to sabotage Teresa by charging that she was seeking personal advantage.[17] From such experience she "derived a very beneficial insight" about the terrible paradoxes of wealth and power (which she had the nerve to communicate directly to her hostess), wisdom she would continue to draw upon in her teaching and writing for years afterward:

> I observed the solicitude [the nobility] had for preserving their composure in conformity with this status, which doesn't allow them to live, obliging them [even] to eat without rhyme or reason because everything must be done in accordance with their status and not with their bodily constitution. (They have often

---

[14]"She herself had solicited his theological opinion on the question but was not persuaded by the reply she received; she thought it contained too much arid theology and not enough evangelical spirit. "In this case," she said she told him, "he did me no favor with his learning." *Life,* 35:3-4.

[15]*Life,* 35:6.

[16]*Life,* 34:3.

[17]*Life,* 34:5.

to eat food that is more in harmony with their position than with their liking.) As a result, I totally abhorred any desire to become a lady . . . —God deliver me from faulty composure! . . . I pitied [doña Luisa] . . . when I saw how often she had to go against her inclination in order to fulfill the duties of her state . . . *This is a kind of subservience that makes calling such people "lords" one of the world's lies, for . . . they are [nothing] but slaves to a thousand things.*[18]

Teresa's experiences and encounters during her six-month stay in Toledo were decisive in reworking her vision of the style of life and purpose of St. Joseph's.[19] On a more personal level, however, the visit was no less important. "While I was there," she later recalled, "it happened that a certain religious came to that city, a person from the nobility with whom I had sometimes conversed many years previously."[20] He was Fray García de Toledo, an attractive, charming courtier, a fine theologian, and a Dominican *letrado* who had been subprior of St. Thomas in Avila in the mid-1550s. There he had served as one of Teresa's confessors. Their paths had not crossed for years.

When she suddenly spotted him saying Mass at the church near the Dominican convent in Toledo, she could barely contain her emotions. She was invaded by "a great desire to know the condition of his soul" since she "wanted him to be a great servant of God." After an intense interior struggle about the propriety of approaching him (she actually returned to her seat the first time she got up, sharply telling herself not "to meddle"), she called him to a confessional. Within that privileged privacy, she wrote, "we began to question each other . . . about our lives."[21]

According to Teresa, none of the tremendous aversion she usually felt upon opening her soul to confessors clouded her conversation with García de Toledo that day. Indeed, each seemed

---

[18]*Life,* 34:4, emphasis added. On other occasions Teresa was equally frank with her aristocratic female friends. See for example, *Letters* I, 55, 62.

[19]At doña Luisa's palace, Teresa also entered into discussions about the reports of Protestant and Catholic clashes in France, events that also colored her view of the importance of the reform project.

[20]*Life,* 34:6.

[21]*Life,* 34:6.

powerless to hold anything back from the other.[22] But it was also obvious that the theologian had not made the same spiritual progress she had in the intervening years; and that night, while at prayer, Teresa was wholly occupied in setting out for God the case of her friend with the "good mind" and many "gifts and talents for doing good," who had still to learn how "to . . . give himself totally to God."[23] Not satisfied that he excel in God's service by using that mind, not even satisfied that he be "good," she begged God to make him "very good," insisting: "Lord, You must not deny me this favor; *see how this [man] is fit to be our friend.*"[24]

Teresa reported that during that same night God gave her "words" to say to him, apparently a rather candid message that caused her to feel nervous and embarrassed. She disliked being an intermediary, she claimed, perhaps because she was worried that García de Toledo's sense of honor and propriety might be pricked by the uninvited ministrations of a woman. To be certain that he understand her role as simply God's amanuensis, she copied the message out on paper and delivered it to him. As it turned out, he took it all extremely well and, according to Teresa, before long he completely amended his life and gave himself over to prayer with great determination. He became "so occupied with God that he no longer seemed to live for anything else on earth."[25]

Teresa probably revelled not only in the spiritual and emotional support he gave her but also in the intellectual stimulation he surely provided. Although she had no use for intellectualism, she was drawn to vigorous intellectuals, and all the more excited by how useful and fruitful learning always was when joined to a fer-

---

[22]*Life*, 34:7.

[23]*Life*, 34:7-8. See also the closing paragraphs of her cover letter upon sending him the manuscripts of *Life, Letters* I, 37.

[24]*Life*, 34:8, emphasis added. In a letter to don Pedro Castro y Nero, a *letrado* and famous preacher with whom Teresa also had a spiritual friendship, she voiced a similar concern for his growth in holiness and seemed particularly concerned that his holiness be put to service in a big way in the Church. " . . . I send you a wish; and if you do not do what you can to grant it to me it would have been better for me never to have known you, so keenly should I feel it. My trouble is that I am not satisfied that you should go to Heaven; I want you to become a person of great influence in the Church of God. I have begged God earnestly today not to allow you to use so keen an intellect as yours for any other end than that." *Letters* II, 892.

[25]*Life*, 34:11.

vent spirituality. Hence her delight in García de Toldeo, who appeared to her to be heading straight toward the goal she so highly prized. Even more to be cherished, however, was the fact that with him she believed she could also enjoy, to a greater degree at least, the mutuality that had been impossible to hope for in nearly all her relationships with male superiors and confessors up to that point.

They became disciples of one another and friends; he the *letrado,* the priest, the confessor, a man, consulted her, the nun, the *espiritual,* the penitent and directee, a woman, about his interior life. Teresa claimed that it greatly embarrassed her to find him "listening with so much humility to some things I was saying about prayer,"[26] but in truth she was overjoyed. She called him "my son" and was certain that the man's conversion had come about through the means of her loving, formative conversations with him as well as her insistent prayers on his behalf.[27]

It seemed to Teresa undeniable that God had indeed heard her prayers and even more importantly, that God was truly the bond that united her to her friend. In a remarkable ecstatic confirmation of the goodness of their conversations and growing friendship, Christ, with "awesome majesty and glory," showed Teresa *his* "great happiness over what was taking place." As if to quell lingering scruples about the emotional strength of her attachment to García de Toldeo, Teresa said that Christ "wanted [her] to see clearly that He was always present in conversations like these" and took great pleasure when anyone delighted in speaking about him.[28]

Christ's delight seems no greater than Teresa's own; it is a "wonderful" thing, she wrote happily:

> when a sick person finds another wounded with the same sickness; how great the consolation to find you are not alone. The two become a powerful help to each other . . . What excellent backing they give to one another, since they are determined to risk a thousand lives for God and they desire the opportunities for losing them.[29]

[26]*Life,* 34:15.
[27]*Life,* 16:6; 34:17.
[28]*Life,* 34:17.
[29]*Life,* 34:16.

That affective spiritual relationships, especially with confessors, were not without their dangers for persons vowed to a chaste and celibate life was something Teresa also believed and understood through experience. But for her, the dangers never amounted to a reason *not* to "find satisfaction in being with persons with whom I discuss my soul and whom I love." To resist or suppress such feelings, she wrote, would be tantamount to the insensitivity shown by a sick person in danger of death who knew "a doctor was curing him" yet "failed to love and thank the doctor."[30]

Moreover, just as "one of the worst trials on earth [is] contradiction on the part of good men," so one of earth's greatest blessings is to be "understood through experience."[31] She believed that like-minded, spiritual people are mightily attracted to one another and speak a common language unintelligible to those without experience. But more than anything else, they unselfishly and tirelessly seek each other's good, and that good is none other than the "perfection" of the friend in the love and service of God.

Bemoaning her early false starts along the path of the spirit, for example, Teresa pinpointed one of the most important reasons why she failed to make progress: she was *alone*. She wrote, "A great evil it is for a soul to be alone in the midst of so many dangers. It seems to me that if I should have had someone to talk this all over with it would have helped me . . . not to fall again . . . "[32] Especially at the beginning, then, "friendship and association with other persons having the same interest" is crucial. One need not fear "vainglory" in these conversations either, for their object is not self-aggrandizement but stabilization and deepened friendships with God. Conversation is for the sake of mutual encouragement, instruction, and help. Discussing one's "joys and trials" for the sake of friendship with God benefits both parties; for although the friends will probably never know just how it happened (not seeing any virtue or wisdom in themselves), each will have truly built up the other.[33]

Moreover, since sensationalistic spiritual pursuits are more in

[30]*Life,* 40:19.
[31]*Life,* 30:5; 30:4.
[32]*Life,* 7:20.
[33]*Life,* 7:20.

vogue than authentic and serious ones, according to Teresa, all the more do like-minded people need each other:

> There is so much sluggishness in matters having to do with the service of God that it is necessary for those who serve Him to become shields for one another that they might advance. For it is considered good to walk in the vanities and pleasures of the world, and those who don't are unnoticed. If someone begins to give himself to God, there are so many to criticize him that he needs to seek companionship . . . And if he doesn't seek this companionship, he will find himself in much difficulty.[34]

Perhaps that is why, she continued, "some saints used to go to the deserts," for opportunities to be near others pursuing the same end and to be separated from those who have no understanding of or appreciation for that pursuit. Besides, she noted, "it is a kind of humility" to believe, and act upon the belief, that "through those with whom one converses God will help and increase charity while [charity] is being shared." Teresa had "powerful experience" of the good that derives from such sharing of love, and she begged her readers to test her assertions themselves by being humble enough to believe *her,* "the most wicked of all human beings," when she extended the hand of friendship to them by offering advice about the worth of spiritual bonds. Fortunately for Teresa, bereft of human companionship at such a critical point of her journey, God acted as her spiritual friend, and it is to God she gave the glory: "For in falling I had many friends to help me; but in rising I found myself so alone that I am amazed I did not remain forever fallen. And I praise the mercy of God, for it was He alone who gave me His hand."[35]

That terrible early experience of isolation intensified Teresa's conviction about the need for human companionship along the way of perfection, even if that companionship turned out to be on many occasions imperfect and, ultimately, disappointing. What mattered was the way God could work through these bonds of love, doing good to the partners in spite of their weaknesses.[36]

[34]*Life,* 7:22.

[35]*Life,* 7:22.

[36]See *Way,* 7:5.

Perhaps the most beneficial aspect of this love was its drive toward truth; the lovers cannot be insincere with each other. Even though at times spiritual friends must be indulgent and patient with respect to the faults of their loved ones,[37] flattery never glosses over the imperfections each sees in the other; rather, because the lovers desire that their friendship endure throughout eternity, each helps the other to clear the path. Indeed, one friend is "always fearful lest the soul it loves so much be lost and the two be separated forever."[38] Thus, to García de Toldeo she declared:

> I beg your Reverence that we may all be mad for love of Him who for love of us was called mad. Since your Reverence says that you love me, prove it to me by preparing yourself so that God may grant you this favor; I see very few who do not have much more discretion than is necessary for their spiritual progress. It could well be that I am the one who abounds in this . . . Don't allow this to happen to me, my Father (since you are also like a son) . . . Disillusion me with truth since these truths are seldom made use of.[39]

The solidarity of community

Teresa also cherished a vision of friendship as the cultivation and development of human community on a trajectory towards God. Believing, for example, that the *devil's* friends were busy "in these times" helping each other by "gather[ing] in secret against His Majesty to prepare wicked deeds and heresies," she wanted *God's* friends to meet on behalf of the cause of holiness. Therefore she wrote to her earliest group of spiritual friends:

> I should like the five of us who at present love each other in Christ . . . to gather together some time to free each other from illusion and to speak about how we might mend our ways and please God more since no one knows himself as well as

[37] *Way,* 7:7.
[38] *Way,* 7:1; also *Way,* 7:4.
[39] *Life,* 16:6.

others who observe him if they do so with love and concern for his progress.[40]

Teresian scholars are not completely certain who these five were, but it is likely that the group included García de Toledo, Francisco de Salcedo, doña Guiomar de Ulloa, and Gaspar Daza; in other words, a mixed community—a theologian and friar, an *espiritual* and cleric, a nun, a married man, and a laywoman who was a widow—all embarked together on the way to perfection.

Teresa strove also to impress the ideal of community as the matrix of the search for God upon the thirteen nuns of St. Joseph's, with whom she shared the perils and the profits of conversion and reform in the first discalced endeavor.[41] The monastery of St. Joseph was founded exclusively to house the life of prayer, she stressed, and prayer was to be the only "language" spoken there. Its inhabitants were to speak it among themselves; likewise they were to speak it to anyone who sought them out. It was a language made up not only of words but also of their daily routines and mutual service. Thus, they were to *treat* each other in the same way they prayed, with genuine, selfless, determined, creative, and grace-laden love.

Their language and their treatment of one another would be incomprehensible to those not yet joined to them in this community (like *algarabía,* she wrote, the garbled, hispanicized Arabic language spoken by *moriscos).*[42] But in the same way, the lan-

---

[40] *Life,* 16:7. Note the contrast Teresa established here between her group and other such cells gathered for what she thought were less noble purposes. She may have had in mind Spanish Protestant groups, perhaps the Valladolid conventicle, uncovered and dispatched by the Inquisition during the period of *Life's* composition. See Tomás Alvarez, "Santa Teresa de Avila, Hija de la Iglesia," *Ephemerides Carmeliticae* 17 (1966): 310; and José Luis González Novalín, "Teresa de Jesús y el Luteranismo en España," *Actas del Congreso Internacional Teresiano* I (Salamanca, 1982): 354–55.

[41] For the following reflections, see especially *Way,* 20:3-6. See also the fine treatment of this topic in Tomás Alvarez, "La oración, camino a Dios. El pensamiento de Santa Teresa," *Ephemerides Carmeliticae* 21 (1970): 164–68.

[42] *Moriscos* were the descendents of the Muslim Moors who had conquered Spain in the eighth century and against whom the Christian population had waged an intermittent crusade of reconquest, finally overthrowing the last Hispano-Muslim stronghold in Granada in 1492. *Moriscos,* Moors who remained in Spain after the *reconquista,* were subject to varying degrees of repression and discrimination by the Spanish Christian powers. During the Golden Age, when Spain was continually confronted with the aggression of North African Muslim states, some of them clients of the much-feared Ottomans, *moriscos* were regarded as a serious internal security risk, since their first loyalty was believed to be, and often was,

guage spoken by those "in the world" was *algarabía* too, the vehicle of communication for a community living by values and criteria different from the community of St. Joseph. There, the spirit of solidarity among all the sisters was the very solidarity each had with God, and *vice versa*.

Teresa regarded mutual love (along with detachment and poverty) as one of the indispensable foundations of prayer. In *Way,* therefore, she gave the nuns instruction about the precise nature of the love they were to demonstrate for each other, and for all those who figured in their development as women of God. Through several chapters, Teresa labored to distinguish among sensual, spiritual, and "mixed" forms of love. Even more vital than the actual distinctions and illustrations she offered in those pages, however, is her profound grasp of love's power to transform human individuals and its ability to join them in networks of mutual service, support, accountability, and creativity. She insisted that although the nuns were not to be dominated by attachments to any particular person, they were nonetheless to be guaranteed the freedom to associate with and authentically to love *anyone* whom they could help or who could help them.[43] With respect to the charge that such love was utilitarian and bloodless, Teresa responded that, on the contrary, it was an "impassioned" love, a love designed to unite the lovers not merely in this life, but also forever, a love full of tenderness and compassion toward all.[44]

Clearly audible too in these sometimes convoluted and hedged affirmations about the different kinds of love is Teresa's persistent perplexity about the powerful forces of her own affectivity and the manner in which her most important friendships seemed often to begin and end in a certain disquiet about their purity. Although she tried to maintain an even love for all her sisters and friends, she recognized that it was impossible not to love some people more than others, having clear favorites herself among

---

to Islam. Philip III expelled them from the Spanish kingdoms in 1609. Teresa referred to the practice of ransoming Christians taken captive by the Barbary corsairs in *Song,* 3:3-4. Her collaborator Gracián was himself captured and held for ransom, according to his *Peregrinación.*

[43]See for example the strong statement to this effect in *Way,* 7:4.

[44]*Way,* 6:5-8; 7:1.

both men and women.[45] Teresa also experienced deep and even depressing disappointments in her loving relationships that sorely tried her faith in the possibility of *enduring* human intimacy. Thus, along with the assertion that human friendship and community are vital to the spiritual pilgrimage, one also hears Teresa declaring frequently, and not merely conventionally, that *no one but God* can ever be trusted to provide the necessary love and support all along and to the very end of the journey. But even the painful data of unrealized hopes (and the growing suspicion that human friendship as she had conceived it might be realizable only in the reign of God) did not stop Teresa from forming friendships and proclaiming the fundamental goodness and necessity of relationship, love, and human community in search of God.

The "Véjamen"

Teresa's vision of the mutual support and solidarity spiritual friendship provided was deeply influenced, as we have seen, by her personal experience of both the efficacy of such support and the fearsome difficulties created when one lacks it. But although friendship was for Teresa a serious business, her relationships were always marked by humor; and although she aimed at respect and appropriate decorum in all her dealings with others, she balked at earnestness and laughed away both her own and others' occasional lapses in polite convention. Teresa liked things simple. Although her personal, social, and ecclesial circumstances often required that she become adept at ironic subterfuge, especially in her writings, both by temperament and by spiritual persuasion she preferred *llaneza*—simplicity, directness, naturalness, and unadorned affability.

Although the mature Teresa took herself quite seriously as an expert in the affairs of the spirit, confident of her prowess in directing others and of the potentially universal value of her extensive written counsels, she was often amused when *other people* were excessively solemn about her expertise or when they wished

[45]See for example her admission to María de San José, *Letters* II, 573, that "not all the nuns appeal so much to my nature" as did the prioress; and her declaration to Gracián that love for him produced in her a "natural weakness" that made her resentful when others said negative things about him, *Letters* II, 811.

to make of the spiritual life too ponderous and earnest a thing. Her instinct in these situations was to deflate and poke fun, helping her spiritual friends to keep things simple, level, and true. For example, while in Toledo during the latter part of 1576, Teresa reported that God spoke to her the words, "Seek yourself in me." That locution stirred her deeply, and she pondered its meaning for some time. She also sent the words to her brother Lorenzo, who had returned from his soldiering and business ventures in America the year before and had since become his sister's disciple. Lorenzo's spiritual capacities were apparently not yet adequate for deciphering the divine words, and he turned for help in the challenge to Teresa's spiritual partners in Avila, including John of the Cross, the "holy gentleman" Francisco de Salcedo, the priest who would become her travelling chaplain, Julián de Avila, and don Alvaro de Mendoza, the bishop of Avila. The nuns of St. Joseph's were also brought into the venture.

They decided to convene a small conference on the matter. When it ended, the participants agreed that their discussion of the meaning of the locution had been the poorer for Teresa's absence. Accordingly, the bishop hit upon the idea of recording all the participants' responses and sending them to Teresa in Toledo. She was to be the judge of which of them came closest to unfolding the profound secret of the sacred message.

It is difficult to ascertain the spirit in which the contest was declared; but if it was entirely in earnest, her friends' eagerness tickled Teresa's funny bone, for her formal reply was laden with irony and crafted in the satirical style of the *véjamen,* a kind of "roast" held at Spanish universities to fête the student upon whom a doctorate was about to be conferred. Teachers and students alike participated in these mock defenses and judgments in which all the candidate's declarations were subject to merciless, albeit good-natured, ridicule in an often hilarious send-up of the pedantry and pomp cherished by academicians of every place and time.[46]

"I have no intention," Teresa announced in the course of her critique, "of saying anything good about what the contestants

[46]For a brief overview of university life and customs during the Golden Age, see Marcellin Defourneaux, *La vida cotidiana en la España del Siglo de Oro* (Barcelona: Argos Vergara, 1983), 158–183. This book is also in English, with the title, *Daily Life in Spain in the Golden Age* (Stanford, Calif.: Stanford Univ. Press, 1971).

have written.''[47] Nor did she. Starting with a kind of formulaic literary prologue typical of those with which she began her own books on the spiritual life, she claimed with tongue in cheek piety that obedience alone had forced her to accept the role of judge—a role that in fact she quite obviously relished, for she proceeded vigorously to dispatch each of the contestants with consummate acumen.

The worst thing about Salcedo's reply, she wrote, was that after "quoting again and again through [his] paper the words of Saint Paul and the Holy Spirit" in illustration of his opinions, he concluded with a flourish of humility in which he characterized everything he had written as a welter of "stupidities." Tripping over himself to display his holy ignorance, he had failed to exempt the sacred words of Scripture from the blanket disavowal of worth. For that blasphemy, Teresa declared, she was ready to denounce him to the "nearby" Inquisition[48] unless he recanted. If he didn't, she menaced, "he will see what happens.''[49]

In Teresa's estimation, Julián de Avila's response also contained many "errors"; he would not be awarded the prize either. But, she added, he was to be forgiven his trespasses, for at least he "did not go on at such length as did my Father Fray John of the Cross.''[50] She commended John's doctrine, but judged it more fitting for Jesuits than "for what we have in mind.''[51] He was too extreme, convinced that everybody had to be "dead to the world" before the attempt to seek God could bear fruit. In humorous but barbed protest of his perfectionism, Teresa prayed:

---

[47]*Critique*, 3.

[48]Its headquarters were in Toledo, the city from which Teresa was writing.

[49]*Critique*, 4. Teresa revealed in this single short paragraph her grasp of the difficult and often dangerous world in which she carried on her work and taught her spiritual doctrine: anyone who wrote on the spiritual life and cited the Bible had to be prepared to have words twisted, propositions lifted from the explanatory contexts and judged, innocent mistakes treated like weighty heresies. Teresa's own experience of constant censorship and self-correction comes through in her gleeful satiric pounce upon Salcedo's carelessness of expression (so automatic were such protestations of worthlessness and submission to the Church's judgment) and in her adoption of the inquisitorial *persona* in her demand that he retract his words "or else." It is difficult to imagine that Teresa was oblivious to the *self*-satire also implicit in her lampooning of the "holy gentlemen," for she herself composed many a humble disclaimer of precisely this quality in the course of her career as an author and teacher.

[50]*Critique*, 5.

[51]*Critique*, 6.

"God deliver me from people so spiritual that they want to turn *everything* into perfect contemplation."[52]

She thought her brother Lorenzo was in way over his head, having "spoken of more than he understands."[53] Teresa acknowledged, however, that his opinions had at least provided her with much "recreation"—a jibe Lorenzo took poorly and for which Teresa felt it necessary to offer an olive branch in subsequent letters to him.[54] Finally, to the bishop she recommended that he oblige all the contestants to "make amends" for their replies. In her qualified judgement, none was satisfactory; they had all gone "beyond what was asked by the question" and failed to answer the question itself.

The *Critique* is a string of ironic put-downs to be sure, but throughout, one senses the energetic, honest engagement with real human beings typical of all Teresa's friendships. Humorous prodding was for her as effective a means of spiritual development as the most somber counsel or pious exercise. When all was said and done, no matter the mode or circumstance, authentic friendship meant real concern for the total welfare of the friend. It nourished itself with a shared ideal and was endlessly creative of practical help to achieve it. True friendship longed for, sought out, and deeply relished personal encounters and conversations among friends that could leave the "soul fired anew with the desire to serve the Lord."[55] Friendship was a vital experience of love, punctuated by great bursts of joy felt right in the heart of flesh for every step a friend took toward the goal, but overshadowed too by a weary dread felt in the spirit, muting joy in this world's good and lovely gifts, whenever a friend turned back, away from God.

Lofty ideals guided friendship, and its primary object was to secure each friend's health of soul. But day to day and down to earth, love of friends was shown as well by things as simple as

---

[52]*Critique*, 7, emphasis added. It is interesting to note that Teresa based her refutation of John's "you must be dead to the world" ideas upon the example of three biblical women, Mary Magdalene, the Samaritan woman, and the Canaanite. These women seemed to her to have grasped the authentic meaning of the mystical life as one long record of God's undeserved mercies, a way of *living*, not simply a "state."

[53]*Critique*, 8.

[54]*Letters* I, 429.

[55]*Life*, 34:15.

recommending remedies for their physical ailments. For example, to her beloved Prioress of Seville, the scholar and writer María de San José, Teresa recommended daily doses of powdered rose hips to alleviate a urinary ailment and suggested "fumigation with sulpher-wort, coriander, powdered egg shells, a little oil, a very little rosemary and a little lavendar," a home remedy that she herself had used to good advantage for fever and "green sickness."[56] She also warned her insistently away from sarsparilla, perhaps because it was believed to be an aphrodisiac![57] Concerned on another occasion that the often headstrong prioress might harm herself with corporal penance, Teresa admonished:

> But we do not want you to be doing penances just now: we want you not to be ill, for that would be inflicting a penance on the whole community, and (we also want you) to be obedient, and not to be the death of me. I can say truly that I should feel the loss of no prioress as much as [you]: I don't know why I love you so dearly.[58]

Deep and persevering gratitude also marked Teresa's love of friends. Her fierce loyalty, however, especially toward those who had rendered service to the cause of the reform, was a trait she acknowledged to be at once honorable and dangerous, for it sometimes bound her to defend them in their troubles even when their troubles were richly deserved. For example, during a prolonged controversy involving some young nuns of the community at Seville, Teresa more than once took the side of the priest Garciálvarez when, according to E. Allison Peers, "by any objective standard, [he] seems to have been greatly to blame. But she could

---

[56]*Letters* II, 761; I, 377. See also II, 794 and 879 for more concern about San José's health and Teresa's prescriptions for alleviating her ills.

[57]*Letters* II, 275, 300, 324.

[58]*Letters* II, 844. Teresa's profound affection for this beautiful and intelligent former lady-in-waiting to doña Luisa de la Cerda never waned, despite the sometimes serious clashes of will that occurred between them. María de San José could be difficult, but so could Teresa, a fact she acknowledged in a subsequent letter. "When I really love someone, I am so anxious that she should not go astray that I become unbearable." *Letters* II, 704; see also I, 252 and II, 727. A recent article treats of the friendship between Teresa and María de San José, Joseph Crawford, "Teresa and Friendship: María de San José," in *Spiritual Life* 33 (1987): 202–12.

not forget the help he had given her when they started their work together in Seville.''[59]

This man had been stirring up the nuns at Seville for years by ignoring both Teresa and the other legitimate superiors of the house on matters pertaining to the hearing of the nuns' confessions. He had even once been deposed from his office at the convent by the local bishop. Teresa was well aware of his inadequacies, but her gratitude for past help enlarged her patience beyond all logic, and perhaps even beyond good sense, and she knew it. Acknowledging that her gratitude was more vice than virtue, she vigorously pleaded Garciálvarez's case in tones that betray both the tenacity of her loyalty and her pain at the harm it was obviously causing:

> . . . For the love of our Lord, daughter, I beg you to suffer and be silent. None of you must try to get that Father turned out, however many trials and annoyances he may cause you, for they are not so serious as to offend God, and I cannot bear our being ungrateful to anyone who has been good to us. I remember how, when some people were trying to cheat us . . . , he opened our eyes to it, and I can never forget . . . what trouble he saved us from. I have always thought him . . . a well-meaning man. I fully realize that this gratitude of mine is not in the least a sign of perfection: it must be my nature—I could be bought with a sardine . . . [60]

Although she was often frightfully demanding of them and critical of their faults with a directness that at times may seem severe, Teresa could also be indulgent and sentimental toward her many friends. But in every case, she strove with all her might to foster them also as the friends of God. She loved them to the end, even when they greatly disappointed her. Among the most important of these strengthening, illuminating, and deeply vexing friendships, her intense relationship with Jerónimo Gracián best illustrates her struggle for a love thoroughly and perfectly human *because* thoroughly and perfectly rooted in and oriented towards the divine.

[59]*Letters* II, 760, n. 3. But see also her generous disposition with respect to the kind and careful treatment this nun and her companions were to receive at the hands of the community, *Letters* I, 645–652.

[60]*Letters* II, 602.

A marriage well-arranged

When Teresa of Avila met Fray Jerónimo Gracián for the first time in the provincial border town of Beas, she was sixty and had been a Carmelite nun for forty years.[61] Already she had established eight monasteries for women and two for men. She had written two substantial books on the spiritual life, other short works, legislation for the reformed convents, and she had also begun to record their history. Two years earlier she had received the grace of spiritual matrimony.

For thirteen years, her "very determined determination" to pursue union with God had flown in the face of a prevailing theology that tended to deny the value of mental prayer, finding it particularly objectionable for women. In those years, in spite of the pauline prohibition constantly trotted out by her detractors, she taught mental prayer to anyone who would listen and established settings where women could learn to practice it in an orderly way. She put their virtue to work on behalf of a beleaguered Church and gave them a sharper ecclesial identity. She emphatically connected the practice of contemplation with the apostolate, addressing personally and institutionally the question of female credibility and efficacy in the mission of the Church and providing an outlet for a self-acknowledged envy of preachers and priests that might otherwise have embittered her.

At the time of the first meeting in the Andalusian spring of 1575, Gracián was thirty, three years a Carmelite, just under two years professed.[62] Although still wet behind the ears as a discalced friar, he was already something of a prodigy, a superior with reforming authority over the Carmelites in that southern province. Soon after his meeting with Teresa, his powers were extended to Castile as well.

Possessed of considerable culture and learning, he had grown up in a humanist household where the ancient authors were read in Greek and Latin and whose windows were open upon the Empire. His father Diego had been a secretary to Charles V; one of

---

[61]For Teresa's version of her meeting with Gracián, see *Foundations*, 23 and 24.

[62]Gracián recounted his version of the meeting, his work for the reform, his fall from grace and subsequent adventures in his *Peregrinación* and in *Scholias y adiciones al libro de la Vida de la Madre Theresa de Jesús que compuso el Padre Doctor Ribera* (hereafter, *Scholias*), republished in *El Monte Carmelo* 60 (1960). See also *Tiempo y vida*, 534–745.

his brothers was in similar service to King Philip. Gracián had taken his doctorate in theology at the once-progressive University of Alcalá where, according to his not very self-effacing autobiography, he was showered with honors. At Alcalá in 1570 he was ordained a priest.

By his account, his entry into the Carmelite novitiate two years later was preceded by a fierce vocational struggle between his attraction to the service of the Virgin Mary and the economic needs of his family, a large brood whose well-being was precariously dependent upon the royal smile. Perhaps believing he was called to loftier things and trusting that God would provide for his family, Gracián chose the poverty of the discalced over the security of a benefice which could have provided a steady income to ease his family's finances.

He always claimed that it was Teresa who had, with her persistent prayers, finally delivered him into the arms of the reform. In *Foundations,* however, Teresa gave the credit to the nuns of Pastrana for praying him into the habit of our Lady.[63] Self-serving as Gracián's version might be, it is nonetheless true too that Teresa was always on the lookout for promising candidates for the reform and was capable of exerting more than supernatural pressure to get her man.

Gracián, she had been told, was a refined spirit with an instinctive grasp of the significance of the reform; a man who charmed everyone with his sweetness, eloquence, and extraverted good humor; a man of true learning, not half-baked like that of the men who had done her so much harm;[64] a man, moreover, with just the sort of political connections the reform was in need of. As far as Teresa was concerned, he was just what the doctor ordered.[65]

But whatever she may have heard, whatever impression she formed from his enthusiastic reports on the successes of his visitations in Andalusia, Teresa seems to have been not at all prepared for Gracián in the flesh. Their three-week encounter in Beas was the start of a love that in that extraordinary spring seemed to her to be capable of anything at all and of everything good.

[63]*Foundations,* 23:7-8.
[64]*Life,* 5:3; 13:17; 14:21; *Castle* V, 1:8.
[65]*Foundations,* 24:1-2.

Immediately after Gracián's departure from Beas, Teresa wrote to a prioress who had already met Gracián and, apparently, had not been too impressed:

> . . . If only you could have been here . . . these last few days! . . . Without exaggeration, I think they've been the best days of my life. Father-Master Gracián has been here . . . ; and although I've gotten to know him . . . I haven't begun to fathom his worth. I think he is perfect; we couldn't have asked God for a better man for our needs. [B]eg God that he be named our superior. If that happened, I'd be able to take a rest from overseeing these houses, for I've never yet come across anyone at once so perfect and so gentle . . . I wouldn't have missed . . . getting to know him like this for anything in the world.
>
> [Everyone] is so taken with him . . . He preaches beautifully. I'm sure he's gotten much better since you saw him . . . [66]

Teresa was habitually generous with praise for people she liked; still, her report of Gracián in this letter is extravagant. Her correspondence of the next several weeks is studded with less rapturous but still strikingly unclouded appraisals of him. Taken together, they reveal a Teresa enthralled. She seems convinced that she has found the mirror of her own soul; like her, he wanted "to do the most perfect thing always." Even more, on every point about the reform, they were in complete accord.[67]

In the face of severe criticism, Teresa had always clung to the conviction that sanctity did not subsist in dourness, that the pursuit of perfection need not muffle the laughter of licit joy. Like many in the prayer movement of her day, she had also taught repeatedly that the learned churchman was of little use unless he was also authentically spiritual. And for a long time she had had need of a Carmelite friar who not only wanted to lead (there were plenty of them) but also shared her vision down to the last detail.

---

[66]To Madre Inés de Jesús, Prioress of Medina, 12 May 1575, my translation. Cf. *Letters* I, 174–77 for complete text. See also her letter to María de San José (who was also not as taken with Gracián as Teresa was), *Letters* I, 362–64. On Gracián the preacher, see *Letters* I, 302, and n. 2.

[67]*Letters* I, 173–74; 178–184; 187–88; 189–191; 191–96; *Testimonies*, 39.

Apart from John of the Cross and a handful of others, a good number of the first friars of the reform were a motley, willful bunch. No wonder, then, that Teresa was overjoyed, encouraged, and disarmed by the conjunction in Gracián of so many needed "worldly" qualities and the highest spiritual and ascetical ideals, a sweet demeanor, and complete dedication to her cause.[68]

For his part, Gracián recalled the meeting as a time of intense spiritual interchange in which Teresa had opened her soul to him, "holding nothing back," and he entrusted to her his own interior life. They discussed the history, ideals, and vicissitudes of the movement, and the spiritual life proper to it. Looking ahead, they talked of ways to sustain that spirit in the generations to come.[69] Teresa never hid the fact that she loved to be loved, and Gracián, unlike the unruly friars who paid so little attention to her authority, was at her side and acting like she really mattered.

Not long after this momentous encounter, confident in his confidence in the reform and gratified by his devotion to her as its guiding genius and by the candor with which he revealed his soul, she chose him as her confessor.[70] Teresa was a veteran of many confessor-directee relationships of varying quality and duration. To Gracián, however, she vowed what she had never vowed to anyone: "to hold him in the place of God" for life. She was casting her ultimate lot with a man as yet untested by events, but the interior conflict that shows up in her confidential memos of this period did not center on Gracián's lack of experience.

Rather, she found it bothersome that the impulse to bind herself to him kept overtaking her in the form of visions; and visions, she knew, could have other than a divine origin. The memory of previous devoted confessors who had counseled her not even to credit visions, much less to act on them, made her feel uneasy, perhaps even a little disloyal. But when the happy assurance she felt as a result of the visions did not fade; when each time she doubted, the visions recurred, she gradually concluded that they were indeed from God.

But even that certainty was hard-pressed to overcome Teresa's natural resistance to binding herself to the degree implied by the

---

[68]See for example her remarks in *Foundations*, 24:12-13.

[69]*Scholias*, 125; *Peregrinación*, 125, 226.

[70]For what follows, see *Testimonies*, 35, 36, 39.

vow. The vision had represented God as a divine matchmaker, joining her hand to Gracián's in an unmistakable imitation of betrothal. To make that vow was to make a marriage of sorts, and Teresa had rejected marriage, once even congratulating herself and her discalced sisters, as we have seen, on having escaped the "subjection," the denial of freedom and the claustrophobia that often came, in her view, in the same package as a husband.[71]

Of course, there remained the question of personal attraction to Gracián. Teresa aspired to objectivity, claiming to have put aside "her love for this Father," her attraction to "his good qualities," and to have "considered the matter as though it regarded a stranger." But she is fairly transparent about the strength of that attraction; only with "a person who so pleased her" could she have handed herself over for God's sake.[72]

One cannot escape the poignancy of Teresa's hope that, through the vow, "this going about consulting different minds with different opinions was now to end." Even the best of her other confessors had never fully understood her; there had always come a parting of the ways, physically or emotionally. In Gracián, she wished to discover a director and friend whom God had created *for her*. Insofar as her interior life was concerned then, she hoped for a simplified and sympathetic consistency. With respect to the reform, she anticipated that Gracián would be an extension of herself and relieve her of the difficulties inherent in her public action on behalf of the discalced, particularly the friars. In both cases, she thought that she would learn much from him, because God had ordained his human and spiritual qualities and given him to her for that end.

For seven years, until her death in 1582, her union with Gracián brought her spiritual benefits. In the extant correspondence many passages reveal how much Teresa longed for his company to talk with him about the state of her soul and how envious she felt towards others he was directing. She experienced deep spiritual relief through her confessions to him. Her vow, she reflected, had joined them in the work of bringing souls to God, and her

---

[71] *Way*, 26:4. See Chapter 3 above.

[72] *Testimonies*, 36:6, 8.

spirit soared to think how greatly God was pleased, and how much she was meriting as a result of having decided to make it.[73]

Apart from these general affirmations, however, little in Teresa's correspondence, nor even in *The Interior Castle* (composed during the period of their association), sheds light on what his positive contributions to the development of her mystical life actually were. Had we his letters to her, perhaps we might better appreciate his handling of her soul, although Teresa's frequent complaints about how miserly those letters could be suggest only slim pickings.[74] As things stand, it is not evident that crucial developments in the trajectory of her interior experience resulted from his insights, skill, or prudence as a director.

In various documents, however, Gracián made it plain that he did take his director's role very seriously. As her father-confessor, it was understood as incumbent upon him to test Teresa, exercise her in humility and other virtues by imposing mortifications upon her, and sanction all her activity. But Teresa's spiritual friendship with Gracián was far more complex than he or subsequent hagiographers have described. That complexity shows up best in their work together for the discalced reform.

Not merely an aspect of their relationship, the consolidation of the reform was the very context and ground of their mutual esteem and discipleship. At the time of their meeting, discalced successes had buoyed the spirits of Teresa and her collaborators with perhaps inflated promises of more to come. Gracián encouraged that optimism with his reports of possibilities for expansion in Andalusia. He had been there and had seen for himself what fertile, open fields awaited their labors.[75]

As intimated above, Teresa's instant affection for him was in direct proportion to how clearly she saw God's hand in Gracián's appearance on the scene. While it was a love deeply and authentically personal, with all the earmarks at the outset of human in-

---

[73]See especially *Letters* I, 400–01; II, 531–35, 640, 661. Unfortunately, Gracián's letters to Teresa have not survived. Our glimpse into the relationship is, then, undoubtedly skewed to some extent in Teresa's favor.

[74]Teresa was always anxious about Gracián's letters for he did not, it seems, write her often enough (although it is likely that at least some of his letters were lost *en route);* and when he did write, his letters were, in her estimation, too short or too careless. See for example *Letters* I, 241, 297, 315; II, 807, 827, 859, 871.

[75]For what follows, see *Tiempo y vida,* 534–543.

fatuation, it was never other than or different from her love for what he, with his talent and dedication, could do for the discalced movement.[76] She would have need of that faith in him; they were all mistaken about the road ahead, and it was an immediate rude awakening.

One of Gracián's first decisions was to overrule the disposition of the Father General of the Order and force a foundation of discalced nuns in Seville. Teresa disliked, even feared, the plan. In the face of her objections, Gracián affected impartiality; but seeing how adamant he actually was, Teresa declined to push for her own way, even though she had received a locution that was not at all in line with Gracián's ambitions. It was a decision that cost her the confidence and support of the General (a devastating personal loss), and a strategic blunder of near-irreparable consequence.[77]

During the following six years, the discalced leaders and pioneers found themselves drawn increasingly into an escalating struggle to retain control of the reform, at times caught in, at times shrewdly manipulating the competing royal, papal, and Religious Order jurisdictions and interests at issue in the protracted fight.[78] Gracián fought too, giving himself over totally to this rescue of the reform, enduring repeated slander and a brief period of house arrest. He played a major role in finally securing a separate province for the discalced, and governed it as first provincial superior. With Teresa he founded new houses; he directed souls, preached, wrote, and planned. Teresa believed that he was doing incalculable good, and her love for him, the servant of the reform, kept pace.

The character of that love, however, ought not be romanticized. Teresa had to defend it not only against those who saw in it something other than angels ascending together to the realms of light, not only from the sniping of priests and female companions who

[76]Teresa was aware that she loved him *personally* "in the Lord" *and* because of the gain to the reform he represented. See for example her declaration to him during the deliberations about the best candidates for election to the provincial's office, *Letters* II, 811.

[77]Her letters to Rubeo attempting to repair the rift are in *Letters* I, 178–184, 220–26. Cf. *Foundations*, 24.

[78]For a succinct summary in English of the misperceptions, power struggles, and conflicting loyalties that issued in a battle royale for the direction of Carmelite life in Spain throughout this period, see the introduction to St. John of the Cross, *The Collected Works of St. John of the Cross*, tr. and intr. Kieran Kavanaugh, O.C.D. and Otilio Rodríguez, O.C.D. (Washington, D.C.: ICS Publications, 1979), 20–26.

felt she was neglecting them as a result of her devotion to him.[79] More than anything else, she had to defend it from her own disappointment; persevere in it when it was carelessly unrequited; keep it kindled when Gracián's actions showed that he did not know how to love with a mature affection that attended to the finer points of human need and to the subtle degrees that mark the difference between dedication and ambition, heroism and protagonism, righteousness and inflexibility.

Teresa's love for Gracián made her overestimate his worth at the outset; she continued to misjudge him and sometimes excused his obvious defects to others in unadmirable tones. But since that day when she had understood in a vision that God had joined them in a "marriage well-arranged," her love for him was inseparable from her love for the discalced reform.[80] She saw his perfection as crucial to the reform's progress, and she kept after him. She could not give up on him any more than she could on the great ecclesial work she believed God had given her to do.

Her letters tell the story. Repeatedly she urged him to sleep; he must not kill himself with overwork. She suggested that instead he leave something for *God* to do. Reminding him of the importance of rectitude of intention, she hinted at his self-sufficiency and his tendencey to substitute planning for prayer. She reprimanded him for failing to keep her properly informed, even wondering whether he was deliberately holding out on her.[81] Poignantly she registered Gracián's neglect of her in remarks such as this:

> Angela . . . has no consolation [but your friendship] and . . .
> she . . . gets distressed when she thinks [her affection] is not

---

[79]For example, her correspondence with M. María Bautista, *Letters* I, 191–96, and Gracián, *Letters* I, 368. In another letter to M. María Bautista, Teresa alluded to a perceived conflict of duty and devotion involving Rubeo, Báñez, and Gracián, *Letters* I, 211. See also *Foundations*, 23:11, in which she seems compelled to justify her spiritual intimacy with Gracián to posterity.

[80]Teresa acknowledged that the matchmaker (God) had tied the knot (arranged her "marriage" with Gracián) very well in a letter to him in 1577, *Letters* I, 400–01. See also her exhortation to María de San José: "the Lord chose him to begin our work," *Letters* I, 362.

[81]For example, *Letters* I, 241, 399–400, 485–86, 495, 508–09; II, 541, 582, 673, 782, 807. In one letter she complained that she never knows his whereabouts and that he changes the code in which they were forced to communicate without telling her, with the result that his letters are too cryptic, *Letters* II, 584.

requited . . . Your Paternity must please tell that gentleman that, careless though he may be by nature, he must not be careless with her; for where there is love, it cannot slumber so long.[82]

She felt his physical sufferings in her own flesh and worried constantly about his safety;[83] but she had also to remind him that he was not the only one to pay the price of persecution. In fact, compared to John of the Cross, who had been kidnapped and imprisoned by the reform's opponents, Gracián had gotten off lightly. Since Gracián had become so despairing under tolerable circumstances, she wondered if he could ever have worn John's shoes.[84] Teresa was also alarmed by the cowardice that had made him deaf to her advice to make a direct, obedient approach to the Father General after the Seville fiasco and help bring about a badly needed reconciliation.[85]

More ominously, she warned him about the dangers of playing favorites and about how a religious superior ill could afford the inconsistent, autocratic, and headstrong behavior others noted in him.[86] He was not to tempt fate by treating too severely the recalcitrant friars under his jurisdiction. For the sake of the reform he must learn to act strategically. She told him, too, that she was "shocked" to hear that he had arbitrarily imposed new rules upon the nuns in Valladolid and warned him never again to interfere with the minimalist Constitutions that sufficed to regulate their lives.[87]

In the letters Teresa wrote him indefatigably, there are hints aplenty of Gracián's inability to leave well enough alone. On one occasion, when falsely accused of indecencies with women, Gracián made a fool of himself producing documents in his own defense. Teresa had begged him in vain not to dignify the accusations with a response. Breaking with her custom of speaking only well

[82]*Letters* II, 683. Angela is a code-name for Teresa. "That gentleman" is obviously Gracián. For the pseudonyms found in Teresa's ocrrespondence see *Letters* II, IV. Index to Pseudonyms Employed by St. Teresa, 1003–04.

[83]Examples of this solicitude, *Letters* I, 202; II, 525, 531–32, 591–95, 839.

[84]*Letters* II, 600.

[85]*Letters* I, 208; II, 614–15.

[86]For example, *Letters* I, 287.

[87]*Letters,* I, 194, 197, 255 and n. 5, 283, 287; II, 571–72.

of him to others, she expressed her consternation to a collaborator: "Our Father," she wrote, "is acting unwisely and demeaning himself in the most dreadful way."[88] Repeatedly she counseled him about his tendency to plunge innocently but recklessly into compromising situations. She urged him to respect the special character of their friendship by not reading aloud to others the intimate passages of her letters.[89] With so little sense of proportion and so much apparent need to play the protagonist, Gracián risked causing worse troubles still for her and the movement.

Although unable on account of her sex to take a direct public role in the formation of the discalced province, Teresa acted decisively behind the scenes through friars, courtiers, and ecclesiastical officials sympathetic to her work. But most of all, she relied on Gracián. Her letters laid out what to say and when to say it, who to approach and who to avoid, what to insist upon and what to bargain over. She frequently deferred to Gracián's ideas and left many decisions in his hands but never hesitated to insist on her own vision or even tell him curtly, "Your Paternity will make a note of my wishes."[90]

Although some wondered whether Gracián was truly the man for the moment, she continually made allowances for him, defended him, demanded special treatment for him, and commended him to all as the one thing necessary for the reform. She campaigned to get him elected provincial and when he won, she praised Providence for the outcome. Teresa's letters are rich in praise of him. Many moving passages of admiration and gratitude show that Teresa doted on him, nearly exploding with happiness when he termed himself her "dear son."[91] She even once demanded to

---

[88]To Ambrosio Mariano de San Benito (a friar who caused her no small vexation in his own right), *Letters* I, 446–47. See also *Letters* I, 359, 345–46, 441.

[89]*Letters* I, 345–46. See also, for example, her warning about being "less simple" and trusting: calumnies often result from naiveté, a lack of shrewd dealing even with "good creatures." *Letters* II, 639–640. Apparently referring to Gracián's excessive candor and to the Andalusians' reputation for duplicity, she also warned him: "Do not meditate turning yourself into an Andalusian: you are not of a temperament to live among them. As for your sermons there, I earnestly beg your Reverence once again to be very careful what you say . . . " *Letters* II, 967.

[90]*Letters* II, 702. See also 583–87, 591–95, 603–05, 633–34, 669–670, 809–811, 813–16, 818–820. Her insistence on her right to an authoritative opinion, coupled with a rebuke of his presumption, is striking in *Letters* II, 810–11.

[91]*Letters* I, 372.

know whether he loved her better than his own mother.[92] With delicacy, she received his confidences about aspects of his interior life that troubled him, and with good humor she bore his occasional imperiousness. Frequently she lauded his "skill" and "shrewdness" in the affairs of the Order.[93]

But her last communication with him is noticeably restrained and contains serious talk about failings of his that directly affected the well-being of the province. This weary letter is also her last of many recorded complaints about him for abandoning her with no justifiable reason at a time when she needed him most. So keenly did she feel his having left her "at such a time" that she lost the desire to write to him at all, "so I have not written," she told him in hurt tones, "until today, when it is unavoidable.[94] Her marriage well-arranged had turned out to be a rocky one. The sharpness of her rebuke of him seems to indicate the depth of her resignation to a failed hope.

Gracián's behavior was but one of several personal betrayals and painful hardships that lend to Teresa's final days an air of appalling bleakness, a sense of something slipping away. But if on some levels the relationship had failed to satisfy the expectations she had placed upon it, it still managed to fulfill its purpose as a boost toward God. For Teresa the moral of the story was clear, and in that last long letter to her friend she spelled it out:

> Teresa[95] has borne it well. She was deeply disappointed that [you] did not come. We didn't tell her [the news] until now. In a way, I'm glad [you have disappointed her], because now she will start understanding that one can place but little trust in anyone but God—*and it has done me no harm either.*[96]

Nonetheless, even this hurt and disappointed Teresa did not see in Gracián's confusing behavior toward her a reason to aban-

---

[92]*Letters* I, 285.

[93]*Letters* I, 341.

[94]*Letters* II, 965. Complete text, 964–971.

[95]This Teresa was her niece (the young daughter of her brother Lorenzo) who had become a discalced nun in Avila.

[96]Letter to Gracián, 1 September 1582, my translation and emphasis. Cf. *Letters*, vol. 2, 965. See a similar expression about the inconstancy of human friendships, this time with reference to Báñez, in *Letters* I, 362: "Blessed by [God]," Teresa concluded, "Who, when we seek His friendship, is *always* our true friend" (my emphasis).

don him or the unfinished project that was their friendship. Faith-fully, maybe even foolishly, she stuck by what she believed God had begun. In the same letter, at the very end, she exclaimed: "Oh, my Father, how oppressed I have been feeling lately! But the op-pression passed off when I heard you were well."[97] Even chastened by the experience of his vacillations, the mere thought of him and of his work for the sake of their shared endeavor continued to be enough to raise her spirits.

It is not known what Gracián felt upon receipt of this letter. We do know, however, that his decision to go south rather than accompany Teresa to Burgos deprived them both of the chance to bid each other good-bye, for a month later at Alba Teresa died.

[97]*Letters* II, 970.

5

Seeing with God's Eyes

For Teresa, seeking God in prayer and in the realities of daily experience, accompanied by the stalwart companions God provided, was a response to a divine invitation. By means of prayer the soul entered a realm of clarity about who God is and who humans are. That clarity of vision and knowledge formed in turn the indispensable matrix for right action in the world; as divine intimacy grew, so did moral vision.

At times, God enlarged the horizon of the mystic's clear-sightedness to include the future; more often, however, God sharpened the focus of the present and taught the soul to take its meaning in, free from illusion and the blur of self-interest. Through contemplation, a person eventually was granted something akin to the vantage point of God and became, as a result, more thoroughly committed to the world and to the men and women God loved in it, since it was the arena of redemption and the chosen dwelling of the incarnate God. But at the same time she became more acutely and critically perceptive with respect to "the world," that sphere of human experience and striving that was estranged from God and which she called "worldly," full of false, deceptive values and rewards.

Through divine intimacy, the spiritual person gained the courage to proclaim and act upon the new vision. She learned also to suffer redemptively the painful consequences of finding herself, at least some of the time, decidedly and publicly at odds with convention, a stranger in a life that no longer fit her frame. The contrast between what God held dear and that which was precious to the world could even be at times too great for the soul to bear, and the anguished soul would long to die and be with God, finally delivered from the pain of seeing rightly in a world perversely bent on averting its eyes.[1]

Of course, the bold claim to have gotten things right by seeing with God's eyes is not made lightly by anyone in any age. In Teresa's day it could cost a reputation or a life. Nonetheless, her experience of God led her to make it and to teach others how to enter into that realm of new clarity, not for the sake of harnessing some esoteric *gnosis* conferring spiritual superiority upon the soul, but in order better to accomplish God's authentic will of freedom and justice, and serve all the needs of the women and men beloved of Christ.

That is not to say, however, that by means of the contemplative life Teresa was easily able to shed her own particularity and transcend completely the selective awareness that characterized people of her class and condition. She remained always a literate, urban Castilian, from a well-to-do middle-class *converso* family with aristocratic pretensions. Scholars have noted, for example, that in her writings laborers make only brief appearances, an omission that betrays an ingrained class bias; typically such folk were regarded with studied indifference or outright disdain by the solidly middle class.[2] The ubiquitous begging poor are also ignored, even though she claimed in an early private account of her conscience to have overcome her repugnance toward them through "a gift given by God."[3] And although generally scornful of the attention paid to status and family connections in her culture, she was not above rejoicing when her nephew made a marriage that was, to her surprise, a good deal better than she had dared to hope.[4]

Still, throughout her long rich life as a founder, spiritual leader, and contemplative, Teresa engaged in a running critique of important aspects of what in her day passed for reality, both in the

---

[1] For example, *Life*, 40:3. "There was left in me [as a result of this vision] a keen desire to speak only those things that are very true, that reach beyond what is dealt with here in the world; so I began to experience the pain of living in the world."

[2] "El linaje," 163.

[3] *Testimonies*, 2:4. The year was 1562.

[4] *Letters* II, 791–92. For other instances of Teresa's contradictory behavior see "Historical Setting," 180, n. 171.

life of the spirit strictly speaking and in the arrangements that governed people's social and religious lives. Her reports of her own spiritual experience, as well as the history of her decisions, activities, and friendships, are studded with breakthroughs, flashes of transcendence, and daring applications of old themes to new situations. These constitute in part the fresh way of seeing, and thus of living, that Teresa as a teacher of the spiritual life wished every person to attain, through the mercy of the One who was reality itself.

"How differently we will understand"[5]

Early in 1571, after difficult negotiations, a discalced Carmelite monastery for women was established in the small Castilian backwater of Alba de Tormes.[6] Teresa had not been eager to make a foundation in such an out-of-the-way castle village, owned and operated, we might say, by the powerful House of Alba. Foundations in urban centers could usually count on a supply of alms to form the basis for an independent convent economy. Nuns in cities were better able to live in the complete poverty Teresa had set as the norm for her new communities, free from the strings attached to endowments. But in a village like Alba, a convent was unlikely to thrive without a subsidy provided by some noble or wealthy family.

Teresa had always been wary of entanglements of this kind. From previous experience she knew that the pious deeds of the nobility were rarely pure. One could count on a fair measure of caprice and self-interest in the dealings of the high-born, who, for their honor's sake and their soul's salvation, would haggle down to the dime.[7] Not surprisingly, one of the sticking points at Alba was agreement on a suitable income for the convent. The benefactors' idea of generous support did not, apparently, extend to the provision of basic elements of survival. Teresa had to convince them that the amount they had in mind would not sustain the number of nuns designated for the community. Thankfully,

---

⁵*Foundations*, 20:3.

⁶*Foundations*, 20.

⁷In *Way*, 19:4, Teresa referred to a "gentleman" she knew who was indeed actually *killed* in "a quarrel over a few dimes."

when the donors "finally became reasonable," they threw into the bargain even the house in which they were living.[8]

We learn little more, however, about the particulars of the difficulties, for Teresa was reluctant to be completely candid about such benefactors when her work was, like it or not, tied to their goodwill. Instead, her account concentrates on the miraculous happenings that had reportedly shaped the life of the convent's patron, Teresa de Layz. Chapter 20 is an edifying tale fashioned to wrap the foundation in a cloak of supernatural predestination.

We read, for example, that the convent is by implication willed by God from the moment the infant "foundress" (Teresa de Layz) miraculously spoke up in a servant's arms to declare herself a Christian, causing her mother devoutly to pray that she might live long enough to see "what God would do with this child."[9] God's purpose is revealed when, later, the patron's troubling childlessness is explained in a dream: her sterility is providential; she will see spiritual children, the nuns of an unnamed Order. The place they will one day inhabit is also shown to her in a lovely pastoral vision hosted by a disguised St. Andrew.[10]

Obstacles to the mission arise when learned and reasonable people convince her that her plans to found a convent are foolish. Teresa de Layz and her husband then try to arrange a marriage between her nephew and his niece, with a view to bestowing upon them the resources once earmarked for the monastery. But God intervenes again; in a matter of two weeks, the nephew is taken ill. Within a few more days he is dead, and the chastened couple return to the original plan with renewed determination.[11]

In this chapter, Teresa de Layz's supernatural experiences are structured to illustrate traditional religious notions about the way

[8]*Foundations,* 20:14. The foundation at Alba was made with the consent of the Duchess, but the endowment was provided by the *contador,* or administrator of the ducal estates, the talented (in all probability, *converso)* Francisco Velázquez, and his wife, Teresa de Layz (also spelled Laíz), whom Teresa described as an old Christian of noble stock. Only the insistence of her longtime friend and confessor, the Dominican theologian Báñez, secured Teresa's agreement to accept the offer to establish the monastery with *rentas,* or fixed income. He cited the authority of the Council of Trent (which had recently ruled about convent finances) to make her relent. Báñez had always opposed absolute poverty.

[9]*Foundations,* 20:4.

[10]*Foundations,* 20:7.

[11]*Foundations,* 20:11-12.

God undermines assumptions, reverses expectations, contradicts worldly values, and carries out the divine will, no matter how determined to thwart it are the forces of human myopia and the devil's wiles. The learned and wise are in fact foolish;[12] physical barrenness becomes the condition of possibility for spiritual fecundity;[13] humbly embracing relative obscurity (as when Teresa de Layz's husband accepted a position in the Alba household) secures a lasting, holy prominence as a helper of the friends of God.[14]

These piously predictable instances of reversal and the upending of human values are as much emblems as they are events, occurring regularly in saints' lives and other edifying stories. Teresa seems to take them for granted as she tells the tale of Alba's foundation. One detail of the story, however, serves to connect the reader with the violent realities of life among even the upper classes of Teresa's day. In a chilling disclosure made at the beginning of the narrative, we discover that Teresa de Layz was the fifth female baby of her family, and such was the consternation of her parents that they had given birth to yet another girl for whom one day they would have to provide a dowry, that the infant was for all practical purposes exposed, simply neglected, and left to die.

Teresa de Layz's family, old Christian *hidalgos,* were bound by codes of honor to maintain the ostentatious appearance proper to their noble lineage. Yet, like so many others of their class, they had been dragged inexorably out to sea in an undertow of debt. To limit public knowledge of their reduced circumstances, they had moved to the countryside where they were, in Teresa's words, without access to "Christian doctrine and . . . many other things that are means to the enlightenment of souls." A disapproving Teresa noted that these foolish nobles were willing to starve their spirits and risk their souls rather than "fail even one iota in those punctilios that accompany what they call honor."[15] They were also willing to sacrifice their fifth daughter, one more drain on their scant resources, to the very same ends.

[12]*Foundations,* 20:11-12.
[13]*Foundations,* 20:7-9.
[14]*Foundations,* 20:10.
[15]*Foundations,* 20:2.

Reading this narrative, one is reminded that Teresa of Avila was the granddaughter of a merchant, a city woman whose urban bias is easy to hear in her disdain of the poor and backward villages of Castile. Moreover, her disgust at the sordid folly of *hidalgo* pretense cannot but reflect the painful experience of watching her own father struggle to maintain a purchased honor and noble appearances as he slid into penury. But Teresa's full fury is reserved for the treatment afforded the infant girl.

Although it is clear that Teresa was shocked by the parents' turning their back on the girl, what she denounced first was the attitude of cold expediency that led to the near-fatal neglect of the child. Indeed, Teresa's report of the parents' actual "cruelty" seems almost mild in comparison with what she thought of their distressed reaction to the *sex* of the newborn child.[16] What exercised her was the parent's inability to receive from God what God ordained, and, by implication, to understand that girls were as much a divine gift to them as boys. Going to the heart of the matter, her comments have a searing edge:

> . . . [H]uman beings do not know what is best for them and are totally ignorant of the judgments of God and of the great blessings that can come to them through daughters or of the great sufferings that can come to them through sons. It doesn't seem they want to leave the matter to the One who creates their children and understands everything, but they kill themselves over what should be making them happy. As people whose faith is asleep, they do not reflect or recall that it is God who thus ordains, and so they do not leave everything in His hands . . . Oh, God help me! How differently we will understand these ignorances on the day when the truth about all things shall be understood. *And how many fathers and mothers will be seen going to hell because they had sons and how many will be seen in heaven because of their daughters.*[17]

This devaluation of girls was a fact of life in sixteenth-century Castile. Here, however, speaking as one who claimed to know the mind of God, Teresa declared the axiom that sons were of greater value than daughters to be at odds with the divine view-

---

[16]*Foundations*, 20:4, 2.

[17]*Foundations*, 20:3, my emphasis.

point. In the end, she announced, worldly judgments will be unmasked as lies; humanity's eyes will be opened to the ignorant absurdity of presuming to judge as inferior that which God has empowered for good.

Teresa's denunciation of the ignorance and lies of the world with respect to the value placed on the sexes touched a sore reality in her world. More than the miraculous paradoxes of fruitful barrenness and foolish wisdom found in edification stories such as this one about the Alba foundation, her assertion that girls and boys were equally capable of revealing God's blessings illuminated and questioned contemporary assumptions governing *ordinary experience.* For most people, and especially for the theologians, if sexual equality existed at all, it obtained solely in the realm of the soul; in the reality of the social and economic order ordained by God, however, real men and real women were not of equal worth and were not meant to be. Ordinary experience in the real world decreed the inferior valuation of girls.

That real world was precisely the backdrop against which Teresa declared her condemnation of Teresa de Layz's parents. Her denunciation came in the context of a very pressing social and economic problem for the family, a superfluity of females; and the judgment she made on the attitude of the parents encompassed their social motives, namely honor, money, and appearance. Teresa was concerned not with some theory of equality of souls but with the realities of boys and girls, of what in fact constituted blessing and suffering, good fortune and ill. Her strong affirmation that girls could be a source of blessing and redemption for their parents and that attitudes such as the ones exhibited by Teresa de Layz's parents were signs of sleeping faith and contrary to God's will was at once a message to her culture, busy measuring human worth by external yardsticks rather than by the judgments of God. And it was through her intimacy with God that she claimed to have hit upon this knowledge of who God really is, and, consequently, of *the way things really are,* knowledge revealed to God's friends now, and to everyone "on the day when the truth about all things shall be understood."

Certainly Teresa's experience of God was shaped in large measure by the religious and cultural traditions in which she was nurtured and expressed in metaphors like Lord and King, Savior and Spouse. Nonetheless, as this incident illustrates, Teresa's picture of God and of God's view of reality was often sharply personal, original, and countercultural. Her experience of God sent her beneath platitudes to the bedrock of human perversity with its drive to subordinate, devalue, and instrumentalize the other; to the wellspring, too, of the graciouss God before whom every breath drawn, male or female, was a precious chance for love. By placing herself squarely in the way of this God, she began to "understand differently."[18]

As Teresa's friendship with God matured, the world began to look and feel different. She noticed things askew, and began to have a great deal to say about the discrepancies that kept cropping up between her experience of God and what others were claiming to be God's nature and plan. Her accounts of these instances yield wonderful glimpses of who God was for Teresa. They are lucid descriptors of her life with the one she called her friend. They demonstrate as well that the loving knowledge of God with which the mystic is illuminated in her journey is a knowledge as public and social in its dimensions as it is intimate and personal, a knowledge of justice and a determination to rectify its scarcity upon the earth. We turn now to some vivid examples of Teresa's ability to see contemplatively through and beyond the world's arrangements and to posit, through her actions especially, an alternative vision.

"Ask them if they can tie my hands"[19]

The year of 1570 ended on a note of deep disappointment and chagrin for Teresa of Jesus. Elections for prioress were to be held at the discalced convent of Medina del Campo, and the Carmelite provincial, Angel de Salazar, was brazenly interfering in the election. Preempting the traditional privilege of nuns to choose

[18]*Foundations,* 20:2. This is not to say that Teresa believed that males and females were equal in *all* respects. She recognized differences between the sexes and accepted basic cultural definitions of "the feminine" and "the masculine." But her *practical* understanding of and positions on the "question about women" was quite complex, as several of the incidents used to illustrate points made in this volume should serve to demonstrate. Thus it is just plain wrong to state uncritically and universally, as Stephen Clissold does, for example, that "Teresa firmly believed . . . in the inequality of the sexes" and held a universally "low opinion of woman's natural abilities and status . . . " *St. Teresa of Avila,* 111-12.

[19]*Testimonies,* 15.

their own officers, he installed a candidate of his own as prioress, a nun from the Incarnation of Avila unsympathetic to Teresa's reform.[20] At the same time, he took sides against Teresa in a dispute about the disposition of an inheritance. Then, in an apparent bid for undisputed authority, he ordered her off the premises of the monastery she herself had founded. According to the chronicles, Teresa obeyed at once. In the middle of the night, her humiliating exit from Medina was accomplished by the only means available, a water vendor's mule.

Later she learned that sometime before her expulsion a leading citizen of Medina had, in a public forum, compared her with Magdalena de la Cruz, the Franciscan nun of Cordoba whose mystical prowess had attracted the attention and devotion of, among many others, the Inquisitor General and the Queen, but whose eventual confession of trafficking with Satan had turned her name in Teresa's time into a byword for spiritual fraud.[21] In response, Teresa is reported to have agreed that she was, like Magdalena, a great sinner but to have denied emphatically that her sins included deliberate deception. All the same, Teresa well understood the implication of the charge; as a woman out of enclosure, her freedom of movement was an anomaly, and despite all the permissions she had been granted by her superiors and all the backing of influential men (such men had also flocked to Magdalena), she could still end up badly.

Such suspicion of her integrity and motives was by no means new, but that kind of talk coupled with her provincial's transparent play for control at Medina was alarming. Her authority over the reform was being wrested from her, and the autonomy of the discalced communities was endangered. Not surprisingly, the assault was being mounted in the name of God's will for women, as expressed by Paul. The injunction that women should

[20]One of the principles Teresa insisted on with energy and determination throughout her career as founder and legislator was the right of nuns to elect their own superiors. Ironically, monastic obedience once required of her that she allow herself to be imposed as superior on a group of nuns who had not been free to elect her, or anyone else. The rioting that occurred at the Incarnation when Teresa arrived in Avila to be installed as that convent's prioress had, it seems, less to do with the nuns' dislike for Teresa and her reformism (a large faction probably would have voted for her, given the chance) than with the nuns' ire at having their traditional privilege rescinded so heavy-handedly. See *Tiempo y vida,* 447-455.

[21]Magdalena's sensational disclosures about a childhood pact with the devil occurred in 1546.

be silent in the Church was in Teresa's day normally applied also to the cloistering, or enclosure, of nuns. Teresa, herself actually a proponent of strict enclosure even before the Council of Trent mandated it for all nuns, was caught in a classic bind: in order to obey what she believed to be God's will and continue the reform, she was transgressing norms also believed to be of God. Thus, even though she was operating under license from ecclesiastical authorities, the mere fact of her activity outside convent walls rendered her continually vulnerable to charges of everything from lascivious behavior to benighted foolishness to heresy and fraud.

A few months after her unceremonious departure from Medina, while still apprehensive about the fate of the reform and her own reputation, she began experiencing in prayer the indwelling of the Trinity in a sublime new way. It was, she wrote of similar experiences in the seventh mansions of *Castle,* as if Christ had removed a "blindfold" from her soul. She perceived that the three divine Persons were "very habitually present" within her, and somehow she felt that she actually understood "how God is three and one." She marvelled that a human soul was capable of absorbing so much divinity, like a sponge becoming saturated with water. Moreover, during these encounters she experienced profound connections among herself, God, and the cosmos. Not only did each of the Persons grant her gifts of authentic love and a capacity for suffering, but also from within her very soul, the eternal three-in-one "were communicating themselves to all creation without fail, [even as] they [did not] fail to be with me."[22]

Such was her profound delight in the overwhelming mystery that she began to wonder whether "those who thought it wrong for [her] to go out to found monasteries" might indeed have a case. Against her activity, they had been arguing that nuns should "be always occupied in prayer."[23] Teresa certainly agreed that

---

[22]*Testimonies,* 13 and 14. Teresa's initiation into this mystery was by way of the "intellectual vision" (an experience in which "infused contemplation directly affects the mystic's intellect without the aid of sensible images of the normal use or the internal and external senses" resulting in simple, intuitive knowledge of great immediacy and certitude. *Christian Mysticism,* 308.) In subsequent years, her apprehension of the trinitarian mystery was sharpened by means of "imaginative visions" (visions that occur in the mystic's creative imagination with greater clarity and realism than normal physical perception). See for example, *Testimonies,* 29; 42; 51.

[23]*Testimonies,* 15.

nothing could compare with solitude and the enjoyment of the "intimate sharing between friends" she called prayer.[24] What could be better than to remain fixed on the mystery of the triune God, now revealed to her in this new compelling way, and seek nothing else?

Her health was, as always, terrible, and she dreaded the tremendous physical hardships associated with establishing reformed convents. Were there not signs aplenty that her critics were right after all? Had she been misreading God? Deep within her consciousness she found the answer to her anxiety, a reply she attributed to God and recorded in her private notes: "While one is alive," she quoted the divine message, "progress doesn't come from trying to enjoy me more, but by trying to do my will."[25]

Teresa heard God enunciate a principle of spirituality that, were it not for its context, is hardly remarkable. Most spiritual teachers would have agreed that the purpose of asceticism, prayer, and the practice of the virtues is to discern God's will and conform the human will to God's so that the divine plan would be played out on earth in God's service, in love of neighbor. Teresa taught repeatedly that the enjoyment of God was not to be sought at the expense of one's scrupulously discerned duties of charity and the building of community.

That "God walks among the pots and pans" was her way of insisting that even the humdrum activity required by a life of service in love to the community is revelatory;[26] spiritual experience of a dramatic sort was not, in her view, intrinsically more valuable than the encounter to be had with God in the day-by-day doing of God's will. Indeed, spiritual maturity, or what she called "perfection," was not to be measured by visions and locutions or disciplines and fasts but by things as basic as, for example, authentic sociability in a sometimes difficult community of women.[27] What marked the soul truly on the road to perfection was not the quest of even licit and salutary spiritual gratification; rather, the humble seeking after God's will in prayer, in the community, in obedience

[24]*Life*, 8:5; also *Life*, 7:1.

[25]*Testimonies*, 15.

[26]*Foundations*, 5:8.

[27]In *Way*, 41:7, for example, Teresa remarked that "the holier [the nuns] are, the more sociable they are with their sisters."

to the superior, even in "the signs of the times," as we might say, and the disciplined ability to embrace it as one's own—these were the hallmarks of perfection.

Yet it is important to note that this valid and necessary spiritual principle was applied by clerical authorities in a particular way to women, whose presumed sensuality and curiosity was seen as leading them to seek devotional experiences for their own sake, or even, in the case of certain visionaries, to fake them in order to achieve notoriety and a measure of authority in a society avid for unusual phenomena and awash in spiritual sensationalism.[28] Countless sermons and tracts, for example, denounced women's voracity for new and insubstantial devotional practices, and pointed to its inevitable seeds of rebellion: great numbers of married women neglecting husbands and loitering in churches, making repeated trips to the confessionals; unmarried women-turned-*beatas* traipsing shamelessly around the countryside in the train of charismatic clerics; nuns (like Teresa) claiming conversations with God and divine missions as pretexts for rejecting enclosure or teaching spiritual doctrine in public like men. In short, women were perceived as abusing devotion by treating the practices of the spiritual life as means to escape male controls, evade household responsibilities, and get out of the recessed rooms to which they were supposed to be confined.

For example, like all other Christians, wives were told that in order to be saved, prayers had to be offered daily. But wives were also instructed to attend to their devotions only when all their other duties were fulfilled, and then, to pursue them privately, in the home. God's will was mirrored for them primarily in their husbands, and husbands, like God, came first. Attending to their needs, or simply obeying them if they happened to refuse permission to attend church, took precedence even over the general Christian obligation to hear Mass and confess.[29] So clearly did

---

[28]In numerous cases of fraudulent *beatas* and female mystics, it must be remembered, high-ranking churchmen and nobles were often among the women's most ardent devotees. The same persons who generally regarded women with spiritual pretensions as flirting with demonic danger seemed to be able to put aside those concerns in the case of "their" holy woman, prophet, or healer—at least until such time as she was revealed, through intimidation, jealousy of a rival, or an authentic change of heart as a "fraud."

[29]Teresa seems to have held to this principle herself. See *Life,* 13:17 where, in the context of explaining the harm foolish or inexperienced spiritual directors can do, she offers the ex-

the authorities wish to convey the moral dangers involved in the
contravening of God's will and good order exemplified by frivolous female devotion, spiritual avarice, and the lack of supervision implied in church-hopping that their rhetoric often steams
with a submerged violence against women all too casually or flip-
pantly passed over by subsequent commentators. Nuns and *beatas,* wives and single women, young and old, were all admonished
to eschew novelty, to curb their curiosity, and, above all, *to stay
put,* to find and carry out God's will for them not through direct
religious experience, but in duty.[30]

The message Teresa reported from God espoused the same fundamental principle, namely that trying to do God's will is the beginning and end of the road to spiritual perfection. What this
message also drove home, however, was the *freedom of God* to
determine finally what is to be included under the rubric of God's
will. It implied that although the disposition to listen to one's superiors and to heed the general wisdom of the tradition is required,
simple acquiescence to law or custom does not always guarantee
that one has grasped God's will.

Teresa's report of the locution continues:

> I thought that [my detractors'] recommendation would be
> God's will because of what St. Paul said about the enclosure
> of women . . . The Lord said to me: "Tell them they shouldn't
> follow just one part of Scripture but that they should look at
> other parts, and ask them if they can by chance tie my hands."

ample of a confessor who "when dealing with matters in the home if the person is a married
woman . . . will tell her that it is better to remain in prayer even if it displeases her husband." In the same vein, she declared it unwise that a confessor advise a nun to obey himself
rather than her legitimate superior. The point is that the prudent director will encourage the
performance of the duties of one's state in life as a means to perfection in the discernment
and carrying out of God's will.

[30]Note the suggestion of violence embodied in the popular contemporary saying, "An
honorable woman: at home with a broken leg," a sentiment echoed by Francisco de Osuna
(Norte de Estados, my translation): "Whenever you see your wife going from church to church
. . . and affecting sanctity, lock the door, and if that doesn't work, break her leg . . . She
can get to heaven limping from inside her own home without having to cast about for a suspect sanctity [outside]. One sermon is enough for a woman, and if she wants more, let a
[devotional] book be read to her while she spins . . . for were she a nun, she could act like
a nun, but since she is married let her act like a wife." For a compilation of texts by Spanish
authors of the sixteenth century on the topic of women, see Julia Fitzmaurice-Kelly, "Woman
in Sixteenth-Century Spain," *Revue Hispanique* (1927): 557–632; see also P. W. Bomli, *La
femme dans l'Espagne du siècle d'or* (The Hague, 1950).

Teresa had been tempted to bow before her opponents since they adduced Scripture as proof of their position; surely what the Apostle wrote as *word* of God in the New Testament was also the *will* of God for believers! Yet the locution seemed to indicate that the will of God is not always to be found through the unthinking repetition of injunctions ripped from the pages of the Bible. God instructed Teresa not to acquiesce to a proof text but to question the prevailing interpretation, in fact *to reply with a hermaneutic of her own.* She was to tell "them" that what St. Paul enjoined in one passage was to be placed in the context of other divine words in order to be understood as God intended.

In a world in which the laity, and women in particular, had no authority to determine the meaning of God's word in the Bible and in which attempts were made strictly to control access to Scripture in the vernacular, the command to "tell them" that they had too narrowly interpreted and applied Paul's ruling about women's roles seems daring. But if Teresa followed through on the command, it would not have been the first time that she questioned a conventional interpretation or application of Scripture and attempted to correct what she perceived as unwarranted harshness or unjust behavior on the part of God's picked men. Her experience of the freedom of God emboldened her. That experience is wonderfully expressed in the final challenge laid down by God in response to her anxiety. Even if the argument about reading particular Scripture passages in light of the whole should fail, the voice seemed to imply, God is free to do whatever is required to advance the divine cause; "and ask them" God ordered her in a "so-there!" tone of conclusion, "if they can by chance tie my hands."

Discerning God's will was for Teresa a delicate and often subtly complex process that required attention to law, custom, Scripture, circumstances, and the teachings of duly constituted authorities as well as a fundamental disposition to obey. But she insisted that if one is to know truly what it is God desires, one must at the very least also *put the question directly to God.* In prayer, in the lifetime give-and-take of a constantly developing intimacy, in the habitual presence of God, one could learn respectfully to weigh and measure the Church's tradition and law, to evaluate and see correctly human opinions, to interpret Scripture in all its profound range of possibilities, and, at every turn, to be startled and refreshed by the ultimate freedom of God.

In this case, that freedom decreed that she should not just then set up a booth on the mountain to enjoy perpetually her solitude with a fascinating God. Rather, she was to continue the work, and let God find her, as God seemed unfailingly to do, no matter where, how far, or into what entangled business she had to go. While she lived, progress was not to be found in enjoying God exclusively but in sharing her experience of and creating the conditions for divine intimacy, especially for her sisters of the discalced movement. That was, it seemed to her, the unconventional but authentic will of God that had at all costs to be done on earth as it was in heaven.

Mud for bricks and adobes[31]

Teresa's gradual assumption of what she understood to be God's point of view set her on a collision course with prevailing opinion and practice on another contemporary issue of immense social significance, namely the matter of pure blood and lineage. Although not the first nor the only religious leader of her day to resist the nearly irresistible social pressure to embrace laws of racial purity, Teresa was courageous in her opposition to such statutes and sharply critical of the arrogance that lay beneath them. Her refusal to allow adoption of pure blood regulations for the discalced reform risked bringing her entire movement into dangerous disrepute.[32]

In part, her adamant stand was rooted in awareness of her own *converso* heritage; in part, too, it stemmed from her knowledge of the rancorous divisions caused in other Religious Orders by

[31]Cf. *Way*, 27:6.

[32]Teresa's refusal to permit statutes of pure blood to rule the admissions process and the fact that the earliest members of the female reform especially were *judeoconversas* in high numbers exacerbated an already popular suspicion of Carmelites in general. Otger Steggink reported that *calced* Carmelite friars had already earned a reputation for looking too much the other way when *conversos* presented themselves for entry. During the Carmelite General Rubeo's tour in 1566, some friars even charged that Carmel was getting the castoffs from other Orders whose laws were stricter. *La reforma*, 205 (the context of the complaint was lax standards of admission generally, the admission of *moriscos* and *judeoconversos* particularly).

questions of pure blood and family status, divisions she was determined to forestall among the discalced. In the last analysis, however, she understood her fierce opposition to her culture's obsession with racial purity and good family as a point of simple fidelity to the gospel; a question, in the end, of whether one was truly living one's membership in the only family that mattered: the all-inclusive family of Jesus that counted God as its Father.[33]

Firm as she always was on the matter, in practical situations involving, for example, to what extent she should rely upon known *conversos* to finance her work, Teresa was at times caught between the desire to stick by her principles and the pressing need to secure public prestige for the reform so that it could flourish without hindrance. It took a sharp encounter with God once and for all to clarify her vision and shore up any weakness in her that could cause her to buckle. Ironically, that moment of truth for Teresa occurred in Toledo, the city through whose streets her father and his father had once trudged from parish church to parish church seven Fridays in a row garbed in the special tunics, or *sambenitos,* with loud green crosses painted on the backs; the costumes that announced to the public eye the grave sin of apostasy, the outrage of *converso* judaizing for which they had been sentenced by the Holy Inquisition to such humbling penitence.[34] Toledo was the seat of her own secret, the place that held the memory of her own tainted blood; in the church of St. Leocadia, the Sánchez *sambenito* might still have been tacked to the wall.

Moreover, as we have seen, ten years earlier the archbishop of the city, Bartolomé de Carranza, had been imprisoned by the Inquisition for advocating, among other things, the *espirituales'* program of interior prayer and access to Scripture in the vernacular. His memory still divided the city, and his supporters included several groups of women who continued agitating well into the 1570s for the release of the leader they revered as an ideal bishop of deeply evangelical spirit. The atmosphere in Toledo was not

[33]See for example *Way,* 27:5-7.

[34]Judaizing could be detected by actions such as changing into a clean shirt on Fridays, stripping excess fat from meat, or holding a traditional Jewish valedictory supper before setting out on a journey. Inquisitorial records also show that judaizers were known to recite psalms without adding the customary Christian doxology *(Gloria Patri)* at the conclusion of each. It is not known what judaizing "crimes" Teresa's grandfather came forward to confess in 1485.

ideal for Teresa. She had come to establish a new discalced convent, a convent for women whose primary occupation would be the exercise of mental prayer, a convent whose founding members would include some of her own relatives, a convent whose doors would be wide open, as nearly all other religious foundations were not, to receive young women from Toledo's new Christian families. It was to be a convent, moreover, established exclusively with new Christian money.

Teresa had been promised the entire, considerable inheritance of one Martín Ramírez, merchant.[35] Negotiations with the family's representatives were under way, and although Teresa was presented with a series of conditions she "didn't think [she] could readily agree to," she was confident enough about the outcome to go ahead and try to rent a place of temporary residence for the nuns she had brought with her from Avila. She could find nothing suitable; moreover, and more alarming still, the expected license for the foundation failed to materialize.[36]

Previously, officials had refused her licenses for her foundations because they disapproved of her intentions to establish poor, unprovided-for convents. That a convent about to enjoy full-fledged patronage would fail to receive permission to open its doors was puzzling. Not even the already high number of Toledo's religious houses for women sufficed to explain the delay, since nearly all of them were rich and well-provided for. The answer lay instead in the intrigues of Toledo's most prominent noble citizens, whose honor was insulted by this attempt by the upstart Ramírez family to secure, in one of the best neighborhoods of the city, a foothold on the privileged mountain of the established nobility, and under false pretenses to boot.

The pressure they exerted upon Toledo's governor was mighty, and so was the dizzying round of lobbying Teresa underwent at the hands of interested parties for and against the idea of the Ramírez patronage. Teresa wanted very much to make a foundation in Toledo; and although she was not one normally to be swayed by reasons of prestige or social correctness alone, she may

[35]For the discussion of the Toledo foundation that follows, I rely on the now-classic analysis of Francisco Márquez Villanueva ("El linaje") as well as on *Tiempo y vida*, 340–362. Teresa's account of the foundation, made in 1569, is in *Foundations*, 15.

[36]*Foundations*, 15:4.

have wavered momentarily. Certainly she had misgivings of her own about the patronage agreement, since it smacked of the pattern of family-convent symbiosis she had repudiated in her first foundation in Avila. Moreover, the whole matter was complicated by the fairly obvious *converso* origin of the Ramírez family. Here was no *bona fide* noble house looking to secure its spiritual well-being by patronizing a religious institution. Rather, here were new Christian *hidalgos* attempting to emulate the traditional behavior of the nobility in order not only to secure their spiritual well-being but to enhance their social prestige as well. Teresa must have been quite unhappy with what she considered pathetic, if familiar and even understandable, new Christian pretensions; they constituted exactly the sort of behavior she regretted in her own family.

Teresa was for some time at a loss about what to decide.[37] In the end, however, prayer resolved her confusion into clarity. The fundamental issue was one of bigotry, and it was to that point she was to address herself:

> While I was at the monastery in Toledo, some were advising me that I shouldn't give a burying-place to anyone who had not belonged to the nobility. The Lord said to me: "You will grow very foolish, daughter, if you look at the world's laws. Fix your eyes on me, poor and despised by the world. Will the great ones of the world, perhaps, be great before me? Or, are you to be esteemed for lineage or for virtue?"[38]

Teresa experienced this locution as "a severe reprimand" from God "for listening to those who spoke [about social class and lineage]."[39] She became "very humbled" and determined to proceed in her agreement with the Ramírez family.[40] The negotiations would take further twists and turns, resulting in one of the most protracted and difficult settlements in which Teresa would ever take part; but in the end, the foundation was well made. Teresa was convinced that had she "paid attention to the vain opin-

[37]*Foundations*, 15:16.

[38]*Testimonies*, 5.

[39]*Foundations*, 15:16.

[40]A complicated contract eventually governed the convent's foundation; its complexity was in part the result of Teresa's dogged efforts to limit the extent of the family's actual influence over the foundation. See "El linaje," 143–45.

ions of the world, it would have been impossible . . . for us to be so well provided for, and I would have offended the one who with so much good will did this charitable deed for us."[41]

In her account of the foundation, Teresa chose not to expose the more fearful and threatening aspects of the Toledo affair. In doing so, she also minimized the moral and even physical courage it must have taken for her to bow obediently before the voice of conscience and choose a path of action that flatly contradicted the tenacious socioreligious dogmas of caste-conscious Toledan society. The voice that spoke so authoritatively in the recesses of her heart, however, was, in her allusive account, the voice of the Lord who himself came from an irregular family of the lower caste, who owned nothing, had nowhere to lay his head, and died a poor man vilified by many as an aspirant to things above his station, shedding blood that could hardly have been, Matthew's genealogy notwithstanding, the blood of kings. What wealth or pride could stand before him? Christ was the source of Teresa's courage, the son of the God who created humans all of muddy earth alike.

Mud makes bricks, and mud makes adobes, Teresa had once reminded her sisters: it is as good for one as for the other, and anyone who would choose to dispute about the relative merits of brick mud and adobe mud was simply wasting time. Worse then, the sister who is concerned about lineage, making her blood out as better than another's, is a Judas in the company of Christ's followers, an ingrate daughter in the household of his Father. No one in any of Teresa's houses "was to speak of any other father but him." The experience of Toledo confirmed that early view: in the end, the only boast that anyone should make is the upside-down delight of resting sure in the open arms of the God of Christ, the outcast one who always was what he did not seem to be.[42]

---

[41]*Foundations,* 15:17.

[42]See *Way,* 27:6.

6

I Would Do Very Noble Deeds

Convinced that she had been granted a vantage point from which to survey reality through God's eyes, Teresa became, as we have seen, a perceptive critic of some of the assumptions upon which her world turned. Her critique was grounded not in a detached moralism but in a passionate affinity for God. Teresa's mystical union with a God she experienced as immensely compassionate and unreservedly committed to the well-being of creatures conveyed to her an intense longing for others, for their immediate and ultimate good. It conveyed to her a determination to do everything in her power, including the acceptance of suffering, "to help souls."[1]

The ways in which Teresa set about helping souls were many and varied—new religious foundations, efforts toward sacerdotal reform, spiritual direction, books on the spiritual life and other writings, her own prayer and miracle-working. Just as remarkable as the *creativity* of Teresa's apostolic spirit, however, is the unflagging *energy* of that spirit, particularly in light of the adverse circumstances that attended all her efforts—chronic ill health, pervasive misogyny, bitter power struggles within the Carmelite Order, the sheer difficulty of sixteenth-century travel, recurring financial crises, and the ever-present possibility of trouble with

---

[1] It should be noted, however, that for Teresa, the Christian virtue of charity and the works of service that flow from it do not make their appearance only as a *result* of achieving maturity in the life of prayer. They are also exercised at the outset of the spiritual journey, since charity is one of its foundation stones. See for example *Way,* 4. Love and its "works" continue to be exercised throughout the journey, imbedded in the very structures and dynamism of spiritual-mystical growth. Still, it is true that a remarkable *increase* in zeal and creative service nearly always characterizes the fullness of interior life.

the Inquisition. Although she frequently complained about these hardships to God and to others, she also embraced them, at times with surprising lightheartedness, as the built-in cost of zeal. And she overcame them through the inexhaustible strength she possessed—the experience of God that engendered within her a superabundant vitality "over which circumstance had no power."[2]

"I envied him greatly"[3]

When Saint Joseph's, Teresa's first foundation, was officially opened by the bishop of Avila in August of 1562, Teresa was present at the ceremonies, but she was not one of the handful of nuns who settled in that day to form the inaugurating community. Her superiors refused to release her from the Incarnation until they had had a chance to examine and, if necessary, reprimand her for her part in the establishment of the new house. Fresh from a battle with scruples that "the devil stirred up" in her about her clandestine, temerious, perhaps even disobedient behavior,[4] Teresa spent the following four months at the Incarnation listening to similar charges from her superiors and some of her sisters, and waiting anxiously as her clerical supporters tried to calm the uproar over St. Joseph's that had broken out in the city.[5]

Teresa finally entered St. Joseph's in December, taking with her four more nuns from the Incarnation. At the new convent

[2]Evelyn Underhill, *Mysticism* (New York: E. P. Dutton, 1961), 429. Underhill believed that spiritual fecundity (such as Teresa's "begetting" of the discalced) and superabundant energy mark all genuine mystical life that has entered the unitive period. The mystic's productivity is not mere activity carried out "for God" alongside of or in competition with the inner life of union with God but real participation in the "incarnation of the Eternal in time," 432-33.

[3]*Foundations*, 1:7.

[4]*Life*, 36:7-10.

[5]*Life*, 36:5-23. Even though Teresa believed that founding St. Joseph's was God's will, she admitted the merit of some of the charges: she had been (too?) "determined"; "she was worse than other [nuns]" in keeping the rule; her efforts amounted to "promoting novelties." But in a chapter of faults she accused herself more grandly "as one who was very much to blame." Then she remained silent, recalling, of course, the silent Christ *unjustly* judged. She also *pretended* to feel "grief" and "disturbance" at the charges so as "not to give the impression that [she] didn't take to heart what they said." After showing her submissiveness, however, she spoke to the provincial "more freely." She then got permission, "once the city quieted down," to join her own foundation.

she was greeted not only by her sisters, but also by Christ. Teresa reported that she saw him (who "seemed to be receiving [her] with great love") while at prayer in the convent church. Whatever trials she had endured were, in her view, amply compensated when in that vision Christ placed a crown on her head and thanked her for what she had done for his mother. On another occasion, Teresa saw Mary herself, "clothed in a white mantle," sheltering under it all the women living in the house.[6] Before long, she revealed in *Life*, even the townspeople who had so violently opposed the foundation came to be "very devoted to this house," generously supplying it with alms. Writing not long after the event, Teresa noted with an air of vindication that "there isn't anyone at present who doesn't think it was right to let the house be founded."[7]

Enjoying the first stretch of uninterrupted solitude she had ever known, Teresa set to work organizing the internal life and structures of the new community. By 1566, she had committed her vision of the meaning of discalced life to the permanence of writing in the *Constitutions* and, more extensively, in *The Way of Perfection*. She also wrote a version of the *Meditations on The Song of Songs* aimed at encouraging the nuns to aspire to the promises of love and intimacy she believed that biblical book contained. In this tranquil period she completed the final version of her spiritual autobiography, sending it to the Andalusian reformer Juan de Avila, whose programs of priestly education, popular catechesis, and affective prayer made him a respected authority on matters of spiritual renewal. His favorable comments about *Life* heartened her personally and, as she knew it would, helped establish her credibility as a woman of authentic divine gifts.[8]

Teresa always regarded the years she spent at St. Joseph's with deep affection and wrote of them later in life with near-romantic

---

[6]*Life*, 36:24. The nuns of St. Joseph belonged to the Carmelite Order, but the house had been placed under the jurisdiction (the "obedience") of the local bishop when the Carmelite provincial withdrew his sanction early in the planning process. The house was finally withdrawn from episcopal supervision and placed under Carmelite obedience in 1577.

[7]*Life*, 36:25.

[8]*Letters* I, 36–37; also 40–50 for correspondence with doña Luisa de la Cerda regarding the safe delivery of the manuscript; *Maestro* Avila's letter to Teresa (12 September 1568) is in Luis Sala Balust, ed., *Juan de Avila. Obras Completas* (Madrid: BAC, 1953), vol. 1, 838–841. Her reaction to his approval is in *Letters* I, 54.

nostalgia, even when acknowledging the frightful hardships—episodes of starvation, winter freezing, debilitating melancholy, and even madness—the members of that first community struggled through.[9] She admired the first nuns' courage and perseverance in the face of serious trial, "certainly not characteristic of women,"[10] considered too weak physically and too fickle emotionally for such sustained purpose. Teresa's contemplation of "the riches God placed in them" led her to conclude that they were all meant for "some great purpose."[11]

In late summer of 1566, the intense routine of the monastery was interrupted when a Franciscan friar named Alonso Maldonado de Buendía paid a visit to the young community.[12] For ten arduous years he had been a missionary in New Spain. Like most other Christians of the sixteenth century, Fray Alonso was formed in the conviction that hell awaited those who were not baptized into Christ. A man of uncommon (some would have said extremist) zeal, his missionary career had been marked both by an indefatigable eagerness to preach to, baptize, and educate the indigenous population so that those souls, beloved also of God, might not be doomed, and by a burning indignation at the cruel exploitation of the native peoples by the ruling *conquistadores*. On these painful subjects he surely spoke at length and with characteristic energy to the nuns of St. Joseph's.

Maldonado's plea for their prayers and penance let loose in Teresa a flood of feeling that, according to her account, kept her in anguished tears for days on end. The thought of "the many millions of souls that were being lost there" for want of preachers and catechists wounded her deeply. Her reaction is noteworthy for its dramatic and prolonged sorrow that souls destined in creation for God might never reach their destination. She echoed this sorrow, perhaps also hinting at the "bestial" conduct of the *conquistadores,* as late as 1570 in a letter to her brother Lorenzo

[9]*Foundations,* 1:1; also *Tiempo y vida,* 207–08.

[10]*Foundations,* 1:6.

[11]*Foundations,* 1:6.

[12]*Foundations,* 1:7-8. See also Pedro Borges, O.F.M., "Un reformador de Indias y de la Orden franciscana bajo Felipe II: Alonso Maldonado de Buendía, O.F.M.," *Archivo Iber-Americano* 20 (1960), 281–337; 487–535; 21 (1961), 53–97.

who was, at the time she wrote, making remote preparations to return to Spain from his lengthy sojourn in Quito.[13]

But this passage is even more noteworthy for the apostolic frustration it reveals; Teresa informed her readers that she "greatly envied" Maldonado his ability to "transfer his [desire for the good of souls] into deeds." They were no different in their desires, she said; God had also given her "the inclination" to convert and win souls. She and the Franciscan differed only in that he was able *to do something* about them in the active mission field and she, because she was a woman and a cloistered nun, was not. As a result she demanded from God that at least, in her words, "my prayer would do some good since I wasn't able to do anything else."[14]

Years earlier, she had received other distressing reports of souls being "lost" unnecessarily on account of Calvinist inroads in France and the Netherlands, and then too she had "begged God that [she] might remedy so much evil." It seemed, she wrote, "that I would have given a thousand lives to save one soul out of the many that were being lost there." But she could not just pick up and go to where the trouble was. "[T]he useful things" she desired to do were not permitted to her, and Teresa knew why: "I realized I was a woman," "incapable" of the active apostolate, "wretched" because of her sins and her sex, unworthy of public action on behalf of Christ's cause despite her huge desires and her considerable talents.[15]

Teresa frequently acknowledged both her drivenness to be useful in God's service and her frustration at being locked out of the full range of apostolic possibilities. She chafed at her restrictions "like one who has a great treasure stored up and desires

---

[13]*Letters* I, 75. It is a great irony that Teresa frequently depended for financial support on this brother whose fortune had been made, without doubt, as a consequence of the exploitative practices of the Spaniards in the Americas, practices that included the wholesale enslavement of the indigenous peoples into a ready labor force. *Conquistadores* like Lorenzo who had *converso* blood were eagerly upwardly mobile; in the New World, the immense Indian labor force and the *encomienda* system that provided continuous and abundant revenue for the European masters made them not only wealthy but also elegantly indolent. They lived not from manual labor but from *rentas,* in the manner of the Castilian elites they aspired to emulate. Thus was their own "tainted" honor papered over.

[14]*Foundations,* 1:7.

[15]*Way,* 1:2.

that all enjoy it, but whose hands are bound and unable to distribute it."[16] These desires were, she reported in an account of her soul written in 1560, the direct result of her intense encounters with God in prayer: "[D]esires to serve God come upon me with impulses so strong I don't know how to exaggerate them, and there is also pain in seeing of what little use I am." The pain at having no "power" to serve God was excruciating; unable to put her desires into practice because of her "body" and her "state" (her ill health perhaps, and certainly her sex and status as a female Religious, "no good at all for serving God"), she felt unfairly trapped: "What I want I am unable to procure." Moreover, she asserted, were she not so "bound" by gender, "I would do very noble deeds insofar as my strength would allow."[17]

Toward the end of her life, even after years of finding effective and constructive outlets for her zeal, Teresa remained both envious of priests—preachers, theologians, and missionaries—and indignant that women were excluded from the Church's active mission. In *Castle* she noted with unmistakable personal overtones that *women* who have entered the sixth mansions, a very advanced stage of contemplation, face a particularly difficult spiritual dilemma. The closer they move to the center of the castle where complete union with God is bestowed, the greater grows their thirst for souls. A woman in this stage of prayer, Teresa wrote, "is distressed by the *natural hindrance there is to her entering the world,* and she has a great envy of those who have the freedom to cry out and spread the news abroad who this great God of hosts is. Oh poor little butterfly, bound with so many chains which do not let you fly where you would like!"[18] And to Gracián she exclaimed in December of 1576, referring to the power and effectiveness of his preaching, "Oh, how envious I am when I think of the sins your Paternity . . . will prevent from being committed! And here I am, with nothing but my good desires!"[19]

[16]*Foundations,* 1:6.
[17]*Testimonies,* 1:4.
[18]*Castle* VI, 6:3-4, emphasis added.
[19]*Letters* I, 369.

"Sons of Adam and all of them men"[20]

This sense of confinement and deprivation permeates a great
many of Teresa's remarks about her own ambitions in the service of God. Many subsequent interpreters of Teresa's writings
have been understandably reluctant to ascribe to a saint feelings
of anger and bitterness, and have therefore frequently spiritual-
ized her observations about female marginalization. But the men
who read and censored her works during her lifetime certainly
sensed the realism and the danger in her many sharp, sometimes
ironic pained expressions.

The censor who obliterated a strong passage about women and
the Church's mission from the first version of *Way*[21] knew exactly what she was getting at—in the face of dire pastoral need,
the Church was being deprived unwisely and unjustly of the gifts
of women because of short-sighted men. This passage is the most
direct statement in all her writings of Teresa's grasp of what we
would today call sexism. It echoes her chagrin at her own confinement, her deep love for the Church of Christ, her anguish
at *its* deprivation, and her intimate conviction that such a state
of affairs could not possibly be the will of the just and compassionate God whom she has met face to face in prayer.

In the course of an explanation of why the nuns of St. Joseph's
should not be reluctant to believe that they, despite their gender
and state of life, could play an important role in defending and
reforming the Church through the perfection of their own contemplative lives and their unceasing intercession for theologians
and priests, Teresa abruptly shifted to the discourse of prayer and,
like a priest interceding for the people, declared:

> Since You, my Creator, are not ungrateful, I think you will not
> fail to do what [these nuns] beg of You. Nor did You, Lord,
> when you walked in the world, despise women; rather, You al-

[20] *Way*, 3:7.

[21] *Way*, 3:7. See also Tomás Alvarez' fine article, "Santa Teresa y las mujeres en la Iglesia: glosa al texto teresiano de *Camino*, 3," *El Monte Carmelo* 89 (1981): 121-132. In the
introduction to the facsimile edition of *Way* prepared by Alvarez and Simeón de la Sagrada
Familia [Santa Teresa de Jesús, *Camino de Perfección* (Vatican City: Tipografia Poliglotta
Vaticana, 1964-65), 2 vols.], see the discussion of the various redactions of this work and
the history of its extensive censorship and revision.

ways, with great compassion, helped them. [And you found as much love and more faith among them than You did in men. Among them was Your most blessed Mother, and through her merits—and because we wear her habit—we merit what, because of our offenses, we do not deserve. Is it not enough, Lord, that the world has intimidated us . . . so that we may not do anything worthwhile for you in public or dare speak some truths that we lament over in secret, without Your failing to hear so just a petition? I do not believe, Lord, that this could be true of Your goodness and justice, for You are a just judge and not like those of the world. Since the world's judges are sons of Adam and all of them men, there is no virtue in women they do not hold suspect . . . I do not speak for myself . . . but because I see that these are times in which it would be wrong to undervalue virtuous and strong souls, even though they are women.][22]

Both prayer and protest, this striking passage reveals Teresa's dismay at the way the cards were stacked against women of spirit, virtue, and talent, both in the Church and in the world at large. With an implicit grasp of what today we might call "sisterhood," or female solidarity, Teresa spoke as a woman, situated among women, speaking on their behalf, adducing the example of women, and demanding for women relief from their unjust situation. In this case at least, Teresa saw the collective problem: women as a group, and only because they were women, were being restrained by a prohibitive male community holding firmly in their hands the reins of freedom and authority. In Teresa's vocabulary in this passage, the way of "patriarchy" (as we might term it) is the way of "the world"—a world arranged by and for men. This is the world that has "intimidated" women so that no public activity is available to them, nor can they openly instruct or admonish its leaders.

Only "in secret" can women speak what they have perceived as "truths," lamenting what they see. The silence and submission required of females also comes under fire, then, in the course of this complaint to God that in God's Church and in the public

---

[22]*Way,* 3:7 [V and E]. The bracketed phrases are those deleted by the censor from the first version.

sphere there is no room for the exercise of an active ministry by women. A sense of the evil, or at least the un-gospel-like character of this marginalization is strong in Teresa's choice of the term "world" to illumine the nature of the problem.

Teresa is emphatically clear that, in her view, justice is at stake: her prayer on behalf of women is a "just petition"; God's "justice" is too great for it to be denied. God is a "just judge" unlike the judges of the world who, because they are human and sinful ("sons of Adam"), but more especially because they are males ("and all of them men"), hold all women's virtue suspect simply because it is *women's virtue.* Teresa shared, of course, the common caution about human nature: no one "deserves" anything entirely by his or her own merit, for all are sinners; yet she also believed that people *do* deserve what is just, because God is just. And it was *not* just, in Teresa's view, to marginalize women simply on account of their sex.

If it is right and proper, Teresa continued, that women be allowed to place the full range of gifts God bestows upon them in service of others, it is also *necessary.* Echoing the teaching of some *espirituales,* she argued that women have always loved Christ and the Church, and that their faith was recognized by Christ himself as greater and more steadfast than that of men. Certainly they were not to be spurned for ministry in the world when Christ had not refused their personal ministry to him. Teresa held up a picture of a Church in desperate straits: Protestants gaining ground in Europe, priests and Religious abandoning their vows, souls by the millions lost and brutalized in the Indies, and Catholics in Castile mired in lukewarm indifference to God and the values of God's reign. These were not times, she observed, to measure the value of people's contributions to the cause of Christ with the yardstick of gender.

"A little woman as useless as I"[23]

As a child, fascinated by saints' lives and their heroic deeds, Teresa had fantasized about martyrdom as a cruel but swift and sure way of attaining eternal glory. As an adult, she continued

---

[23]*Foundations,* 2:4.

to envy the martyrs the heroism (and *finality!)* of their witness[24] but often found herself suffering instead, as one historian aptly termed it, "the martydom of feeling useless."[25] Behind many of Teresa's apparently deprecating remarks about her own femaleness, one can detect traces of that suffering.

She complained, for example, that God was wasting precious gifts by pouring them into her broken bottle. But it was not only on account of her vileness as a sinner that she seemed to herself bound to squander God's gifts; it was also because God had placed them in the hands of a person "of so little importance" in the eyes of her society, a person who "cannot make use of them to win over anyone." "In sum," she added referring to herself, " . . . a woman."[26] She felt the bind especially keenly when it came to the contemporary debate about the merits of contemplation and the example of God's mercies her own life might provide for others, dearly wishing that she had "a great deal of authority . . . so that I might be believed,"[27] and declaring emphatically that "though being what I am, I would like to shout and argue with those who say that mental prayer is not necessary."[28]

Teresa was certain of the truths she wished to proclaim, certain that they would be for the good of souls[29] and certain that she was, with God's help, ready and able to act, even though "the Apostle and [her] incapacity" prevented her from preaching and teaching "with words," that is, in public.[30] In a strong outburst of feeling in *Life* (for which she felt compelled to offer a subsequent disclaimer, as if conscious of the potential effrontery of her remarks),[31] she declared herself willing even to appear before

[24] Note that her admiration for Magdalene and Augustine is great because, once converted, they *stayed* converted, in contrast with Teresa's sense of herself as vacillating and ungrateful in the face of the mercy she had received. See *Life,* 9:2, 7-8; and 19:5, in which she probably was alluding to some of her favorite intercessors, Paul, Peter, Magdalene, and Augustine, all saints who fell and then remained true to God.

[25] "Private prayer," 3.

[26] *Life,* 18:4.

[27] *Life,* 19:4.

[28] This exclamation was edited from the second redaction of *Way* (22:2).

[29] For example, the heading of *Life,* 40; also *Life,* 18:8.

[30] *Way,* 15:6.

[31] *Life,* 21:4: "I am becoming very bold. Tear this up if it sounds bad to your Reverence

Christian kings so that through her testimony to her experience of God, they might have a better understanding of their divinely ordained responsibilities. Kings should strive for contemplation's heights in order to ensure from the top down the spiritual health of their kingdoms, all for the glory of God: "For one fraction of an increase in faith and for having given some light to the heretics such a king would be willing to lose a thousand kingdoms— and rightly so; for the gain would be far greater: a kingdom without end."[32] If the world's potentates would take seriously their spiritual obligations and get to know the great King of kings, Teresa believed that they would feel the same thirst for souls and the same intense need to act that she herself experienced; for "once a soul has reached [the fourth degree of prayer], what it possesses for God is not only desires; His Majesty gives it the strength to put these desires into practice. There is nothing that comes to mind that it thinks would be of service to Him that it wouldn't venture to do."[33]

Teresa knew full well that she would never be called upon or permitted to teach formally in public, much less preach in courts to kings. Embedded in her over-excited rhetoric of zeal are the poignant realities of a hemmed-in, untried public vocation:

> O Lord! Were You to give me the office by which I could shout this aloud, they would not believe me, as they do not believe many who know how to say this better than I; but at least it would be satisfying to me . . . In spite of what I am, I experience great consuming impulses to tell these truths to those who are rulers. When I can do no more, I turn to You, my Lord, to beg of You a remedy for all . . .
>
> The trouble is that for persons as useless as myself there are few opportunities to do something. May you be pleased, my God, that there come a time when I may be able to repay You even one mite of all I owe You. Ordain, Lord, as You wish, how this servant of Yours may in some manner serve You. Others were women, and they have done heroic things for love

. . . I would say it better in person if I could, or if I thought they would believe me, for I very earnestly commend them to God and would like to be of some help."

[32]*Life*, 21:1.

[33]*Life*, 21:5.

of You . . . Cost what it may, do not desire that I come into
Your presence with hands so empty . . . [34]

This was the feeling of uselessness and the desire for productivity with which Teresa had once begged God that she might be
of some help to souls in America.[35] It was an overwhelming affliction, but God had a remedy. Teresa testified to a confident
and comforting reply: "Wait a little, daughter, and you will see
great things."[36] What those great things were, and what role she
would play in effecting them, Teresa claimed not to know. But
the words remained "fixed in [her] heart" in an unforgettable
way, like a promise to Sarah, a presage of fruitful generation.

"The little that was in my power"[37]

Teresa's writings reveal a lifelong awareness of the tension between the dictates of the "natural reason" in use in her culture—
"that a useless little woman as helpless as I . . . couldn't do
anything"—and what she embraced as her personal inclination
as well as God's will for her—that "when these [apostolic] desires
come to a soul [from God], it is not in its power to put them
aside."[38] The striking proto-feminist passage of *Way* analyzed
above, however, is the only extended instance in Teresian writings in which Teresa was completely and unmistakably direct in

[34]*Life*, 21:2, 4-5.

[35]In light of Teresa's strong desire to help souls in the New World, it is ironic that her
Carmelite opponents once plotted to assign her to "the Indies" in order to get her out of
the picture once and for all, or so it was rumored. Teresa reported the rumor with a kind
of grim humor in *Letters* I, 354: "I thought that was a beautiful idea about sending me to
the Indies. God forgive them: the best thing they can do is say so many things (about me)
at once that nothing they say will be believed by anyone."

[36]*Foundations*, 1:8. Teresa believed that her concern for the Indians was answered when
the Carmelite General Rubeo gave permission for new discalced foundations for women
throughout Castile. In them more nuns could dedicate themselves to the orational activity
without which Teresa believed that public evangelism aimed at converting the indifferent,
the immoral, the ignorant, and the heretic could not hope for success. See *Foundations*, 2:4:
"And thus in seeing the strong desire of our Most Reverend General that more monasteries
be founded, it seemed to me I saw them founded. Remembering the words our Lord had
spoken to me, I now perceived what before I could not understand."

[37]*Way*, 1:2.

[38]*Foundations*, 2:4.

her criticism of the low esteem in which women's virtue and talents were held. Normally, she expressed her feelings more subtly, making consummate use of irony to subvert some of the features of the female stereotype of her day.[39]

But Teresa's response to the situation in which she found herself was not limited to protest, envy, complaints to God, and ironically surbersive turns of phrase. Even though she continued throughout her writings to express in these ways her dissatisfaction with official exclusion from any sort of public role, she did not accept victimization. Instead, she acted on the basis of a simple axiom: "Faith and the love of pleasing God make possible what to natural reason is not possible."[40] Impelled by the great energy and creativity of a person who experienced herself as possessed of and by the divine, she seized on "the little that was in [her] power"[41] and simply did it, often transgressing the very boundaries she lamented, convinced that those incursions were both mandated and sanctioned in heaven.[42]

Teresa was sensitive to the possibility that her enormous desires to be and to do everything and anything for God could be subject to sin; the devil, she believed, could be behind some of them, and she knew well the danger of "building castles in the air."[43] And although she always possessed and encouraged great determination and lofty desires, she also counseled that one should begin one's activities within the realm of the *possible*. The practical realism and spiritual insight she had developed on the basis of her extensive experience of human nature had taught her that many people aim high as a way of never having to do anything at all.

Moreover, achieving the *impossible* lay in the realm of *God's* will and power; the job of the faithful soul was to start right where

[39]See Aurora Egido, "Los prólogos teresianos y la 'santa ignorancia,' " *Actas* II, 581–607, and "Santa Teresa contra los letrados. Los interlocutores de su obra," *Criticón* 20 (1982): 85–103. The ironical diminutive (e.g. *mugercilla*, or "little woman") is a device Teresa favored in her writings for its subversive rhetorical effect. Alison Weber examines Teresa's writings and shows that Teresa made extensive use of this and other stylistic devices to defend her positions. *Teresa of Avila and the Rhetoric of Femininity* (Princeton, N.J.: Princeton Univ. Press, 1990).

[40]*Foundations*, 2:4.

[41]*Way*, 1:2; *Life*, 32:9.

[42]Cf. *Testimonies*, 15.

[43]For this reference and the brief discussion that follows, see especially *Castle* VII, 4:14–15.

she was and do first "the task at hand." To be content with having desired the impossible while leaving undone the possible, desiring to benefit the whole world all at once and failing to serve those who are in your company, Teresa told her sisters, is foolishly to think that God values more the magnitude of one's deeds than the depth of one's love. "By what you do in deed—that which you can—His Majesty will understand that you would do much more . . . And if we do what we can His Majesty will enable us each day to do more and more." Teresa began, then, with "the little that was in her power" and very close at hand. And by the time she was through, her "little" amounted to a prodigious lot.

At the outset, doing what was in her power meant that she would live her religious rule with as much perfection as she could muster, trusting in the mysterious efficacy of even the hidden life of the cloistered contemplative. Her own resolve soon included others, however, as she began to formulate a vision of a new kind of Carmelite praying community stressing contemplation as its "whole reason,"[44] and encouraging the transformation of even familiarly recited vocal prayer into a genuine personal and affective encounter with God. Fidelity to such a vocation was, she asserted, "fighting for God" and advancing the divine cause just as truly and effectively as did the theologians, preachers, missionaries, and teachers of the Church when they engaged in their public ministries. More importantly, *without* the contributions of the praying women of Carmel, Teresa believed that the public ministries of the Church were likely to flounder on the shoals of unsupported and uncentered activism.

Therefore, she secured permission to begin a great work of monastic reform and renewal in service of the ideals she understood to undergird her "glorious" Order. At once a continuation of the late medieval impulse toward a return to the sources and to strict observance and a creative new form of religious life, the Teresian reform must also be understood as Teresa's way of externalizing, extending, even institutionalizing her own ongoing friendship with God, an intimacy that caused her to adopt God's interests as her own. The reform, because it would invite people to understand prayer as apostolate, could become their way, too, of fighting for God and renewing the Spanish Church.

"*Life*, 32:18.

But it would also mean that she herself would have to be far more active than she had once thought her vocation required, often having to forego long quiet periods of prayer and, instead, engage in all the harried, tangled, and tedious activities associated with establishing convents. To the nuns who found it hard to believe that by entering discalced convents they were also enlisting in the spiritual army of God and reforming the Church, Teresa taught that contemplation is a form of action. But that was not to be the whole story. She also understood and taught, particularly by example but also by her word, that *action arising from divine intimacy,* whether public (such as establishing reformed monasteries) or more intimate (like service to a sick nun in a convent infirmary), is also a form of prayer and praise for God.

Teresa taught from experience that at the culmination of the mystical journey God creates in the person a form of life so full and deep that its "outward" and "inward" dimensions pose almost no contradiction to each other. "Inebriated" with the wine of God's strong love, "enveloped" in their communication with the divine, indeed totally "unaware" even of what they are saying, souls are led to a life of service that is heedless of the world's opinions—service that does, in Teresa's opinion, "much good."

In her meditation on the scriptural passage from *The Song of Songs,* "Sustain me with flowers and surround me with apples, for I am dying of love,"[45] Teresa explained her understanding of the deep connection between contemplation and action, intense love and fruitfulness, purity of spirit and the benefit of others:

> I understand by these words that the soul is asking to perform great works in the service of the Lord and its neighbor. For this purpose it is happy to lose that delight and satisfaction. Although a person's life will become more active than contemplative, and one will seemingly lose if the petition is granted, Martha and Mary never fail to work together when the soul is in this state. For in the active—and seemingly exterior—work the soul is working interiorly. And when the active works rise from this interior root, they become lovely and very fragrant flowers.[46]

[45] *Song,* 2:5.

[46] *Song,* 7:3.

For Teresa, the key is to act exteriorly out of the impulse of love, active works rising from an interior root. Souls who act out of their union with God lose interest in their own benefit, "[t]hey look only at serving and pleasing the Lord." "Because they know the love God has for us better than anyone else" (since through prayer they are profoundly identified with God's loves), "they like to leave aside their own satisfaction and good so as to please Him." They also act as counselors and teachers to others, telling "souls beneficial truths by the best means they can." So as to please God more, they "forget themselves for their neighbor's sake, and they lose their lives in the challenge, as did many martyrs . . . These souls do much good."[47]

Thus Teresa entered the arena of reform. Perhaps because she was so aware of the disdain with which she was regarded by some churchmen on account of her "unfeminine" high public profile, Teresa was drawn to the New Testament figure of the Samaritan woman.[48] In the chapter of *Song* we have just cited, for example, Teresa seems to take enormous comfort in her example. She wrote, "I recall now what I have often thought concerning that holy Samaritan woman . . . *How well she must have taken into her heart the words of the Lord, since she left the Lord for the gain and the profit of the people of her village.*"[49] Right in the pages of the New Testament, then, Teresa could cherish an example of a woman whose face-to-face encounter with Christ had led her to "leave" him (as she would have so often to leave her cloister) and, impelled by the love and gratitude of that meeting, engage in the public announcement of the good news of salvation.

The story of the Samaritan woman presented Teresa with a soulmate. Although Teresa may have been unaware of the similarity, the modern reader is struck by the fact that both Teresa and the *Samaritana* were women whose tribes were objects of social and religious marginalization; they shared also a capacity for facing and accepting the full truth about themselves, unable to hide behind the shield of wealth or aristocratic standing; both were

---

[47]*Song,* 7:5.

[48]See *John* 4:39-43. In *Life,* 30:19, Teresa mentioned the woman in connection with "the living water the Lord told [her] about" and added, " . . . I am very fond of that gospel passage." Teresa brought a sacred picture of this gospel scene from her home in Avila and placed it on the wall in her cell at the Incarnation. *St. Teresa of Avila,* 24-25.

[49]*Song,* 7:6, emphasis added.

women who *because* they listened to the Lord, because they spoke with him face to face in a daring dialogue, were entrusted by Christ with the message of salvation and brought it, actively and publicly, "shouting through the streets," to their people. Even more astounding, and for Teresa undoubtedly reassuring, the Samaritan woman, even though she was a woman, *"merited to be believed and see the wonderful good our Lord did in that village."*[50]

Teresa's admiration for the reception given the woman's announcement to her kin is reflected in her insistence on the fact later in the same passage:

> This holy woman, in that divine intoxication, went shouting through the streets. What amazes me is to see how the people believed her—*a woman.* And she must not have been well-off since she went to draw water. Indeed she was very humble because when the Lord told her faults to her she didn't become offended (as the world does now, for the truth is hard to bear), but she told Him that He must be a prophet. In sum, the people believed her; and a large crowd, *on her word alone,* went out of the city to meet the Lord.[51]

The lesson of the Samaritan woman could serve Teresa well not only for her personal situation as founder, legislator, and administrator of an increasingly large number of new religious houses; it also served all the discalced contemplatives who might have feared that they were "losing" something when the needs of their sisters and the day-to-day vicissitudes of their austere, demanding lives required them to engage in work within their cloister that took them away from, or left them little time for, the exclusive contemplation of God. Even though the practice of prayer was, in Teresa's view, "the whole reason" of these communities, prayer (or any of the other spiritual and ascetical practices that Teresa used and encouraged) was never to be an end in itself. Indeed, it was no good at all if in the end, when the needs of the neighbor or the community called loudly for remedy, it had not cultivated in the soul the talent of service. A person of *authentic* spirit is never purely a Mary or exclusively a Martha,

[50]*Song,* 7:6, emphasis added.

[51]*Song,* 7:6, emphasis added.

in Teresa's view, but always both at the same time.[52] Thus the nuns of the reform were to believe that, once they had irrevocably fixed their hearts on God, their prayer was always service, and that their service, especially the day-to-day attention to the immediate needs of their sisters and their communities, was always like a prayer.

But it was not enough for Teresa that she establish reformed communities dedicated to the life of contemplation-as-apostolate (each new convent church, she believed happily, offering to God a compensation for a Catholic building or tabernacle desecrated by "the Lutherans").[53] It was one thing to pray for the workers of the vineyard (theologians, preachers, missionaries) exposed to the heat of the day; it was another that the laborers themselves be persons of deeply cultivated spirit. This goal too was never far from Teresa's plans and visions, for like other *espirituales* she was acutely conscious of what she felt to be the mediocre state of the clergy and seems to have perceived that such moral and spiritual waywardness had contributed to the contemporary "havoc" of a confused and divided Christian Church. By herself and with other reformers, her discalced sisters and brothers, and friends clerical and lay, Teresa engaged in a personal and collective apostolate, decrying ignorance among the clergy, restoring fervor to religious life, introducing theologians to contemplation, exhorting preachers to preach the gospel's "madness," and instructing knowledgeable, skilled, and experienced confessors and spiritual guides.[54]

She also engaged in a lifelong ministry of healing. Less well-known and appreciated in our own day, Teresa's ability to intercede with God on behalf of both the living and the dead was apparently a matter of popular acclaim in her own lifetime; and Teresa as miracle-worker and healer of ailing bodies and, especially, unhealthy spirits, was an important aspect of the hagiographical portrait developed after her death, overshadowed

[52]See especially *Castle* VII, 4, 12–13.

[53]E.g., *Foundations*, 18:5; 3:10; *Way*, 3:3; 33:3; 35:3.

[54]For Teresa's concern about the state of the clergy and her pastoral attention to particular priests see for example *Testimonies*, 3:7; *Foundations*, 14:12; *Castle* Epilogue, 4; *Life*, 5:3–6; 13:21; 31:7–8; 38:14, 38:23. See also "Private Prayer," 8–9; Emmanuel Renault, *L'idéal apostolique des Carmélites selon Sainte Thérèse d'Avila* (Paris: Desclée de Brouwer, 1981), 60–74; *Tiempo y vida*, 115–17; *Biografía*, 74, 166, 250, 268.

only by the emphasis placed on her "seraphic" mysticism of love and her "sublime" mystical doctrine. She herself was quite candid about her powers:

> It often happens that our Lord draws souls away from serious sin and also that He leads others to greater perfection because of my beseeching Him. The Lord has granted me so many favors by freeing souls from purgatory and doing other noteworthy things that I would tire myself and tire whoever reads this if I mentioned them all. He has granted much more in regard to the health of souls than He has in regard to the health of bodies. This has become something well-known, and there are many witnesses to it.[55]

That God would thus empower her on behalf of others was a result "solely . . . of His goodness," and she declared that "it doesn't bother me" to believe that God would do anything at all that she asked, for God knew that she would never ask anything that was not "in conformity with His glory."[56] Teresa was not afraid of vainglory in connection with her miraculously efficacious petitions on behalf of others; on the contrary, she noticed that the positive effects of her intercession made her deeply grateful. The more God did through her, the more she was indebted to God. "[T]he fact that He does this," she wrote to her confessor, "quickens my love and causes an increase in my desire to serve Him."[57]

Teresa the privileged intercessor before God began her ministry of healing and reconciliation early, with the moral miracle of conversion worked while she was recuperating from the desperate illness that had forced her to leave the Incarnation not long after entering. With the aid of her prayers, the young priest of Becedas broke the spell of seduction in which a local woman with a bad reputation was reportedly holding him enthralled.[58] The Teresian tradition holds that she later performed a miracle of resurrection when she revived her nephew Gonzalo after part of

---

[55]*Life,* 39:5.
[56]*Life,* 39:1.
[57]*Life,* 39:5.
[58]*Life,* 5:3-6.

the roof or wall of the house that was to become St. Joseph's fell and struck him an apparently fatal blow.[59] On another occasion, her prayers obtained vision for a blind friend (someone to whom she "was obligated"), even though she was at the time afraid that her sins would prevent the Lord from hearing her. In spite of her sins, the man got his sight back before "eight days passed."[60] At another time, she reported:

> there was a person very sick with a painful illness . . . What he suffered for two months was unbearable; the pain was lacerating. My confessor . . . went to see him; he took great pity on him and told me I should by all means go to see him . . . I went and was moved to such pity for him that I began to beg the Lord insistently for his health. In this experience I saw fully and clearly the favor He granted me; the next day this person was completely cured of that affliction.[61]

Teresa's greatest intercessory concerns lay with people in bad moral states. In Chapter 39 of *Life* she recounted several examples of the healing power of her prayer, including one in which she described a devil "who very angrily was tearing to shreds some papers he had in his hands." Apparently, the month of continual prayers Teresa had offered for a person she "loved very much" and who was unable to break free of very "dangerous" occasions of sin had succeeded in snatching him from that devil's hands. Whatever outstanding debts the demon was hoping to collect were cancelled by Teresa's healing power.[62] Her prayers were particularly heartfelt for priests and Religious, and often God gave her messages for them or revealed to her the state of their souls, sometimes exquisite, as in the case of some Dominicans, Jesuits, and nuns and friars of the reform,[63] sometimes horrifying, as in the case of a priest who was celebrating Mass in a state of mortal

---

[59]See testimony about this incident in *Tiempo y vida*, 148–49. Teresa may have employed artificial respiration, warming the child with her own exhalations.

[60]*Life*, 39:1.

[61]*Life*, 39:2.

[62]*Life*, 39:4.

[63]For example *Life*, 34:11, 17; 38:12-15 28-29, 30-31.

sin (Teresa saw two devils whose horns were tightly wrapped around the poor man's throat).[64]

She believed God used revelations to comfort her upon the death of friends or benefactors for whose salvation she feared. For example, because she had so often witnessed the abuses of power that superiors committed and the distractions to which the less spiritual among them were constantly subject, she had made up her mind that ascending to positions of high authority in the Church or in Religious Orders could be an occasion of grave sin for persons whose spirits were not strong with humility and mortification.[65] As a consequence, when "someone who had been [her] provincial" died, even though she knew him to be a person of "many virtues," Teresa "feared for his salvation in that he had been a superior for twenty years," more than enough time to have succumbed to the distractions and temptations of authority. With "much anxiety" she entered the oratory to pray for his soul, offering to God all the good she had ever done in her life on the man's behalf. Very soon God granted her, she reported, a vision of her former superior ascending to heaven "with greatest happiness," his advanced years transformed to glowing young manhood. "I was so extremely consoled," she added, "that his death could never cause me any more sorrow . . . "[66]

Like holy men and women before and after her, Teresa's spiritual authority over bodily ailments and spiritual affliction extended as well to human conflict. A conduit of God's comfort and a reconciler, she acted on behalf of whole communities (once delivering a small town from the ravages of drought)[67] as well

[64] *Life*, 38:23. Teresa used this experience as an object lesson in Catholic sacramental theology. At the same time that she saw the abominable demons strangling the unfortunate priest, she saw the communion host in his sinful hands resplendent with the beauty and majesty of Christ. In other words, the validity of the sacrament does not depend upon the worthiness of the minister.

[65] She was herself reluctant to accept such posts for this same reason. See *Life*, 35:7. See also 40:16: "A person once asked me to beg God to let him know if it would be to the Lord's service that he should accept a bishopric. The Lord told me after I had received Communion: 'When he understands . . . that real lordship consist in possessing nothing, then he will be able to accept it.' With these words He indicated that anyone who is about to receive a prelacy must be far from desiring or wanting it, or at least from striving after it."

[66] *Life*, 38:26-27.

[67] *Relaciones de la M. Ana de S. Bartolomé*, in *BMC* vol. 2, 302, cited in *Tiempo y vida*, 624-25. In that same town on another occasion, Teresa declared that her "recreation was to console the afflicted," *Tiempo y vida*, 629, my translation. She then proceeded to com-

as of individuals, believing that it was incumbent upon her to use unsparingly and unselfishly for the good of others the powerful riches of her intimacy with the divine. Moreover, in line with Teresa's Catholic faith, she extended her intercession on behalf of God's needy beyond the boundary of life into the place of purification. There her prayers performed the charity of assisting the good souls who in purgatory were suffering the painful yet hopeful process of gradual perfection in love, speeding them on their way to the final encounter with God's glory. In all these healings and revelations, in all her miracles and discernment of spirits, Teresa understood herself to be fulfilling her great desire to "help souls."

"I am leaving it in writing"[68]

Teresa's sense of mission and her irrepressible need to be of service also found apt and congenial release in her writings. A woman with a vivid message and a strong vocation to write and to teach, as well as a perceptive grasp of the power of the written word to spark transformation and to perdure, over the last twenty years of her life she produced in fairly rapid succession a series of spiritual classics based on her own experience—instruction, edification, and testimony for a wide audience.[69]

It is well known that others found Teresa's written teachings of great benefit; it is less well acknowledged that she herself was immensely pleased by her own books. She was forever citing herself;[70] and although she frequently engaged in the rhetoric of *mea*

fort a woman who had given birth only to stillborn infants by giving her the cincture of one of the discalced nuns to wear, saying that it was a sign of future "fruit." We are not told whether the woman's next child was born healthy, but the implication of success is strong in the chronicler's remark that "Since that time, all the sorrowing *(afligidas)* mothers of that neighborhood found prodigious consolation in that cincture."

[68]*Way,* 2:3.

[69]In a single work, Teresa addressed an ever-expanding audience: individual confessors and particular theologians; *letrados* in general, "souls," all Christians, married men and women, parents, discalced Carmelites, future generations. On Teresa's audience and other matters related to her literary art, see V. García de la Concha, *El arte literario de Santa Teresa* (Barcelona: Ariel, 1978). Joel Sangnieux, among others, has suggested that writing was for Teresa a substitute for the public preaching and teaching she was otherwise forbidden to engage in. See his "Santa Teresa y los libros," *Actas* II, 760. See also *Life,* 40:24; *Foundations,* 1:6; 19:1; *Castle* VI, 6:3.

[70]For example, *Foundations,* 4:2, 3; 7:1; *Way,* 17:3; 9:6; 31:1; 32:10; *Song, 2:17; 4:1, 3; 7:6; Castle* I, 2:13, 16-17; II, 1:1, 7, 10; *Letters* I, 195-96, 500.

mediocritas, apologizing for her inadequacies both as a mystical theologian and as a writer in a fashion common to much literature of the period,[71] it is evident that in general she liked the way she explained things. In one letter, she unabashedly told a friend that her recently completed *Method of Visiting a Convent* was "made in heaven" and "might have been taught by God";[72] in another she declared that *Foundations* made "good reading."[73] She sent original verses to her brother, confident that they would arouse his devotion (but cautioned him not to tell anyone she said so!),[74] and asked the Prioress of Seville to send a copy of *Way* to a Carthusian friend, in order to give him "pleasure."[75] Even the chapter headings she wrote for *The Book of Her Life* repeatedly reveal her conviction that what she has to say is "important," "noteworthy," "most helpful," and, indeed, "explained very well."[76] Still, when Teresa went so far as to write, at the head of Chapter 18, "This should be read very attentively, for the explanation is presented in a very subtle way and there are many noteworthy things," her censor put a heavy line through it, in some irritation perhaps at her tone of authorial self-assuredness.[77]

[71]If judged by the elite latinate standards of most contemporary theological writing, certainly Teresa had some inadequacies as a writer of which she was well aware ("I have digressed much"). She recognized that the technically precise vocabulary of academic theology, with which she was acquainted, but only minimally, could perhaps have been of service in rendering her insights more subtly. But in general, Teresa preferred her comparative way (It is like a castle; it is like a chess game; it is like a silkworm . . .), a way typical of *espirituales.* Protestations of inadequacy were, of course, also a rhetorical key (as old as St. Paul in the Christian tradition) to the *captatio benevolentiae* (getting the reader's good will and sympathy) considered essential to the good reception of books, certainly all the more necessary in the case of a woman author writing primarily for women. Coupled with this classical device, Teresa engaged in the stratagem of offering minimizing, ironically deprecating explanations to justify the need for a woman to write books for other women. See for example, *Way,* Prologue: 1, 3; *Castle* Prologue: 4.

[72]*Letters* I, 263.

[73]*Letters* I, 231.

[74]*Letters* I, 396.

[75]*Letters* I, 450.

[76]E.g., Chapters 25, 27, and 28.

[77]The censor was the Dominican theologian Báñez who, although supportive of Teresa personally, discouraged her public word since on principle he deeply disapproved of female writing, especially if it had to do with the supernatural. It is possible that he was also trying to shield her from the reactions other official readers might have to such straightforwardness on the part of a woman. It is striking that when Teresa composed the chapter headings, as in *Life,* they are effusive and confident in the manner illustrated above. When they were

Teresa was on the whole a satisfied author, taking great pleasure in the creative rewards of writing but frequently complaining as well of the irksome hardships and stern self-discipline the process of composition entailed. One of her greatest pleasures came from knowing that by writing down and endeavoring to order for the good of others her experience of life with God, she was bringing many souls to the converted life and to the praises of God; and one of her greatest frustrations was the sense that no words could convey adequately the experience she wished to share. Nonetheless she wrote, confident that her words could make a permanent difference in others' lives, especially by teaching them to pray.

While she herself was living, it was primarily by means of her vigorous speech that Teresa could remind her sisters and disciples of all they should know; but after her death, she acknowledged, it would fall to her written words to continue her mission toward them. To the nuns of St. Joseph's she declared, "Sisters, what I am saying [about poverty and trust in God] is so important I want you to remember it after my death—and that's why I am leaving it for you in writing . . . "[78] Even while she was still among them, however, they were to "read often" what she was writing them about prayer.[79] For example, in the matter of relinquishing honor (especially the defense of oneself against insult), Teresa reminded the nuns that she had "often told [them]" in person that they should "run a thousand miles" from expressions like "I was right!" All the same, she wanted "to leave it in writing here so that [they] will not forget it."[80] Christ himself assured Teresa of the enduring character of her books of spiritual teachings. Upon taking up again the much-interrupted composition of *Foundations* in the fall of 1576, Teresa wrote Gracián to say that "Joseph" (their pseudonym for Christ) had informed her that her chronicle "will be to the profit of many souls."[81]

composed for her, as in *Song* and in *Way* (the most scrupulously reworked of all Teresa's texts), they are much more tersely descriptive, like those of the works of many contemporary male authors.

[78] *Way*, 2:3.

[79] *Way*, 4:3. Teresa ordered that a copy of *Way* be kept in every discalced house and read aloud in the nuns' refectory.

[80] *Way*, 13:1; *Song*, 4:1; and especially *Life*, 37:29.

[81] *Letters* I, 294.

Teresa was also aware that the nuns of her convents would never have money enough to buy a great many books to assist them in their spiritual formation. Thus her own writing provided a great service, since they all could afford copies of her manuscripts.[82] But even greater than the practical service her books rendered was the spiritual and psychological permission they gave the nuns to experience themselves, contrary to the contemporary stereotypes of the superstitious, frivolous, or sensual devout lady, as human beings with an authentic capacity for God. By reading her writings her sisters were inducted into a realm of interior liberty that placed them in a privileged position *vis-à-vis* some other nuns and most all other women, especially the married, "in the world." By following the advice and instruction contained in Teresa's books, they could legitimately bypass the restrictions of their gender, allowing their imaginations to linger over Scripture passages and their affections to interpret them freely. Teresa herself set the example. Addressing the nuns in *Song,* she wrote:

> I interpret [this Scripture passage] in my own way, even though my understanding of it may not be in accord with what is meant. For if we do not depart from what the Church and the saints hold (which is why learned men who understand the matter will examine this carefully before you see it) the Lord gives us license—from what I think—just as He does when we think about the Passion . . . And if we do not indulge in curiosity, but accept the understanding His Majesty gives us, I hold as certain that we do not offend Him when we find delight and consolation in His words . . . Nor must we make women stand so far away from enjoyment of the Lord's riches. If they argue and teach and think that they are right; yes that would be wrong. Consequently I am not thinking I am right in what I say . . . But . . . it consoles me to tell my meditations to my daughters . . .[83]

[82]For example, *Song,* 2:7. Once again we are reminded of the fact that Teresa's reform counted heavily (although by no means exclusively) upon women who could *read,* a tiny minority in sixteenth-century Spain, a culture still primarily *oral* and *aural.* We are reminded also that women from *converso* families figured prominently in the reform; such families often regarded reading and university schooling as means of getting ahead in society.

[83]*Song,* 1:8. Note that Teresa set this invitation within the context of observing that the *Song of Songs* is a mysterious and difficult text to understand, *even for the "doctors."* Those learned men have written countless volumes of commentary but have never succeeded in grasp-

With the instruction, encouragement, and personal example Teresa offered them in her books, the sisters could also release themselves from the claustrophobic world to which women were consigned, imaginatively and physically, and ramble at will through the endless rooms and hallways of the castle within their souls, restrained only by the claims of charity. In the Epilogue of *Castle* Teresa recognized this function of her teaching and writing:

> [N]ow that I am finished [writing this book] I admit the work has brought me much happiness, and I consider the labor . . . well spent. Considering the strict enclosure and the few things you have for your entertainment, my Sisters, and that your buildings are not always as large as would be fitting for your monasteries, I think it will be a consolation for you to delight in this interior castle since without permission from the prioress you can enter and take a walk through it anytime.[84]

Even though some of the rooms are not accessible by will, and the soul must await divine pleasure to enter them, she continued, once God has opened the doors the nuns will be able to "walk through them often," reaching at last even the "very dwelling place [God] has for Himself." Moreover, they need not fear leaving the castle when their duties require them to abandon it: "[Y]ou will always find the door open when you return." No one can take from them this hope of constant return.[85] Teresa concluded by reminding her sisters that what she has described is only a fraction of what awaits. In suggestive strokes Teresa painted the lush world to which they could yet aspire: "Although no more than seven dwelling places were discussed, in each of these there are many others, below and above and to the sides, with lovely gardens and fountains and labyrinths, such delightful things that you would want to be dissolved in praises of the great God who created the soul in His own image and likeness." Then she added,

ing its full meaning, she pointed out. It is, then, not only women, with no learning, but also men, with plenty of it, who must allow *God* to reveal the meaning of this mysterious book to the intellect and heart. This observation sheds a new light on all the restrictions with which Teresa hedged the assertion of the nuns' right and ability (in simplicity and love) to perceive for themselves *Song's* secrets. See *Song,* 1:1; 1:8; 6:7.

[84]*Castle,* Epilogue: 1.

[85]*Castle,* Epilogue: 2

"If you find something good in the way I have explained it to you, believe that indeed His Majesty said it to me so as to make you happy . . ."[86]

Over and over again, Teresa claimed never to be writing or teaching anything that God had not given her to experience. But raw experience was of little use to anyone; sorting that experience out and describing it so that it could help others required discernment and skill. Teresa believed herself to be supported fully by God's grace in the task of understanding her own experience and expressing it in a form accessible to many. Consonant with the experience of great authors throughout the ages, she was often amazed when, coming to the end of a work she found that it had, in a sense, mysteriously written itself. That she was able to write what she had hoped to convey and do it so well she attributed to God, the source of all inspiration and the sustainer of every good desire: "For it is," she wrote in *Life,* "one grace to receive the Lord's favor; another, to understand which favor and grace it is; and a third, to know how to describe and explain it."[87] Indeed, God once chided her for failing to make notes of her interior locutions. Teresa had, apparently, a bad memory and sometimes forgot what God had told her in these illuminating moments. God insisted that she be more careful, since, according to Teresa's record of the reprimand, "even though it may not benefit you, it can benefit others."[88]

Thus she understood her mystical experience, her teachings, and her writings as authentic divine charisms. Describing herself at times as God's amanuensis, impelled by a spiritual force so strong she wished she could write with both hands at once to keep up with the generous streams of supernatural insight, Teresa underscored repeatedly the connection between her life of prayer and her vocation as an author, a witness, and a teacher of the spiritual life.[89]

---

[86] *Castle,* Epilogue: 3.

[87] *Life,* 17:5.

[88] *Testimonies,* 48.

[89] For example, *Life,* 39:8; 25:17; 19:15; *Way,* 34:4. Many commentators believe Teresa to have received the mystical grace of automatic writing. Both she and others testified that she wrote at times with trance-like intensity. From her writings and other sources, we learn that Teresa's writing also involved very labored composition, and that she made use of conversations and literary sources in all her works. Although not incompatible with automatic

Pleased with her books as she certainly was, she was also determined that others understand clearly that her primary object had always been to spotlight the protagonism of God by presenting unflinchingly the record of her many sins and base ingratitude alongside and intertwined with a litany of her extraordinary powers of insight and knowledge, her ability to heal and convert, the creative realizations of the discalced reform, and her astounding ability to overcome huge obstacles, and of course her teachings about prayer. In both cases, she wrote so that God's unmerited graciousness toward her might shine more clearly and encourage other souls to trust God and aspire to great things. If she could do it, so could they, because God was ready to be kind to all.

In a letter to Madre María Bautista, Prioress of Valladolid, in August of 1575, Teresa expressed great satisfaction that *Life* and *Way* had escaped condemnation and burning. She indicated too that her experience, contained in those volumes, would "profit many souls." "[A]nd what," she asked, "do I care about anything else? I want my Lord to be glorified and I want there to be many who praise Him, and, of course, I should like people to know what a wretched creature I am."[90] She had originally entitled her spiritual autobiography *The Book of the Mercies of God,* and referred to the subject matter of *Castle,* the magisterial summation of her mystical theology based on her own experience, as "nothing less than the very reality of God."[91] Regarding the founding of the discalced house at Medina, Teresa confided that she decided to write about that vexed endeavor only because by doing so many would come to see that God alone was ultimately responsible for the positive outcome of her efforts; the achieve-

writing by any means, these "human" elements help us create an understanding of Teresa's writings as a *complex product* of her remarkable inner life. This product was transmitted to the public by means both ordinary and privileged, in the manner of genius, *aware that what it has created it has also received.* For a concise definition of automatic writing, see *Christian Mysticism,* 304–320.

[90]*Letters* I, 195. In this startlingly frank missive, the fed-up Teresa also excoriated the prioress: "It is a great mistake to think you know everything, and then say you are humble . . . No other prioress has ever taken up such an attitude with me—nor has anyone who is not a prioress either."

[91]Letter to Gaspar de Salazar, 7 December 1577, my translation. In *Letters* I, 500, Peers translates "no less a thing than the Being of God Himself."

ment seemed to her to have no human explanation for its eventual success.[92]

Teresa's exercise of her vocation as spiritual teacher and author involved her in painstaking self-censorship and collaboration with the (often supportive) theologians and confessors charged with the correction and emmendation of her books. Many authors of this volatile period exercised this same sort of vigilance over their public words more or less as a matter of course; but when women or others among the generally uneducated laity took up the pen, the need to do so was all the greater. Because the Inquisition's judgments about what constituted orthodox discourse and behavior were elusive and shifting throughout the period of Teresa's greatest literary activity, all the more was it necessary to secure the *letrados*' approval and insert protestations of one's attitude of ultimate submission to Catholic orthodoxy. In women's writings, moreover, there occur frequent allusions to the power of obedience to a superior or confessor who "commanded" their female subjects to write. Teresa often claimed, with no small element of irony, that since she was "just a little woman," she had had to be dragged away from sewing, spinning, and praying, the normal and accepted activities of a female Religious, by confessors who for some divine purpose ordered her under obedience to write, something she would never ordinarily have undertaken on her own.[93]

In such an atmosphere, too, it helped to have friends in high places, and one of Teresa's high-placed friends and admirers was none other than Cardinal Quiroga, the Grand Inquisitor, who read her *Life* and attested to its salutary effect upon him. But the times were ripe not only for the denunciation of real heresy, whenever it could be detected, but also for parlaying personal or political grudges into charges of heterodox tendencies. Against such un-

---

[92]*Testimonies*, 6.

[93]For four centuries the idea that Teresa had to be *forced* to write under obedience has been a mainstay of Teresian hagiography. Few modern historians familiar with the Teresian context (the complex workings of monastic obedience, the imposition of a rigid orthodoxy, the cultural prohibitions concerning the "public word" of women, and the more or less conscious recourse to traditional rhetorical devices) would wish today to defend such a view unqualifiedly, even in the face of Teresa's repeated assertions that she was a reluctant writer. Rosa Rossi's incisive article, "Teresa de Jesús. La mujer y la palabra," *mientras tanto* 14 (1982): 63–79, lays out clearly the terms of any serious discussion of this matter.

predictable turns of vindictiveness or opportunism, there was little one could do to secure a shield. It had already been clearly demonstrated, in the case of Bartolomé de Carranza, that not even archbishops were immune to the mean spirit of the day. The calced Carmelite opponents of Teresa's reform seemed to her always on the watch for reasons to denounce her as a disobedient and dangerous woman in order to put a stop to her foundational activity. Run-ins with influential people over their participation in the reform also loomed as potential sources of spite that could result in delations to the tribunals or a ruined public reputation. And the shifting lines of orthodoxy coupled with the apparent radicalization of some preachers and reformers over a period of time put Teresa into the uncomfortable situation of finding her name associated on occasion with men convicted by the Inquisition who had, years earlier, been among the counselors and friends she had relied upon to help her secure the success of her work.[94] Thus even Teresa's sanctioned activity was never completely safe, and she always wrote and taught at a risk to herself and to the good name of her new foundations.

Although it is now apparent, for example, that the manuscript of *Life,* denounced by a disgruntled noblewoman in 1574 and confiscated by the Inquisition in 1576, was never in serious danger of being declared heretical nor its author's spiritual experiences and conduct ever judged by the tribunal as unorthodox, Teresa herself could never be confident of the outcome as long as she lived. And if she and her spiritual doctrine were to fall into discredit, so would the work of her reform. Hence the extreme caution she took in the transport of her letters and manuscripts from one place to another so that they would not fall into the hands of either the enemy or the ignorant;[95] the attempts to pretend that

---

[94]For example, the Doctor Bernadino Carleval, of whom Teresa spoke warmly in a letter to doña Luisa de la Cerda in 1568, *Letters* I, 50. At the time he was denounced to the Inquisition (1572), he was the Rector of the University of Baeza. He and other priests with ties to Juan de Avila were part of an intense spiritual movement in Andalusia which, particularly because it encouraged women to become *beatas* and shared the apocalypticism of one wing of the sixteenth-century Spanish spiritual revival, had come to the attention of the tribunals as possible *alumbrados.* Teresa met Carleval in 1568 and appointed him confessor to the nuns of Malagón. Apparently his turn toward heterodoxy occurred the following year, after the death of Juan de Avila. See *La Inquisición española,* 29–35.

[95]Examples in *Letters* I, 336, 337, 352 (secret modes of sending letters) and in *Letters* I, 390 (secrecy and deliberate care with her manuscripts).

the experiences she was describing belonged to a third person whom she knew intimately;[96] the adoption of pseudonyms in her correspondence in an effort to confuse the prying eyes of the calced and their allies who, she felt, would surely pounce on her words and twist their intent for their own purposes;[97] and, of course, her continual protestations of deference to the teachings of the Catholic Church, at once authentic confessions and prudent stratagems, absolutely sincere and absolutely necessary.

One night in a bad inn

But the price Teresa paid for fidelity to what she perceived as her mission to help souls was counted not only in the coinage of potential damage to her reputation or the discrediting of her foundations. It was counted also in terms of physical deprivation and illness; she was constantly suffering from stomach ailments and head-splitting pain brought on, among other causes, by malnourishment and lack of sleep. She suffered through many a "cure," purgation, cupping, bleeding, and the like, that normally served only to worsen her condition, and she endured bouts of depression and other psychological crises that she recognized as being intimately connected with her physical state.[98]

Teresa spent the last twenty years of her life under constant and, at times, extreme stress. No matter how abandoned her will was to God's, the strain of worry about money and the intense

[96]For example, *Castle* I, 2:2: "I know a person to whom our Lord wanted to show what a soul in mortal sin was like."

[97]The pseudonyms Teresa and her collaborators began using in 1575 included "Great Angel" for the Grand Inquisitor; "Egyptians" and "Owls" to denote the calced enemies of the reform; "Ravens" for the Jesuits; "Seneca" for John of the Cross; "Butterflies" and "Grasshoppers" for various groups of discalced nuns; and "Cyril," "Eliseus," "Elias," "Joannes," and "Paul" for Gracián. Teresa referred to herself as "Angela" and "Laurencia." Christ was simply "Joseph."

[98]*Foundations,* 29:9. Teófanes Egido and Luis Rodríguez Martínez observe that while her major works dwell primarily on spiritual health, her letters are heavily weighted with concern for the health of the body. They note as well that Teresa did not share her society's disdain for the medical profession, a profession associated in the popular mind exclusively with Jews and *conversos,* and recommended consulting doctors even about the use of the homely herbal remedies she so enthusiastically collected and passed on to others, *"Epistolario,"* in *Introducción a la lectura,* 439. For a succinct catalog of some of Teresa's illnesses, see her letter to her sister Juana, *Letters* I, 97. For references to the medical treatments she received, see for example *Letters* I, 426; *Life,* 5:5-7.

concentration of her energies required by continual litigation over her foundations took a terrible toll. In the course of her career as a founder, she had constantly to be on guard against exploitation, especially by unscrupulous house owners who, once they realized that she was interested in a purchase, would greedily raise their prices. Teresa learned quickly to be shrewd in real estate dealings, making a show on one occasion of looking at many houses so that the owners would not think "that we had no other choice."[99]

Many of her convents had to be established in strict secrecy for fear of arousing opposition, especially from other Religious Orders, in the towns where they were made. At times real dread enveloped the stealthy movement of personnel and equipment from one town to the next. In often makeshift, squalid, and uncertain quarters, Teresa and the small group of cofounding nuns spent many fitful nights worrying about being harassed by rowdy students or wondering aloud to each other what would happen if they should die in such horrid places. In Segovia, for example, the opposition of the Franciscan friars to Teresa's little band struck her as unusually virulent. Thus, when the nuns settled secretly and late at night into a house near the Franciscan convent, the fear among them was so great that "every shadow . . . seemed to be a friar."[100]

Making foundations and administering them meant travel under relentless hot suns and bitter Castilian snows, travel that was slow, dangerous, and difficult. No one in sixteenth-century Castile travelled through Spain merely for pleasure,[101] for there was precious little enjoyment to be had on the generally bad roads and in the universally bad wayside lodgings. Indeed, when reaching once for an apt comparison for hell, Teresa settled on the notion of an eternity spent in "a bad inn" and remarked gratefully that

[99]*Foundations*, 29:15.

[100]*Foundations*, 25:7.

[101]Domingo Ortíz, *El Antiguo Régimen: los Reyes Católicos y los Austrias* (Madrid, 1973) 102. See also Teresa's comments about travel in, for example, *Foundations*, 18:3-5. She felt "authentic panic" toward lengthy journeys, and knew that it would be impossible for her adequately to visit and administer far-flung houses. Not surprisingly, the most-visited houses of the discalced reform cluster around Medina del Campo, a veritable crossroads of Castile. See Teófanes Egido, *"Fundaciones,"* in *Introducción a la lectura*, 255.

this life, although troublesome enough, was at least passing, equivalent to just a single night in such a lodging.[102]

On the roads and mule paths of Castile, it was easy as well to get completely lost, as Teresa and her companions frequently did, their wagon drivers and guides notwithstanding. On at least one occasion, the guides not only mistook the route but, once they realized they were lost, also turned on their heels and abandoned the nuns altogether, "saying they had other things to do."[103] It was not unusual to fall into swollen rivers or to get dangerously chilled to the bone in sudden downpours or even to lose the pack mule that was carrying the money![104]

Teresa and her companions usually tried to make the best of these situations. *Foundations* is replete with wonderful accounts of their attempts to amuse themselves in their cumbersome conveyances covered with blankets and veils to keep out prying eyes and maintain a semblance of cloister. Crowded into the wagon with them were statues of saints and other religious paraphernalia destined for the altars and passageways of a soon-to-be-founded monastery. On their way, Teresa and the nuns set up a crucifix, a holy water font, and a water clock in their carriages and crowded accommodations so that at the periodic sound of a little bell they could observe the customary convent schedule. They would sing together (Teresa was a good hand at song lyrics and light verse), tell jokes and edifying stories, and from time to time, try to cheer up the drivers who endured with them the natural hardships of travel but did not share their high ideals and stubborn providential outlooks.[105]

That Teresa was always reluctant to undertake foundational journeys has sometimes been cited as evidence of her humility, as if she did not think it right for so useless a person as herself to be engaged in a project of such magnitude. But any expres-

---

[102]*Way,* 40:9; also 70:4 [E]; *Foundations,* 24:6.

[103]*Foundations,* 30:13.

[104]Teresa's chaplain Julián de Avila told this story in his early hagiography, *Vida de Santa Teresa de Jesús,* ed. Don Vincente de la Fuente (Madrid, 1881), cited in the introduction to *Foundations, Collected Works* III, 49.

[105]Teresa preferred the relatively expensive covered carriage for her journeys with nuns since it was better suited to the sort of community life she tried to maintain on the road. For other modes of teresian travel, including comment on the coaches lent her by members of the aristocracy, see *"Foundations,"* in *Introducción a la lectura,* 256–57; and the introduction to *Foundations, Collected Works* III, 48–52.

sions of reluctance Teresa may have recorded in her letters and books must always be viewed as well in the light of the tremendous hardships of travel with which she was so intimately acquainted. Thus it comes as no surprise that when she was ordered by her Roman superiors to desist from further foundational activities and retire to a convent of her choosing, her initial reaction was nothing less than an exhausted sigh of relief for the respite (it would prove brief) her forced reclusion would afford her from the martyrdom of travel.[106]

But nothing could release her from the "daily martyrdom of writing letters."[107] It was the only way to stay abreast of the development of the convents, and she undertook the tedious task of letter-writing as part of her ineluctable obligation as mother and founder.[108] But her sense of duty did not make the task any less grueling; in addition to a ministry of support and direction, she experienced it as a form of unremitting tyranny.[109] The frequent references to the pressures under which she was writing nearly always include the crush of time; she only rarely composed at leisure. Writing practically every day during the last two decades of her life, she usually had to work very late into the night to finish what she had been unable to attend to during her days of travel, consultation, business, and legal dealings.[110]

Throughout her correspondence, references to the wee hours recur like formulaic refrains: "It must be nearly midnight, and

---

[106]See for example *Letters* I, 211–12. Teresa always freely admitted that founding convents was a great "bother," but the bother seemed, of course, all the greater as she got older. But since it was, in her mind, undoubtedly the divine plan that she do so, she went on with it. As a somewhat younger woman, she had approached foundational work with a bit more idealism, *Letters* I, 73: "[T]iring though I find the work, these houses do so much good in the town where they are founded that my conscience tells me to found as many as I can."

[107]*"Epistolario,"* in *Introducción a la lectura,* 428.

[108]For Teresa's sense that her letter-writing was an important aspect of service, see for example, *Letters* I, 259, 395.

[109]Only occasionally did she admit to enjoying letter-writing. See for example her letter to Gracián, *Letters* I, 281, in which she declared that writing him is "relaxation." It was also a relief to turn to friendly correspondence after having penned numerous business letters. See *Letters* I, 52. But in general the "worry" of letters was "killing" her, and driving her "crazy" (the effort she expended did in fact contribute to the severe depression she underwent in 1577), *Letters* I, 322, 285. Letter-writing also kept her from prayer, but that gave her "no scruple" since it was time also occupied in God's service, *Letters* I, 395.

[110]In *Letters* I, 88, she referred to a rare moment in which she could permit herself to write at length because she had completed the day's other pressing correspondence.

I am very tired, so I will not write any more."[111] "I have written a great deal today and it is late; I am not going to write any more now."[112] "I am having to write this so quickly that I shall not be able to say all I should like. I had been just about to begin it when I received an urgent visit, and now it is late at night and the letter must be given to the muleteer."[113] Often Teresa drove herself imprudently beyond the limits of endurance, and the resulting exhaustion undoubtedly accounted in large measure for her recurring bouts with headache and her inability to digest food. Finally, doctors forced her to begin using an amanuensis, although letters to much-loved correspondents continued to be penned from time to time in her own hand.[114] She was not proud of her imprudence but was never able to conform completely to common sense on the matter; correspondence was her lifeline as well as her bane.[115]

Teresa wrote not only to supervise the houses and their good ordering; the content of her letters also include spiritual advice to her friends and disciples, family concerns, the cultivation of relationships with persons who could be of service to the reform, and the sharing of her longings and fear with her intimate associates. She wrote to direct the campaign to thwart the discalced Carmelites' enemies, and she prescribed remedies for the common ailments of her day, from headache to melancholy. Her letters, composed in pain and haste, often in the midst of worry and fear, are a precious repository of wisdom, humor, and sometimes startling candor. They are an historian's gold mine as well, bulging with offhand political, social, and economic commentary, observations on contemporary mores. Because she was always so concerned about correspondence—how much it cost, the safest ways to send it, even how best to address the covers—her letters even given the social historian valuable examples of the structure and the vagaries of the sixteenth-century Spanish postal system.

---

[111]*Letters* I, 99.

[112]*Letters* I, 68.

[113]*Letters* I, 365.

[114]*Letters* I, 426, 435.

[115]"I just live for [receiving]letters!'", Teresa once exclaimed to María de San José, one of her most cherished correspondents, *Letters* I, 362.

Whatever else its value, however, the *epistolario* of Teresa of Avila, set alongside the hardships of travel, her illnesses, the slander of enemies, the stress brought on by litigation and material poverty, and the spectre of the possible suppression of her life's work, stands as an enduring witness to the fulfillment of her fondest desire: to be conformed to the very love of Christ, to his patient, enduring service, his sufferings and his death, and to the joy, even the triumph, of the limitless and powerful fecundity of resurrection life. In day-to-day duties, as well as in uncommon achievements, Teresa accomplished those "very noble deeds" toward which she felt so powerfully drawn from the moment she understood through experience that God is love and thirsty for our good.

7

Afterword: Pictures

By her own admission (and by her own adult standards), Teresa had been a vain young woman, succumbing early to preoccupation with her looks—makeup, jewelry, and dresses, the measure of the female honor she was bound to keep. Even as a nun she had at first worn velvet. Her discalced life broke with the outward trappings of that vanity. A way of Christian perfection replaced the code of female appearance and behavior which had been for her, perversely, both appealing and oppressive in her youth.

She did not, however, emulate some female saints whose choice of Christ had led them to deface their flesh and beauty in permanent and painful ways. On solid principle Teresa disavowed what seemed to her extremist practice; it also seems she liked, quite simply, to be clean. She was fastidious in ragged poverty and smelly sicknesses. Even though at times she wrote in wonder of the filth and bloody scars of other-worldly saints, she never counseled anything but hygiene for her nuns.

That Teresa was indeed fine-looking was a fact on which her many friends agreed. They said she always seemed much younger than her age. Her body was regarded for its roundness, her stature neither short nor over-tall; her well-proportioned face admired for three *lunares,* small raised spots that curved in crescent from her nostrils to her lips and chin. She had small ears, small hands, dark eyebrows thick and straight, an air of graceful dignity. It would be strange if she was blithely unaware that by the canons of her age she ranked a beauty.

Only one portrait from life was made of St. Teresa.[1] Gracián ordered it as half a two-pronged plan of mortifying her; he said she dragged her feet about obeying.[2] Did she think it vain? Did she hate the very notion, as her friend reported, that her "memory and figure" would remain forever in the world? I doubt it. It hadn't seemed vainglorious to her to think about her books as mirrors of herself-in-God bequeathed to her posterity. She was pleased with the notion that her sisters were like offspring who would bear her stamp down through the generations, the likeness of encounter with the living God. A painted portrait too could serve the nuns, stirring them to imitate the mother who, all the while she lived, had lived Christ in her body.

Teresa was far more levelheaded about the dangers and advantages of fame than hagiographers will ever be. Never eager for popular canonization in her lifetime, and probably not anticipating the scope of the posthumous acclaim she would enjoy, she was nonetheless a woman aware of her hold on others, frank about her spiritual powers, and not averse to being remembered as one in and through whom God worked mercies. Thus, I am inclined to think that more than modesty, it was the paucity of time that caused her to demur. The sittings were bound to cut too deeply into hours she didn't have to spare.

During that summer of 1576 everyone was hurrying to finish up the renovations of the house that was to be the convent of the discalced women of Seville. Most harried of them all was the Italian friar who had been tapped to decorate the convent church. Just a few days remained before the festive inauguration, and Fray Juan de la Miseria still had work to do on walls and ceilings. He would not quit the job to satisfy the nuns who, on account of Teresa's imminent departure, were pressing hard to have her portrait done. Finally, the paintings in the church complete and Teresa acquiescing, Fray Juan began to paint her—the day before she left Seville.

[1]The portrait, from which numerous copies have been made, remains in the discalced Carmelite convent of Seville.

[2]The other prong was to require that she prepare for a general confession of all the sins of her life. Recalling her ingratitude toward God always pained Teresa deeply, and, according to Gracián's accounts, she begged him tearfully to let her get the confession over with. Gracián prolonged her agony for nearly twenty days, and then at the last moment called off the actual confession. See his *Scholias,* f. 40r, in *El Monte Carmelo* 68 (1960), 131; *Peregrinación,* 229.

His eyes as much upon the clock as on his reluctant subject, the friar painted in the head and face and left for later details he could do from memory. The results of Fray Juan's talents drew some mixed reviews. Gracián thought it a bad likeness.[3] María de San José said it captured Teresa well.[4] Teresa's reaction was harder to decipher. Perhaps she meant her verdict as a good-natured poke at the painter; perhaps it was a cover for slight disappointment; or maybe it was deprecation to deflect her genuine and unexpected pleasure in his work.

With *mucha gracia,* her typical high humor, she told him simply this: "May God forgive you, brother Juan; now that you painted me, you've made me rheummy-eyed and ugly."[5]

* * *

Propped up on my desk I keep a modern image of Teresa made by icon-painter Robert Lentz.[6] She wears a proper Christian halo and the discalced habit, white and black and brown. She stands before a wall of Moorish tiles, blue stars of David: Teresa with a heritage, a place and time. Her mouth has just begun, it seems to me, to smile. Her cheeks are ruddy with that flush remembered by her friends. But no sign of *lunares.* Her head is fully upright; here there is no modest custody of eyes nor gaze gone blank in ecstasy, but frank intelligence and energy. Direct, she is, with every sense alert.

She's making music on a well-worn tambourine. Perhaps she plays to banish bugs.[7] Or keep the beat of respite for the nuns. Or heat the winter corridor with songs of God. It can't be long before she dances.

* * *

[3] *Peregrinación,* 229.

[4] *Libro de recreaciones* 8, 96. Cited in *Tiempo y vida,* 593, n. 140.

[5] *Peregrinación,* 229. My translation.

[6] Reproduction by Bridge Building Icons, Burlington, VT, c. 1986.

[7] Among the many poems, carols, and *coplas* Teresa composed for the nuns is a processional beseeching God to rid their rough woolen habits of *mala gente,* the "impertinent little flock" of parasites that infested them. See *Poetry,* in *Collected Works* III, 409–410.

To mark a favorite passage, I slipped between the pages of a favored book a photo of Bernini's sculpture of Teresa.[8] Transverberation: fleshiest of ecstasies, seraphic virgin ravished. A childlike angel above her unprotected body aims again the golden dart. He looks pleased, coquettishly sweet but maybe smug. The arrow has already spread the heat of God throughout her flesh and snagged her soul. She has folded, languid with divine sensation. The iron point is clean of any clinging fragments of her deepest part. Perhaps they burned in licks of fire. Teresa's half-closed eyes and parted lips are marble moans.

Arising from her sleep with God, she'll find that it is still the day, the night, then day and night again. She'll clasp her shining suffering close and go about her business stupefied.

* * *

In Pastrana, where the princess Eboli was a disastrous nun, the town church boasts a canvas of Teresa in the pose of preacher.[9] The Spirit hovers like a glowing hummingbird above her teaching hand. Mystical doctor: her academic cap lies on the lip of the pulpit. Her left hand rests with some authority upon a book with covers closed. Her fingers curl around its end. By robes and hoods and tonsures, you mark the grave *letrados,* male-only audience below: sons of Francis, Dominic, Ignatius, and Elijah. Hands on hearts, they whisper, "O sublime, sublime!" Off to one side, Dominican and Jesuit, stern, stern rivals for the truth, confer in unaccustomed peace behind a column draped in gauze.[10] Cherubs in a corner hold the coat of arms of Carmel.

A legend partly lost because of ribbon-folds explains the scene:

[8] *The Ecstasy of St. Teresa.* Sculpted in 1646, it is housed in Santa María della Vittoria in Rome. The marble sculpture depicts the "heart-piercing" experiences Teresa reported in *Life,* 29:13-14.

[9] For the story of the princess' attempt at religious life and her troublesome support of one Teresian foundation, see *Foundations,* 17; see also Teresa's letter to Báñez, January 1574, *Letters* I, 128. The painting is *St. Teresa Preaching,* anonymous oil on canvas, presumed to be a late seventeenth-century work. See a black and white photographic reproduction [fig. 54] in Jean de la Croix, "L'Iconographie de Thérèse de Jésus, Docteur de L'Eglise," *Ephemerides Carmeliticae* 21 (1970): 219-260.

[10] I have assumed it is a Dominican, but the white-robed figure talking with the Jesuit might also be a Carmelite.

Teresa teaches her teachers.[11] I notice one more curious detail: this female preacher's mouth is painted closed.

* * *

The statue near the convent of the Incarnation shows Teresa on her travels.[12] She strides, a young strong woman, seasoned walker on easy terrain. Staff planted, her flapping habit is no hindrance as the trailing leg prepares to take the front again, a dozen leagues accomplished with each pace. She is no *wandering* nun, as Sega charged. Wandering is aimless. This nun knows where she is going. Her purpose is to keep on going. Her eyes take in all things and dreams in ample arc to the horizon, she is so tall. The cadence of her step is measuring her heart. Beat by beat she covers every distance, convent to convent, friend to friend, deep unto deep. To God, to God.

Teresa with her sick body never walked like this in all her life. Teresa with her sick body walked like this at every moment of her life.

* * *

I have an article on Teresian iconography that includes thirty-six pages of reproductions, from all the intervening centuries and several lands.[13] Seventy-nine pictures all in all, a fair representation. A magnifying glass has helped me see detail. Some are icons showing Teresa all alone (unless you count the ever-present dove) in attitudes of prayer. Many have her teaching men. Some, twin portraits of the theologians Thomas and Teresa, remain as striking witness to the long (yet only now official) history of acclaim of Teresa as a doctor of the Church. The paintings showing her with Christ and angels illustrate the mercies she described in all her books. One overbearing allegory has the triumph of the Virgin of Mount Carmel: a crowded scene of earth and heaven filled with cardinals, popes, and friars, musician angels, bearded Fa-

---

[11]*S. Theresia ab ipsis edocta docens,* a legend commonly found on the numerous paintings of Teresa teaching and preaching to an assembly of theologians and doctors of the Church.

[12]I do not know the name of the sculptor who fashioned this powerful work.

[13]Jean de la Croix, "L'Iconographie."

ther God and glorious Son; the only women, Teresa and the Virgin.[14]

In fact, in only one of nearly eighty I make out a group of nuns: Teresa kneels with arms outstretched beneath a shower of divinity and grace that falls clear shining from the dove. From her mother-founder's heart beneath her habit two strong branches grow, the end of each a flower. And on the petals of the flower to her right her sons are kneeling, six discalced friars with eyes upraised and praying hands. On the petals of the flower to her left her daughters kneel, six discalced nuns with eyes upraised and praying hands.[15] Here is a start. But why not more?

If I could paint I'd show the Saint *surrounded* by her sisters. In company of strong and faithful women I would show her with her walking staff, her doctor's hat, the arrow of her ecstasy, her swooning flesh, her athlete's step, her tambourine and David's star. Spinning, praying, sewing, writing, teaching, dancing, signing deals on dotted lines, she should be shown for once at least with women all around.

Sister, daughter, mother, names of struggle and of love: women ought to fill the pictures that we use to call to mind the meanings of her life, the pictures that we use to mark our books in places that inspire. If I could sculpt or paint, it's what I'd do.

[14]Nicolás Rodríguez Xuárez, *The Triumph of the Virgin of Carmel,* 1695. Discalced Carmelite Fathers, Celaya, Mexico. Fig. 74.

[15]Matheus, *Teresa of Jesus, Mother of the Carmelites,* early seventeenth century. Cabinet des Estampes, Paris. Fig. 21.

Selected Bibliography

Teresa's Works

I. Modern Spanish Editions

Obras Completas. Ed. Tomás de la Cruz (Alvarez), O.C.D. Burgos: El Monte Carmelo, 1971.

Obras completas. Ed., intro., and notes by Efrén de la Madre de Dios (Montalva), O.C.D., Otilio del Niño Jesús (Rodríguez), O.C.D., and Otger Steggink, O.Carm. 3 vols. Madrid: La Editorial Católica, 1941-1959.

Obras completas. One-volume edition. Ed., intro., and notes by Efrén de la Madre de Dios and Otger Steggink. Madrid: La Editorial Católica, 1962; 2nd ed. 1967; 3rd ed. 1972; 4th ed. 1974; 5th ed. 1976.

Obras de Santa Teresa de Jesús. Ed. and notes by Silverio de Santa Teresa, O.C.D. Vols. 1-9 in *Biblioteca Mística Carmelitana.* Burgos: El Monte Carmelo, 1915-1924.

II. Modern English Editions

The Collected Works of St. Teresa of Avila. Tr. Kieran Kavanaugh and Otilio Rodríguez. 3 vols. Washington, D.C.: ICS Publications, 1976-1985.

The Complete Works of St. Teresa of Jesus. Tr. E. Allison Peers. 3 vols. London: Sheed and Ward, 1958.

The Letters of Saint Teresa of Jesus. Tr. E. Allison Peers. 2 vols. London: Sheed and Ward, 1980.

Selected Biographies

Auclair, Marcel. *St. Teresa of Avila*. Tr. Kathleen Pond. New York: Pantheon Books, 1953.

Clissold, Stephen. *St. Teresa of Avila*. London: Sheldon Press, 1979.

Montalva, Efrén de la Madre de Dios, O.C.D. and Steggink, Otger, O.Carm. *Tiempo y vida de Santa Teresa*. Madrid: BAC, 1968. 2nd ed. 1977. An expanded edition has recently appeared. *Santa Teresa y su Tiempo*. 3 vols. Salamanca: Coleccion Bibliotheca Salmanticensis, 1982.

Papasogil, Giorgio. *St. Teresa of Avila*. Tr. Gloria Anzilotti. Rev. ed. Jamaica Plain, MA: Society of St. Paul, 1988.

Peers, E. Allison. *Mother of Carmel: A Portrait of St. Teresa of Jesus*. Wilton, CT: Morehouse-Barlow, 1944.

Rossi, Rosa. *Teresa de Avila. Biografía de una escritora*. Barcelona: Icaria, 1984.

Studies

Alvarez, Tomás (de la Cruz), O.C.D. "Humanité du Christ: L'école carmélitaine," *Dictionnaire de spiritualité* 7, cols. 1096-10110.

_____. " 'Esta Monja.' Carisma y obediencia en una relación de la Santa," *El Monte Carmelo* 78 (1970): 143-162.

_____. "La oración, camino a Dios: el pensamiento de Santa Teresa," *Ephemerides Carmeliticae* 21 (1970): 115-168.

_____. "Santa Teresa y la polémica de la oración mental: sentido polémico del Camino de perfección," *Santa Teresa en el IV Centenario de la Reforma carmelitana*. Barcelona, 1963.

_____. "Santa Teresa y las mujeres en la Iglesia. Glosa al texto teresiano de *Camino* 3," *Monte Carmelo* 89 (1981): 121-132.

_____. *Santa Teresa y la Iglesia*. Burgos: El Monte Carmelo, 1980.

Arenel, Electa and Schlau, Stacey. *Untold Sisters: Hispanic Nuns in Their Own Works*. Translation of texts by Amanda Powell. Albuquerque: Univ. of New Mexico Press, 1989.

Barrientos, Alberto, ed. *Introducción a la lectura de Santa Teresa.* Madrid: Editorial de Espiritualidad, 1978.

Bilinkoff, Jodi. "The Social Meaning of Religious Reform: The Case of St. Teresa and Avila," *Archiv für Reformationgeschichte* 79 (1988): 340–356.

―――――. *The Avila of St. Teresa: Religious Reform in a Sixteenth-Century City.* Ithaca, NY: Cornell University Press, 1989.

―――――. "Private Prayer, Public Apostolate: The Mission of Teresa of Avila." Paper presented at the Seventh Berkshire Conference on the History of Women. Wellesley College, June 20, 1987.

Boersig, Teresa M. "Teresian Spirituality," *Contemplative Review* 15 (1982): 37–42.

Burrows, Ruth, O.Carm. *Interior Castle Explored: St. Teresa's Teachings on the Life of Deep Union with God.* London: Sheed and Ward, 1981.

Carroll, Eamon R., S.T.D. "The Saving Role of the Human Christ for St. Teresa," *Carmelite Studies* 3 (1982): 133:151.

Deneuville, Dominique. *Santa Teresa y la mujer.* Tr. Fernando Gutiérrez. Barcelona: Herder, 1966.

Dobhan, Ulrich. *Gott, Mensch und Welt in der sicht Teresas von Avila.* Frankfurt-am-Main: Peter Lang, 1978.

Egan, Harvey D. "St. Teresa of Avila (1515–1582)," a chapter in *Christian Mysticism: The Future of a Tradition.* New York: Pueblo, 1984: 118–164.

Egan, Keith J. "The Significance for Theology of the Doctor of the Church: Teresa of Avila," *The Pedagogy of God's Image: Essays on Symbol and the Religious Imagination.* Ed. Robert Masson. Chico, CA: College Theological Society, 1981. 153–171.

Egido, Teófanes. "The Historical Setting of St. Teresa's Life," *Carmelite Studies* 1 (1980): 122–182.

Frs. Thomas and Gabriel, O.C.D., eds. *St. Teresa of Avila: Studies in Her Life, Doctrine and Times.* Westminster, MD: Newman Press, 1963.

Galilea, Segundo. *The Future of Our Past: The Spanish Mystics Speak to Contemporary Spirituality.* Notre Dame, IN: Ave Maria Press, 1985.

Gracía de la Concha, Victor. *El arte literario de Santa Teresa.* Barcelona: Ariel, 1978.

Hamilton, Elizabeth. *Servants of Love: The Spirituality of Teresa of Avila.* London: Darton, Longman and Todd, 1975.

Hellwig, Monica. "St. Teresa's Inspiration for Our Times," *Carmelite Studies* 3 (1982): 212–224.

Herraiz, Maximiliano. "Experiencia y teología. Teresa de Jesús, vida y palabra," *Revista de teología espiritual* 22 (1978): 7–36.

_____. *Sólo Dios Basta. Claves de la espiritualidad teresiana.* 2nd ed. Madrid: Editorial de Espiritualidad, 1981.

Howe, Elizabeth Teresa. *Mystical Imagery. Santa Teresa de Jesús and San Juan de la Cruz.* New York: Peter Lang, 1988.

Llamas Martínez, Enrique. *Santa Teresa de Jesús y la Inquisición española.* Madrid: CSIC, 1972.

Llamas, Román. "Santa Teresa y su experiencia de la Sagrada Escritura," *Teresianum* 33 (1988): 447–513.

Marie Eugene de l'Enfant Jésus, O.C.D. *I Want to See God. I Am a Daughter of the Church.* 1 vol. edition of the 2 works. Westminster, MD: Christian Classics (reprint expected, 1990).

Márquez Villaneuva, Francisco, "Santa Teresa y el linaje," a chapter in *Espiritualidad y literatura en el siglo XVI.* Madrid-Barcelona: Alfaguara, 1968: 141–205.

Pablo Maroto, Daniel de. *Dinámica de la oración. Acercamiento del orante moderno a Santa Teresa de Jesús.* Madrid: Editorial de Espiritualidad, 1973.

Peers, E. Allison. *Handbook to the Life and Times of St. Teresa and St. John of the Cross.* Westminster, MD: Newman Press, 1954.

Pertusi, Pierluigi. "Spiritual Direction in the Major Works of St. Teresa," *Carmelite Studies* 1 (1980).

Quitslund, Sonya A. "Elements of a Feminist Spirituality in St. Teresa," *Carmelite Studies* 3 (1984): 19–50.

Rahner, Karl. "Teresa of Avila: Doctor of the Church," a chapter in *Opportunities for Faith.* New York: Seabury, 1970.

Renault, Emmanuel. *L'idéal apostolique des Carmélites selon Thérèse d'Avila.* Paris: Desclée de Brouwer, 1981.

_____. *Ste. Thérèse d'Avila et l'experience mystique.* Paris: Editions du Seuil, 1970.

Rossi, Rosa. "Teresa de Jesús I. La mujer y la Iglesia," *mientras tanto* 14 (1982): 63–79.

_____. "Teresa de Jesús II. La mujer y la palabra," *mientras tanto* 15 (1983): 29–46.

Ruíz Soler, Luis. *La personalidad económico-administrativa de la Santa Madre Teresa de Jesús.* Zarauz: Editorial Icharopena, 1970.

Slade, Carole. "St. Teresa's Meditaciones sobre los Cantares: The Hermeneutics of Humility and Enjoyment," *Religion and Literature* 18 (1986): 27–44.

Steggink, Otger, O.Carm. *La reforma del Carmelo español. La visita canónica del General Rubeo y su encuentro con Santa Teresa (1566–67).* Rome: Institutum Carmelitanum, 1965.

_____. "Teresa de Jesús, mujer y mística ante los teólogos," *Carmelus* 29 (1982): 111–129.

Truman Dicken, E. W. *The Crucible of Love. The Mysticism of St. Teresa of Jesus and St. John of the Cross.* New York: Sheed and Ward, 1963.

Weber, Alison. *Teresa of Avila and the Rhetoric of Femininity.* Princeton, NJ: Princeton University Press, 1990.

Welch, John. *Spiritual Pilgrims: Carl Jung and Teresa of Avila.* New York: Paulist Press, 1982.

Whalen, James. *The Spiritual Teachings of Teresa of Avila and Adrian Van Kaam: Formative Spirituality.* Lanham, MD: University Press of America. 1984.